D0140858

Thinking About Political Corruption

JX
2249
D45
1993

Thinking
About
Political
Corruption

Peter deLeon

M.E. Sharpe
Armonk, New York
London, England

DAVID L. RICE LIBRARY
UNIVERSITY OF SOUTHERN INDIANA
EVANSVILLE, IN

#27975989
AAW2800

Copyright © 1993 by M. E. Sharpe, Inc.

All rights reserved. No part of this book may be reproduced in any form
without written permission from the publisher, M. E. Sharpe, Inc.,
80 Business Park Drive, Armonk, New York 10504.

Library of Congress Cataloging-in-Publication Data

deLeon, Peter.
Thinking about political corruption / Peter deLeon.
p. cm.
Includes bibliographical references and index.
ISBN 0-87332-838-8.—ISBN 0-87332-839-6 (pbk.)
1. Political corruption—United States.
2. Political corruption—United States—Case studies.
I. Title.
JK2249.D45   1993
364.1′323′0973—dc20
93-4026
CIP

Printed in the United States of America

The paper used in this publication meets the minimum requirements of
American National Standard for Information Sciences—
Permanence of Paper for Printed Library Materials,
ANSI Z 39.48-1984.

∞

MV (c)   10   9   8   7   6   5   4   3   2   1
MV (p)   10   9   8   7   6   5   4   3

CONTENTS

PREFACE

In 1986, when I was doing research for a book that was to become *Advice and Consent* (1989), I was intrigued by the lack of analysis in the literature on Watergate relating the scandal to American politics. There was more journalism, histories, and personal tellings of Watergate than one could shake a stick at—which were all well and good— but nothing that examined how Watergate, as an instance of political corruption, affected the American political system. However disparate these authors' training and purpose, they all seemingly reached the same conclusions: that, in President Gerald Ford's words, the long nightmare of Watergate was behind us and there was little reason for generalization. My disappointing survey, which I now sheepishly admit was probably incomplete,[a] led me to wonder why this (at least to me) obvious gap existed in the literature. It led me to pose broader questions about political corruption and about why there was so little work examining its generic effect on the United States. Which led to the present book.

This book has been a more difficult book to write than I had anticipated. I now have a very intimate appreciation of why the analysis of political corruption is an underattended subject. The subject matter is truly fascinating—the literal stuff of political drama—but the actors,

---

[a] Given the immense library on Watergate, I suspect it approaches the infinite monkeys on infinite typewriters syndrome, e.g., there might be an article somewhere relating Watergate and Hamlet, or Gemstone and Wilkie Collins' *Moonstone* (1868), etc.

their motives, and scenarios are so varied that to weave them together in a coherent pattern required more work than I had ever imagined in the naive days when I proposed the book to a publisher. I am grateful for having written this book; I have learned more than I had bargained for, always a good feeling. Still, I confess that at times I felt as if the book were somehow taking over and writing itself. Perhaps the key lesson could be to respect the market signals: when there appears to be an obvious interest matched by an equally obvious gap, it is circumspect to wonder why.

Writing this book was difficult in another sense. It is important for the reader to know my personal sentiments on the subject of political corruption. I am not a neutral observer. Reading volumes about various incidents of public corruption, watching individuals with motives and standards far removed from mine commit what I consider deliberate violence to the public order, tended to raise my blood pressure. Marginalia in my source books testify that I did not take the culprits' actions lightly or from an academic's detached perspective. However, then to sit back, softly contemplate and analyze corruption from a dispassionate perspective required a very different, more tolerant perspective; to treat these cases as mere illustrations of a larger theme rather than verse for the pulpit was often a difficult struggle. I trust that for the most part, my analytic angel has held the field; if readers should occasionally sense my emotive angel snatching a phrase or two (maybe a page), I hope they will appreciate that even the best analysis should reflect the author's values.

Let me offer a very quick Baedeker for the reader. I am, by profession, an academic. Chapter 2, rather laced with theory, is largely written as dues to my colleagues, payments the general reader might not wish to incur. The less academically oriented may be inclined to read the introduction (Chapter 1), skim (or even skip) Chapter 2, read the case studies (Chapters 3–7), and finish with the conclusions (Chapter 8), and can do so without fear of missing the book's main themes.

* * *

There is one aspect of this book that appears at first glance to be highly partisan in nature—the five cases of political corruption reviewed below all occurred during the Republican administration of President Ronald Reagan. The readily drawn conclusion—that this is a Democrats-inspired, hatchet-job book, written to denigrate President

Reagan and vilify the Republican Party—simply is not true. My selection of cases is strictly an artifact of the study. For relevancy's sake, I wanted recent examples of corruption at the federal level of government. It just so happens that the American voters have sent Republicans to the White House for the last twelve years. We will discuss and again reject this interpretation at greater length in the Conclusion of the book. Until then, I must ask the reader's indulgence that this book has no hidden agenda to tar the Republican Party and its presidents with the pitch of political corruption.

ACKNOWLEDGMENTS

As I confessed in the Preface, this book has had a longer gestation than any diligent author should wish to admit. As a consequence, the book has a lengthy lineage. My colleagues at Columbia University, especially Alfred Stepan (former dean of the School of International and Public Affairs), initially assured me that what I was looking for was right around the next library carrel; that they were mistaken does not diminish their encouragement. More substantively, Professor Susan Rose-Ackerman (then at Columbia's Law School and now at Yale University), who had provided an economist's view of corruption in her *Corruption: A Study in Political Corruption* (1978), kindly shared her more recent thoughts on the subject.

Michael Johnston (Colgate University), whose *Political Corruption and Public Policy in America* (1982) served in many ways as a model, was equally generous with his time and insights. Indeed, an initial inkling of this book's argument was published in a Johnston-edited journal, *Corruption & Reform*, bearing the ungainly title, "Public Policy Effects of Systemic Political Corruption" (1989). Theodore J. Lowi (Cornell University) graciously sent me materials I was having difficulty obtaining. I owe a particular debt of gratitude to Robert K. Merton (The Russell Sage Foundation), less for his seminal thinking regarding corruption than for his personal encouragement; I trust that my reading of his ideas will not embarrass him.

In the summer of 1988, Brian Jenkins, Chair of the RAND Corporation's Political Science Department, hosted a seminar in which I presented an outline of this book's argument. A few years later, I had a similar opportunity with the School of Public Administration and Policy at the University of Arizona. Both seminars, although truly traumatic at the time, have resulted in a more thoughtful analysis.

My University of Colorado colleagues here in Denver have offered quiet enthusiasm that gently urged me through my periods of frustration. Chancellor John C. Buechner's occasional "how's the book going?" greetings provided more stimulus than I am sure he intended, and meant more to me than I am sure he knows. Professor Linda deLeon asked more questions than I probably wanted to field, but every reader should be appreciative of her insistence. Professor Elizabeth Peters (Department of Economics, University of Colorado at Boulder) patiently translated relevant economic theory to me. Graduate students Stephanie Cunningham and Jeff Romine assisted in tracking down elusive research materials.

Finally, Professor Kenneth J. Meier (University of Wisconsin-Milwaukee) read the entire manuscript and provided welcomed encouragement and criticism. On the other hand, Professor Paul A. Sabatier (University of California at Davis) has not read a word of the manuscript. Nevertheless, he has graciously agreed to be responsible for all errors of fact and interpretation; it is only fair that I acknowledge any remaining errors as my own.

It seems *de rigueur* for every author to thank his editor. Let me not flout convention, especially when it is so richly deserved. Michael Weber of M.E. Sharpe has been incredibly considerate as I dithered well past my promised delivery dates. Maybe he should have been sterner, but I am grateful that he was not. I trust the end product rewards his patience.

* * *

There is, happily, a final convention I need acknowledge. I dedicate this book to my wife Linda, not so much for how she has aided me in my scholarship (although that is far from inconsequential), but for all she has done and continues to do for me in so many other ways. She is my very great and abiding fortune.

Part I
WHAT IS POLITICAL CORRUPTION?

1

IT IS SOWN IN CORRUPTION
(1 Corinthians 15:42)

> Corrupt influence, which is itself the perennial spring of all prodigality, and of all disorder; which loads us, more than mills of debt; which takes away vigour from our arms, wisdom from our councils, and every shadow of authority and credit from the most venerable parts of our constitution.
> —Edmund Burke,
> "Speeches on the
> Economical Reforms" (1870)

Numerous authors, political observers, and just plain folk have commented on the presence of corruption in American politics, usually with some admixture of Puritan outrage and world-weary cynicism. Alexis de Tocqueville to Walter Lippmann, Sinclair Lewis to Bob Woodward, Ida Tarbell to Mike Royko, Thomas Nast to Herblock—the list would be endless. Certainly one would not have to look too far for culpable individuals throughout American history and politics, but somehow, we would like to think that political manners and mores "back then"—when politics were hurley-burley, the press less attentive (or less intrusive, depending upon your perspective), and public servants not trained in "good government"—were much more susceptible to wrongdoing than is currently the case.[1]

But this is patently not the case. Corruption often seems omnipresent in contemporary American political systems. No level of government appears particularly sacrosanct. In 1987, New York City had a scandal of such a magnitude regarding the purchase of hand-held computers to write parking tickets that Donald Manes, a former borough president of Queens, committed suicide rather than face charges;[2] subsequently, less than six months later, it was discovered that over $3 million in pocket change[a] was stolen from parking meters by the meter collection company, almost 10 percent of the revenue from the city's 56,000 parking meters.[3] Rural southern law enforcement officers, FBI agents, and even a member of the Justice Department's Organized Crime Strike Force have succumbed to corruption from the millions of dollars culled from illegal drug money.[4] In 1988, Ex-Governor Evan Mecham of Arizona was impeached; a few years later, state legislators were revealed to have accepted bribes from an ersatz gambler cum undercover police officer and then complained of the subterfuge.[5] As if this were not enough for one state, both Arizona U.S. senators were reprimanded for violating Senate rules to keep Charles Keating's crumbling S&L afloat and the current governor is being sued by the government for his role in Arizona's S&L debacle.[6] James Fesler and Donald Kettl relate how "In an FBI 'sting' operation, 105 out of 106 offers of bribes to suspected municipal officials in the State of New York were accepted; the 106th was rejected as too small."[7]

One might think that these cases are all local government incidents, where politics is more personal and less visible, hence more susceptible to corrupt dealings. Unfortunately, the highly illuminated halls of the federal government are also prone to corruption. An embarrassingly large number of Republican administration appointees under President Ronald Reagan (up to and including Attorney General Edwin Meese) were forced to resign for conflict-of-interest reasons. *Time* magazine counted "more than 100 members of the Reagan Administration [who] had ethical or legal charges leveled against them. That number is without precedent."[8] Amazingly, the *Wall Street Journal*, never thought to be a Democratic apologist, went so far as to report how some scholars link Republican administrations with corruption, a trend "explained by the philosophical bent of those who tend to work for Republican presidents—a bent that often leads them afoul of the guidelines of government work."[9]

Nor should one claim that corruption is strictly a public sector phenomenon. The continuing exposés of Wall Street financial institutions, such as Burnham Drexel Lambert and Solomon Brothers, the irrepress-

---

[a] Giving, one suspects, new significance to the phrase "deep pockets."

ible greed of many bank executives that precipitated the disastrous Savings and Loan crisis, and the Pentagon procurement indictments regarding the misuse of inside information for ill-gained profits and falsifying test information would disabuse any such naive notion that the private sector has any particular concern for the well-being of the public sector beyond its anticipated profit margin.

This dour litany is not to suggest that corruption runs rampant or even commonplace in either the private or public sectors, or that scoundrels and scalawags rule the various power roosts. We should not leap to the conclusion that corruption is as pervasive as "Miami Vice" or the *Godfather* trilogy would have us believe, or be swayed by *Time* magazine's emotion as it bemoaned the "scandal-scarred spring of 1987" in which close to one hundred major and minor federal government officials were accused of violating the public trust: "Lamentation is in the air, and clay feet litter the ground. A relentless procession of forlorn faces assaults the nation's moral equanimity. . . ."[10] Even major government scandals, such as Watergate, influence peddling at HUD, or the S&L embarrassments, should not shake the knowledge that government personnel are, by and large, dependably responsible, honest, and well-intended.

Still, the presence of corruption cannot be blithely ignored or treated as a minor social malaise. A 1988 Associated Press survey "found deep skepticism of federal government integrity. In the most critical finding, an overwhelming 70 percent said they thought taking illegal payoffs for favors was widespread. Fully half the respondents called government dishonest overall."[11] If these findings are representative, and I have scant reason to think otherwise, this sentiment can lead to many things, none of them salutary. For instance, the perception of a corrupt bureaucracy could convince legislatures to enact a series of increasingly restrictive measures that, as we will see below, would be counterproductive, that is, they would only serve to increase the likelihood of corruption rather than its intended decrease. A scandal "witch hunt" mentality—what Suzanne Garment calls a "Culture of Mistrust in American Politics"—could develop that would greatly exaggerate minor peccadilloes and cause severe anguish to all those involved, including the political system that is putatively being defended.[12] Or citizens will lose faith in their government at the very time when government is being asked to involve itself in an increasing number of activities. Finally, and most ominously, "corruption in high places, or the mere *appearance* of wrongdoing, cannot only reduce popular trust in leaders and institutions; it may also let citizens off the hook for their own misdeeds. They may ask why they must be better than others are," with the inevitable answer dangerously threatening to rend the social fabric.[13]

I will argue that although corruption might be a little more than a minor malady in the American body politic, it deserves careful analytic as opposed to anecdotal attention, for if left to election box oratory, flaming headlines, and episodic campaigns, its effects could possibly become more than dyspeptic. For instance, the American political ethos is predicated on equal opportunity and access, conditions fundamentally undermined by corrupt practices. To prevent such an ulcerous condition from occurring, we need to understand several specific points regarding public corruption as a recurring condition: For example, what motivates corrupt actions? How are they perceived? Are there different varieties of corruption? What function might they serve? And how can they best be minimized?

The purpose of this book is to address these questions. However, let me immediately register some important reservations. First and foremost, I am dealing exclusively with public sector corruption; private sector corruption, however pervasive (or not) is a separate matter,[14] except in those areas in which the public and private sectors are clearly conjoined, as in regulatory policies or when private sector actors are undercutting government responsibilities. Second, as I have noted above, public sector corruption does have certain ubiquitous qualities, showing little respect for geographical, temporal, or level of government boundaries. The author that dares to tackle this immense body of materials would be hard-pressed to write a coherent book. Or, by great dint of effort and perseverance, if the book could be written, it would be so long and cumbersome a tome as to intimidate, virtually defy all but the hardiest reader. I choose here not to write this encyclopedia—or to construct a veritable cathedral—of corruption. I prefer to be read rather than ritually referenced, thus implying a more modest effort, a chapel if you will, that talks less about indexing every corrupt act since Eve whispered the benefits of fruit into Adam's ear and, instead, proposes, more discretely, ways of systematically thinking about corruption as a continuing political phenomenon.[15]

A third caveat needs to be offered. Corruption, like most political activities, is decidedly dependent on societal and cultural norms. What transpires in a Latin American, Middle Eastern, or Asian nation as legitimate, excusable, or at least accepted business exchanges would be felonies in the United States. Similarly, there are significant differences in what is acceptable within the various regions and states of the United States,[16] and certainly among different cities. Again, to make my (and ultimately the reader's) task more manageable, I am focusing on probably the most visible examples of governmental corruption, those that occur on the federal level. I will, however, refer to a variety of examples cutting across government levels in the United States to articulate and illustrate the general structure of my analysis.

Fourth, some observers have virtually equated the affiliations between political interest groups (or, when dollars are present, "political action committees"—PACs) and legislators as a corrupt (or corrupting) relationship.[17] These interactions can be viewed as a means for wealthy groups to buy votes, and, consequently, ensure themselves of favorable, that is, profitable, government decisions and, concomitantly, for government officials themselves to join the ranks of the wealthy.[18] Without questioning the possibility of this relationship presenting, maybe even fostering, corrupting conditions, this book will not directly deal with the subject, because contributions to political campaigns are a given, a permanent part of the political landscape with which we must operate. Politicians and administrators should work with their constituents; similarly, constituents should be free to express their support of their elected governmental representatives within legally defined limits and procedures. To mandate away these interactions, to separate government officials from their constituents, would be to guarantee a movement toward bureaucratic despotism and still not rid the government of possible corruption. Furthermore, and more to the point, there is presently nothing illegal about accepting political contributions within specified means and amounts. Nor will reforms in election campaign financing be the talisman many would hope. I will argue below that it is not the presence of PACs per se that is the corrupting element; rather, PACs are little more than the medium through which the corruption current flows. As we will see, to eliminate or, more likely, reform one medium would just create other potentially more *sub rosa* channels.[19]

Finally, this is not intended to be a chronicle of all political corruptions that ever occurred in America on the federal level. Conditions, cultures, and professional behaviors extant in the nineteenth and even in the early parts of the twentieth centuries simply are no longer relevant or permissible. However, the history of earlier acts of public corruption is reflected in laws and expected norms of political conduct—for instance, the reforms fostered by the Progressive movement in the early part of this century. Congress would not (perhaps could not) engage in another Credit Mobilier embroglio, nor the executive branch recreate another Teapot Dome scandal. Even the most vivid contemporary example of corruption on the national level—the "long national nightmare" of Watergate—now seems safely distant, a few decades removed, and beyond recurrence; its subsequent "Ethics in Government" legislation, designed to prevent similar scandals, remains intact (if not necessarily in force), as we shall see.[b] The scenario, then, is current, because if we are to suggest ways to reduce corruption, they must fit into the relevant political context, in other words, today.

For these reasons, *Thinking About Political Corruption* will focus on relatively recent—that is, post-Watergate—examples of major corruption on the federal level. Minor infractions, such as accepting dinners from PACs, while worrisome, will not be included since their impacts on the workings of government are barely discernible. However, these limitations are not unduly constraining for at least two reasons. First, there is no paucity of examples to illustrate my primary themes; indeed, some selection and summary even among these will be necessary or again risk the forbidding tome. Second, I have considerable confidence that if we can understand the workings of this relatively constrained set of examples, that knowledge or insight is readily transferable to other government settings if the appropriate differences (e.g., history or form of government) are taken into account.

Some Disciplinary Perspectives

If we can momentarily agree that corruption is an issue of genuine concern for the American voter (an issue I will directly address in the

---

[b] One possibly more lasting effect of Watergate, however, is the tendency within the press to refer to any ensuing scandal as another "-gate," e.g., "Irangate," "Koreagate," "Rubbergate"—the House of Representatives' bank's practice of honoring members' (sometimes egregious) overdrafts, and of course, "nannygate,"—two of President Bill Clinton's nominees for attorney general were disqualified because of their use of illegal child care. The most personalized example of this sorry convention is "Quaylegate," attributed to Vice President Dan Quayle over the allegation that an inmate in a federal prison was placed in solitary confinement when he claimed to have sold marijuana to the young Dan Quayle. (See Mark Singer, "Quaylegate," *New York Times*, October 16, 1992, p. A19.)

next chapter), a very interesting question is why the relevant academic disciplines such as political science, public administration, economics, and public policy research have largely neglected a systematic examination of the subject, let alone proposed effective remedies.

Nobody has disputed Harold Lasswell's definition of politics as the art of who gets what, when, and how.[20] Surely by most any standard, corruption could comfortably snuggle into that definition. So it is somewhat surprising that political science, while developing a sizable literature on political corruption, has hardly made it a central topic of investigation. Writing in the discipline's touchstone publication, the *American Political Science Review*, Tevfik Nas and his co-authors concede, "Despite its frequent occurrence, governmental corruption has undergone surprisingly little systematic investigation."[21] Indeed, political scientists John Peters and Susan Welch inquire with some irony in the subtitle of their article, "If Political Corruption Is in the Mainstream of American Politics, Why Is It Not in the Mainstream of American Politics Research?"[22] After considerable struggle with the very definition of the word corruption (as we shall see in the next chapter), the existing literature falls almost entirely into the categories of political history, political theory, and political reform.

Political history, which provides a rich vein of anecdotes and personal biographies we can mine as our evidential base, offers little in the way of systematic observations or a theory of corruption.[23] Political theory, while much more systematic, addresses the problem of corruption on a philosophical plane that is of little relevance for present purposes. In its desire to be universal, political theory surrenders much in the way of precision that would be necessary to examine the American political scene or develop policies to reduce the incidents of corruption. For instance, in his review of corruption in the western democracies since the Greek city-states, J. Patrick Dobel ultimately concludes:

> Finally, it is absolutely necessary that severe limits be placed upon great accumulations of wealth and hereditary privilege. The entire dialectic of injustice and corruption begins with such inequality. A healthy polity must prevent any effective derogation of its power to private governments and destroy any factions which gain enough power to consistently subvert the law. [24]

True, perhaps, but not very useful for a nation whose politics has traditionally been defined by pluralism, that is, the interplay of political interest groups; whose economy has been characterized by aspirations to (and the occasional achievement of) large personal fortunes; and whose citizenry has rejected even the whiff of such a draconian redistribution of wealth and privilege.

Political reform, while intuitively germane to our tasks here, more often than not views corruption as an outlying, degenerate phenomenon, the result of a few greedy miscreants whose apprehension and possible conviction would cure the problem. Some have characterized this as the "moralist" brand of corruption, which, like any morality play, has an easily identified culprit and, with exorcism, a remedy. Unfortunately, as is the case with most ready remedies, things are rarely (if ever) that simple. For instance, do PACs financially corrupt or support political movements? Moreover, and more disheartening, the solution has been demonstrated to be futile. Corruption has repeatedly reoccurred, despite the many reforms initiated and "bad apples" discovered and discarded. Likewise, political reforms of an institutional nature have proven to be ineffective, as we shall discuss below.

Public administration, almost in its founding tenets, has been dedicated to the establishment and maintenance of "good government," seemingly an insistent invitation to study corruption. Excluding the infrequent nominal nod that almost proves the rule, this invitation has largely been rejected. Gerald and Naomi Caiden, writing shortly after the fever of Watergate, observed that, "The increased visibility of administrative corruption has become a persistent and disturbing feature of our times. Almost every issue of the daily press brings, it seems, fresh examples of allegedly corrupt behavior on the part of responsible public and private figures."[25] However, just two years later, Naomi Caiden was moved to comment that "not long ago, corruption was marked *terra incognita* on the map of pubic administration."[26] The Caidens' observations are equally valid today. James Fesler and Donald Kettl's splendid public administration text has only a few pages devoted to a discussion of corruption, while John Rohr's *Ethics for Bureaucrats* has none.[27] Thus, public administration scholars have been even more remiss in this regard than their political science colleagues, a neglect Simcha Werner suggests is "due primarily to the axiomatic belief of earlier scholars that American public administration was inherently moral."[28]

The public administration literature is quick to point an incriminating finger abroad, to cite illustrations of pervasive political corruption in developing nations. In fact, some authors have suggested that corruption provides invaluable recruitment incentives and workaday perquisites during the tenuous days of a nation's political development.[29] In their view, the availability of personal gain via public corruption recruits skilled personnel into an otherwise unattractive, unrewarding bureaucracy, motivates an otherwise lackadaisical administrative system into the timely actions necessary for economic development, and provides socializing services to otherwise disenfranchised parts of the political system. The last function easily describes how the great corrupt urban American political machines, such as Tammany Hall in New York City and Mayor John "Honey Fitz" Fitzgerald's machine in Boston, assisted in politically assimilating waves of European immigrants into the American polity during the early part of the twentieth century. These arguments give rise to what has been termed the "functional" school of corruption.

Taken at face value, the functional interpretation has a certain plausibility and appeal, claiming that corrupt administration is only a product of hard times and great stress. But, inherent in this interpretation, functionalism also implies that as a nation progresses through something called the political maturation process, it will somehow naturally shed itself of these corrupt practices, somewhat akin to naughty children becoming responsible adults. Again, unfortunately, the historical record has conclusively demonstrated that this is far from the case. Not only is it difficult to decide exactly what political maturity is—let alone when it is reached—but the presence of corruption in all the advanced industrialized nations, whatever their form of government, belies this conclusion.[30] Robert Klitgaard's valuable study of corruption in contemporary Hong Kong, Singapore, and South Korea, modern industrialized Third World nations by most any economic standard, underlines this point.[31] Similarly, corruption in contemporary India is said to be so pervasive that it is "choking" the nation's growth; it is so widespread that "liaison agents" or corruption brokers are emerging to facilitate the transactions![32] More to the point for our purposes, if the functional interpretation were applicable to the United States, the record of twentieth-century or even post–World War II corruptions would render it false.

When public administration chooses to redress corruption in the

United States, its recommendations are largely based on the morality model and therefore can be seen as naively optimistic and ineffectual: a new regulation or inspector general here, a revised code of conduct there, or an Ethics in Government Act would seemingly return the offending agency to its proper administrative disposition and direction. Many have advocated an ethics component to professional training curricula, trusting that "learning" about values and ethics would inoculate the bureaucrat against the corruption virus and thus eliminate unethical or corrupt behavior.[33] These and similar propositions have not had their desired effect—as the number of scandals mentioned above and discussed in Part II give all too immediate testament—nor is there any particular reason to think a priori that they should.

It is a persuasive commentary on the chariness of political scientists and public administrators toward the systematic study of corruption that the single book which most rigorously analyzes political corruption is written by an economist, Susan Rose-Ackerman. Rose-Ackerman sets the rationale for her work with admirable directness: "Whatever else is problematic, societies obviously do not use a single, consistent method to make allocative decisions." Corruption is only one albeit unsanctioned method among many. Based upon the presence of market forces (i.e., economic competition) and, in the economist's jargon, the desire "for corrupt officials to capture all the [economic] surplus generated by the program," Rose-Ackerman scrutinizes the susceptibility of a number of political arrangements composed of different types and combinations of legislatures, interest groups, and bureaucracies.[34] She also examines the conventional solutions for each set of situations, generally demonstrating their fallibility on economic grounds. And, admittedly, there is a certain elegance and detachment to discussing an "optimal amount of corruption" in terms of "marginal social cost."[35]

Other economists have examined corruption using the concepts of "moral hazard" and "principal agents." The first refers to the risk an insurance company takes; its policyholders have little or no incentive to minimize—indeed, they often exaggerate—their reported losses to the insurance company.[36] Principal agents analysis examines the relationship between supervisor and worker (i.e., agent) and how the former can provide sufficient incentives or create inducements (both usually couched in monetary terms) so that the latter will carry out the former's orders with some known degree of fidelity.[37] Both moral hazard and principal agents research concentrate on how management can assure that its mandates are faithfully executed, and thereby could be applied to the obverse, that is, corruption. Economists have brought a wealth of game-theoretic insights to these studies, but because these models are admittedly incapable of capturing the complex political and organizational features of human interactions,[38] Rose-Ackerman's book is almost a singular example of economics treating political corruption.

It is at first blush surprising that economics—a discipline whose hallmark is the allocation of scarce resources without the burden of societal norms—would have devoted so little inspection to this very obvious form of resource reallocation. After all, noted Naomi Caiden, "Corruption is a variant of economic choice, and like any other economic choice is determined by its price in the market." The reason, however, is forceful, largely due to the economist's characteristic unit of analysis, the famous economic, profit-maximizing individuals—that is, "rational beings, capable of assessing their interests according to costs and benefits" defined in purely monetary terms.[39] In the examination of governmental corruption, there are numerous examples of alternative, noneconomic (i.e., political, institutional, and social) forces that have led to or resulted in public sector corruption. These discrepancies in the economic perspective of corruption indicate that there are corruption motives beyond the economic, thereby limiting the applicability and explanatory power of the discipline.

Thus, a strictly economic view of corruption would prove incomplete, hence inadequate because of its focus on corruption "within a model of rational individual choice, with little concentration on the overall impact on society."[40] Again, in the economist's jargon, the "utility" of an economic analysis of corruption cannot be overlooked, but it is only effective "at the margin." Rose-Ackerman ends her book with the open confession that personal and political values undermine the analytic insights into corruption that her discipline has provided, most seriously in terms of what to do to minimize it:

> An effort to use economists' methods to synthesize political scientists' concerns ultimately forces us to recognize the limitations of the economists' approach itself. While information and competition may often reduce corrupt incentives, they cannot completely substitute for the personal integrity of political actors. [41]

These disciplines, then, have chosen to recognize political corruption but, for various reasons, not make the phenomenon a central part of their disciplinary attentions. However, the most interesting question of neglect is why public policy scholars have almost to a person ignored the subject, in terms of its substance and—more tellingly—its effect. Public policy analysts have been intensively schooled to combine efficiency and normative standards in their analyses, a combination apparently violated by the presence of corruption. If political corruption does exist in, say, social welfare or law enforcement programs and can be shown to have deleterious effect on a specific program or, more generally, the body politic, then it surely must affect the nominal policy process and product. Would public policy formulation, policymaking, or evaluation be the same if the hidden "friction costs" imposed by political bribery or nepotism were nonexistent? Therefore, public sector corruption presents important but as yet unexplored grounds for public policy research.

In short, economics seems unable and political science unwilling to address frontally the questions posed by political corruption and, more critically, what can be done to reduce it and its effects. Surprisingly, perhaps, the law is not much better. After reviewing the legal literature, Daniel Lowenstein concludes that "Whatever may be the sins of omission of the social scientists in this regard, they pale beside those of the legal scholars, who have ignored the subject entirely."[42] Although one might regret these shortcomings, they can be excused (barely) because both disciplines are professionally sequestered in the academy; university standards define their achievements. This forbearance, however lenient, is less available to the public policy scholars whose research must pass the scrutinies of real-world relevance and effective policy recommendations. Can analysts realistically propose policy programs if the programs' implementation must survive a sieve clogged with potential corruption or the analysts' evaluations are tainted by illegal payoffs? While we will draw upon the disciplines discussed above for their insights, it is to this last standard, one of policy relevance, that this study aspires.

Organization

This book is organized into three main parts. The first part sets out the problems presented by a policy-oriented study of public sector corruption and proposes a framework for analytically thinking about corruption. The second part examines a series of five contemporary cases of political corruption on the federal level that will serve to illustrate the framework. That they all occurred during President Reagan's administration was probably not a complete coincidence, but this choice is not meant to indicate that political corruption is an exclusive Republican prerogative, regardless of the Wall Street Journal's charge. The incidents are:

- influence peddling in the Department of Housing and Urban Development (HUD);
- the Wedtech scam;
- weapons system development and procurement irregularities in the Department of Defense;
- the Savings and Loan (S&L) scandal; and
- the Iran–Contra affair.

These histories are not intended to be definitive expositions of these events. In some cases, the accounts are still open on what occurred; in the case of the Iran–Contra affair, we may never completely know who was culpable of what. The history of exactly what happened or the extent of the crimes in others of these cases is still highly contentious, such as influence peddling at HUD and the S&L scandal. But for our purposes, exacting detail is not critical, fortunately, for each of these incidents would require a book-length manuscript; indeed, the S&L and Wedtech affairs already are covered by a shelf-full of books and I suspect that Iran–Contra will not lag far behind. Rather, these chapters will simply acquaint the reader with the main features of these cases so that they may be used to illustrate and conceptualize corruption.

The third and final part of the book examines how these corrupt activities can be better explained by the proposed framework. However, we should realize at the outset that there is only so much light these explanations can shed before running smack into the barrier of human nature, a condition notably immune to public policy. As long as politics is the instrument of human beings, we cannot hope to eliminate completely corruption, just as we cannot hope to eliminate all manifestations of human greed. In some intractable way, the two are intimately linked. Why, for instance, would President Richard Nixon, a man at the pinnacle of his dreams, finagle his income tax returns? Or why would Drexel Burnham Lambert's Michael Milken violate Security and Exchange Commission regulations in 1988 when he was already making hundreds of millions of dollars?^c Still, I will propose that within these limitations, there are a number of specific recommendations that could reduce the incidents of governmental corruption.

Before putting the horse of conclusions before the cart of examples, we need to turn to a series of questions, such as What is corruption? Is it as bad as its reputation would have us believe? and Is it sufficiently prevalent to warrant our attentions? If we can answer these last two questions in the affirmative, then I will propose a perspective for realistically thinking about corruption and its possible remedies. It is to these tasks that we shall now turn.

---

^cFor the accountants among us, if we assume Milken's $550 million compensation in 1988 is accurate, that works out to over $1.5 million per day, $62,785 per hour (waking or sleeping), and over $1,000 per minute. Arguably, this is rich beyond the dreams of Croesus and represents actions greed per se cannot excuse or explain.

Notes

1. Many of these are briefly described in George C.S. Benson et al., *Political Corruption in America* (Lexington, MA: D.C. Heath, 1978); and Abraham S. Eisenstadt et al., *Before Watergate: Problems of Corruption in American Society* (New York: Brooklyn College Press, 1978).

2. Andy Logan, "Around City Hall: A Fine Mess," *New Yorker*, Vol. 62, No. 46, January 5, 1987, pp. 74–82.

3. Leonard Buder, "33 Held in Thefts of Parking Coins," *New York Times*, October 16, 1987, p. A12.

4. Philip Shenon, "Enemy Within: Drug Money Is Corrupting the Enforcers," *New York Times*, April 11, 1988, pp. A1, A8. For a more generalized recent discussion, see John Dombrink, "The Touchables: Vice and Police Corruption in the 1980's," *Law and Contemporary Society*, Vol. 51, No. 1 (Winter 1988), pp. 201–232.

5. Arizona State Senator Carolyn Walker was videotaped saying, "I like the good life, and I'm trying to position myself so that I can live the good life and have more money." Quoted in Seth Mydans, "Civics 101 on Tape in Arizona, or, 'We All Have Our Prices,' " *New York Times*, February 10, 1991, pp. A1, A10, at A10.

6. Stephen Labaton, "U.S. to Sue Governor of Arizona," *New York Times*, December 16, 1991, p. C1.

7. James W. Fesler and Donald F. Kettl, *The Politics of the Administrative Process* (Chatham, NJ: Chatham House, 1991), pp. 332–333.

8. Anonymous, "Morality among the Supply-Siders," *Time*, July 25, 1987, p. 18.

9. Gerld F. Seib, "GOP's Legacy: From Grant to Reagan, Scandals Seem to Hit Republican Presidents," *Wall Street Journal*, July 16, 1987, p. 1.

10. Walter Shapiro, "What's Wrong?" *Time*, May 22, 1987, p. 14.

11. Anonymous, "70 Percent in Poll Believe Bribery is Common," *Rocky Mountain News*, May 22, 1987, p. 14. Similar responses were reported by Michael Johnston, "Right and Wrong in American Politics: Popular Conceptions of Corruption," *Polity*, Vol. 18, No. 3 (July 1986), pp. 367–391.

12. This is the thesis of Suzanne Garment, *Scandal: The Culture of Mistrust in American Politics* (New York: Random House, 1991).

13. Johnston, "Right and Wrong in American Politics," p. 388; emphasis in original.

14. For some possible insights, see Lester A. Sobel, ed., *Corruption in Business* (New York: Facts on File, 1977).

15. The intellectual model, of course, is James Q. Wilson, *Thinking about Crime* (New York: Basic Books, 1983); in particular, see his Introduction in which he carefully sets aside entire classes of crime he will not examine, including police and judicial corruption.

16. James Q. Wilson, "Corruption: The Shame of the States," *Public Interest*, No. 2 (1966), pp. 28–38.

17. For a recent account, see Carol Matlack et al., "Special Report: The Money Chase," especially "PACs Bearing Many Gifts," *National Journal*, Vol. 22, No. 24 (June 16, 1990), pp. 1448–1485.

18. This is the major theme of Larry Berg, Harlan Hahn, and John R. Schmidhauser, *Corruption in the American Political System* (Morristown, NJ: General Learning Press, 1976).

19. Michael Johnston, *Political Corruption and Public Policy in America* (Monterey, CA: Cole, 1982), elaborates on the difficulties inherent in reforming campaign financing.

20. Harold D. Lasswell, *Politics: Who Gets What, When, and How* (New York: Meridan, 1958; originally published in 1938).

21. Tevfik F. Nas, Albert C. Price, and Charles T. Weber, "A Policy-Oriented Theory of Corruption," *American Political Science Review*, Vol. 80, No. 1 (March 1986), p. 107. Kenneth J. Meier and Thomas M. Holbrook, " 'I Seen My Opportunities and I Took 'Em': Political Corruption in the American States," *Journal of Politics*, Vol. 54, No. 1 (February 1992), pp. 135–155, characterize "systematic empirical research on political corruption" as "not extensive" (at p. 135).

22. John G. Peters and Susan Welch, "Political Corruption: A Search for Definitions and a Theory," *American Political Science Review*, Vol. 72, No. 3 (September 1978), pp. 974–984.

23. See Benson et al., *Political Corruption in America*, and Berg et al., *Corruption in the American Political System*. Robert A. Caro is perhaps the preeminent biographer of political corruption; e.g., *The Power Broker: Robert Moses and the Fall of New York* (New York: Knopf, 1974).

24. J. Patrick Dobel, "The Corruption of a State," *American Political Science Review*, Vol. 72, No. 3 (September 1978), p. 972.

25. Gerald E. Caiden and Naomi J. Caiden, "Administrative Corruption," *Public Administration Review*, Vol. 37, No. 3 (May/June 1977), p. 301.

26. Naomi Caiden, "Shortchanging the Public," *Public Administration Review*, Vol. 39, No. 3 (May/June 1979), p. 294.

27. Fesler and Kettl, *The Politics of the Administrative Process*; and John A. Rohr, *Ethics for Bureaucrats* (New York: Marcel Dekker, 1989 ed.).

28. Simcha B. Werner, "New Directions in the Study of Administrative Corruption," *Public Administration Review*, Vol. 43, No. 2 (March/April 1983), pp. 146.

29. See Fred W. Riggs, *Administration in Developing Countries* (Boston: Houghton Mifflin, 1964); also Joseph S. Nye, Jr., "Corruption and Political Development," in Samuel P. Huntington, ed., *Political Order in Changing Societies* (New Haven, CT: Yale University Press, 1968); and Michael Johnston, "The Political Consequences of Corruption," *Comparative Politics*, Vol. 18, No. 3 (July 1986), pp. 459–477.

30. Even relatively stable totalitarian governments have been unable to rid themselves of corruption. However, in combating the current rash of corruption in the People's Republic of China, press organs have turned this theory around; the *People's Daily* wrote in a front-page editorial that "Corruption is an inevitable accompaniment of social progress." Edward A. Gargan, "As China's Economy Grows, So Grows Official Corruption," *New York Times*, July 10, 1988, pp. A1, A10. Since corruption even flourished during the days of Mao Zedong's dictatorship, one can question the putative relationship; see Alan P.L. Liu, "The Politics of Corruption in China," *American Political Science Review*, Vol. 77, No. 2 (July 1982), pp. 602–623.

31. Robert Klitgaard, *Controlling Corruption* (Berkeley: University of California Press, 1988).

32. Edward A. Gargan, "Corruption's Many Tentacles Are Choking India's Growth," *New York Times*, November 10, 1992, pp. A1, A4.

33. See Rohr, *Ethics for Bureaucrats*, and Rosemarie Tang, *Ethics for Policy Analysis* (Englewood Cliffs, NJ: Prentice Hall, 1986). A refreshing collection of empirical studies of corruption done by public administration scholars is H. George Frederiekson, ed., *Ethics and Public Administration* (Armonk, NY: M.E. Sharpe, 1993).

34. Susan Rose-Ackerman, *Corruption: A Study in Political Economy* (New York: Academic Press, 1978), pp. 1 and 92, respectively.

35. As in Klitgaard, *Controlling Corruption*, p. 26.

36. For a brief discussion, see Lee S. Friedman, *Microeconomics Policy Analysis* (New York: McGraw-Hill, 1984), pp. 225–232.

37. See John W. Pratt and Richard J. Zeckhauser, eds., *Principals and Agents: The Structure of Business* (Boston: Harvard Business School Press, 1985), especially the chapter by Kenneth J. Arrow, "The Economics of Agency," pp. 37–51; also Terry M. Moe, "The New Economics of Organization," *American Journal of Political Science*, Vol. 28, No. 4 (November 1984), pp. 739–777.

38. As neatly summarized by Donald F. Kettl, "The Perils—and Prospects—of Public Administration," *Public Administration Review*, Vol. 50, No. 4 (July/August 1990), pp. 411–420, at 414–415.

39. Both quotations from Naomi Caiden, "Shortchanging the Public," p. 296.

40. Nas et al., "A Policy-Oriented Theory of Economics," p. 108.

41. Rose-Ackerman, *Corruption*, p. 216.

42. Daniel H. Lowenstein, "Political Bribery and the Intermediate Theory of Politics," *UCLA Law Review*, Vol. 34, No. 4 (1985), p. 785.

2

A MODEL OF CORRUPTION

The purpose of this chapter is threefold: to derive an acceptable definition of corruption, to assess the significance of corruption, and to stipulate a framework useful for thinking about corruption.

First, we need to determine what corruption is before we can outline a way to consider such actions. Although everybody seems to "know" what a corrupt act is in a specific incident and context, this knowledge is widely debated when described in a more generalized context, somewhat akin to U.S. Supreme Court Justice Potter Stewart's widely quoted definition of obscenity: "I don't know what obscenity is but I know it when I see it." Still, an operational definition is critical if we are to agree on what constitutes corruption. Briefly, then, what precisely is a corrupt act in both a generalized and a specified venue? The answer, perhaps surprisingly, is far from straightforward. For instance, at what level does a victimless indiscretion, an easy favor, or the appointment of a family member to an official position become corrupt acts?

Second, before posing a model of corruption, we should pause and ask if such an exercise warrants our attention. Again, the answer to this question is hardly a foregone conclusion, and depends primarily on what type of corruption might be transpiring. In James Q. Wilson's calculation, there is corruption and then there is corruption: "I am rather tolerant of some forms of civic corruption ... but I am rather intolerant of those forms of corruption that debase the law-enforcement process, discredit its agents, or lead people to believe that equal justice is available only for a price."[1] Similarly, Theodore Lowi distinguishes between Big Corruption ("corruption that contributes to the decomposition, dissolution, or disorientation of the constitution") and Little Corruption ("that reflects or contributes to individual moral depravity"), concluding that the latter is "widely, though needlessly, feared." [2] We might refer in common parlance to Little Corruption as scandal.

From our short review of various disciplinary perspectives, we can appreciate why many scholars would look upon corruption as simply another unavoidable but relatively minor cost of doing business, as necessary albeit unpleasant as fire insurance; others declare corruption to be an integral, functional activity of government. If either of these views is substantiated, then there is little reason to continue the discussion, because, on one hand, corruption is an inalienable yet insignificant part of the economics of government, or, on the other, necessary for the very mechanics of government. In short, either it cannot or should not be a candidate for possible reduction and reform. Thus, corruption should evoke little more than a shrug of the shoulders, an "oh well" perspective, and therefore should be scant cause for alarm, examination, or reform.

By much the same argument, if we find that corruption extracts such a relatively small price from the body politic and is as difficult and expensive to exorcise as American history would convincingly demonstrate—that is, if the costs of tolerating corruption were perceived as less than the benefits of eradicating it—then best leave it be. The remedy game would simply not be worth the criminal candle, hence rendering a similar conclusion.

If we can successfully define corruption and demonstrate that it represents a public policy problem worthy of our consideration, we can then turn to the third issue of this chapter, a generalized examination of what factors contribute to corruption. As we will see, these go well beyond the commonly held attributes of personal greed and consider institutional and systemic forces that tolerate, condone, and in some cases, actually encourage corrupt activities.

What Is Corruption?

Surely one of the most formidable obstacles to the study of corruption is the question of exactly what is meant by "corruption." Not unexpectedly, the answer varies principally as a function of the inquiring discipline.

Whatever problem economists might have in explaining corruption is indicated by Susan Rose-Ackerman's definition of corruption as an "allocative mechanism" for scarce resources. When this allocation is somehow shared between a

> market system in which wide inequalities of income are taken for granted, [and a] democratic political system that grants a formal equality to each citizen's vote . . . [P]olitical decisions that are made on the basis of majority preferences may be undermined by wide use of an illegal market as the method for allocation. . . . [C]orrupt incentives are the nearly inevitable consequence of *all* government attempts to control market forces—even the "minimal" state.[3]

Based on two cornerstones of the American political system—the free market and government intervention to protect citizens from market failures—this definition surrenders little in terms of political, institutional, and normative insights or, more seriously, solutions. Rose-Ackerman realizes this shortcoming when she ends her book with the open admission that the personal and political values involved limit the applicability of economists' approach, especially regarding correctives, since economics "cannot substitute for the personal integrity of political actors." [4]

Still, we can appreciate two components of the economic definition. First, Rose-Ackerman emphasizes the systemic nature of the problem, if not her solution. Corruption resides, we can infer, in the interface of the American political-economic system, particularly with what she characterizes as the invariably obscure dividing line between market and nonmarket (i.e., government) allocation schemes, and the inherently disputatious nature of the boundary between the two. The potential for confusion (deliberate or innocent) is enhanced because in some instances the public and private sectors are governed by different sets of rules and expectations. This ambiguity creates the susceptible condition or opportunity for corruption to occur. Second, corruption is endemic as long as there are scarce resources juxtaposed against allocation mechanisms that are vulnerable to the vagaries of political manipulation (or, more benignly, choice). In the economist's hypothesized world of perfect free market competition, these opportunities and vulnerabilities would not exist or, if they somehow did, would be included in the visible transaction costs. But this economist's idealized dream world does not exist, so corruption does.

Political scientists seem to reside at the other end of the definitional stick, with an abundance of definitions. As one might expect amid this opulence, there seems to be little agreement; as John Peters and Susan Welch point out in their review of the political science literature examining corruption, "it becomes immediately apparent that no matter what aspect of American politics is examined, the systematic study of corruption is hampered by the lack of an adequate definition."[5] James Scott demonstrates the confusion by suggesting that there are three bases for defining corruption: legality, public interest, and public opinion.[6] However, as Scott admits and Michael Johnston later details, there are almost as many problems with each of these as there are implied solutions.[7] Legality would seemingly be the key component, but that would imply that only illegal acts are corrupt, an implication we will later see to be shortsighted. Public interest would be central to the issue, but it would force the particular researchers or constabulary to be the protectors of whatever they define as the public weal or standards, a notoriously slippery and often self-serving assignment—witness Richard Nixon's invocation of national security as his exculpatory rationale for Watergate.[a] And public opinion is even more mercurial and unpredictable, to which the 1990 televised congressional hearings on the Iran–Contra controversy provide vivid testimony.

In an attempt to slice through the Gordian knot of complexity, Benson and his co-authors propose a definition of corruption that is general to a fault: "all illegal or unethical use of governmental authority as a result of considerations of personal or political gain."[8] The problem here is just as profound: corruption, by its very nature, is a creature of values and mores, personal and institutional, so a definition predicated on personal ethics and/or political gain is acutely idiosyncratic, a function of who is viewing the questionable activity. Hence, consensus is well-nigh unattainable for any but the most blatant examples.

Finally, in their admitted search for a Rosetta Stone, Peters and Welch

> analyze potentially corrupt acts according to the component elements apparently involved with every political act or exchange. We believe this process can meaningfully be partitioned into the "public official" involved, the actual "favor" provided by the public official, the "payoff" gained by the public official, and the "donor" of the payoff and/or "recipient" of the "favor" act.[9]

---

[a] Or Samuel Johnson's reported definition of patriotism as "the last refuge of a scoundrel."

This definition has the advantage of identifying a number of actors and relationships that must be present in virtually any political exchange; depending on what officials, favors, payoffs, and donors are involved, the action may or may not be considered corrupt. This correctly implies that corruption is an interactive relationship (there is no corruption in isolation), and one that should be judged by a matter of degrees. Unfortunately, this otherwise helpful typology does little to define what some of these terms mean, fails to address the issue of openness or visibility, and largely leaves those worrisome tasks to the parties involved or to quicksilver public interest, a dubious proposition at best.

The obvious (but not very helpful) solution to the babble of definitions is put forth by Arnold Heidenheimer when he colors corruption as either "black" ("which a majority consensus of both elite and mass opinion would condemn and would want to see punished on grounds of principle"), "white" (in which "the majority of both elite and mass opinion probably would not vigorously support an attempt to punish a form of corruption that they regard as tolerable"), or, inevitably, "gray" (which "indicates that some elements, usually elites, may want to see the action punished, others not, and the majority may well be ambiguous").[10] As one might expect, the majority of corruption cases falls into the gray category of disagreement, thereby vitiating the usefulness of Heidenheimer's distinctions, except, once again, in the most transparent of cases. Johnston summarizes the definitional dilemma of his disciplinary kin:

> we should not expect to find a sharp distinction between corruption and noncorrupt actions. Instead, we will find fine gradations of judgment, reflecting a variety of equivocations, mitigating circumstances, and attributed motives.[11]

Or, to borrow from Lowi's admirably succinct manner, "Big C is often justifiable."[12]

To progress any further in our thinking about corruption, we need to leave behind these lexical knots that place a priority on comprehensiveness rather than clarity and, especially, utility. Therefore, let us agree with Naomi Caiden when she observes that "the agonizing over definitions which marked much of the earlier literature has been replaced by broad agreement, which focuses on the illicit use of influence in public decisions. . . . In other words, everybody knows what corruption is, and heart-searching over marginal cases is not worth-while."[13] I am perfectly content to begin with Joseph Nye's (unfortunately jargon-laden) definition, which has proved after almost twenty-five years to be the consensual definition, the one most cited in the political science corruption literature:

> Corruption is behavior which deviates from the normal duties of a public role because of private-regarding (family, close private clique), pecuniary or status gains, or violates rules against the exercise of certain types of private-regarding influence. This includes such behavior as bribery (use of reward to pervert the judgment of a person in a position of trust); nepotism (bestowal of patronage by reasons of ascriptive relationship rather than merit); and misappropriation (illegal appropriation of public resources for private-regarding use).[14]

For purposes of public policy applications, Nye's definition needs to be amended in order to incorporate the abuse of power by authorized individuals for political or social gains into our definition of corruption. These desiderata are in addition to Nye's reliance on "private-regarding"—in other words, largely economic or strictly personal—gains. Drawing upon Arnold Rogow and Harold Lasswell, we can propose that

> A corrupt act violates responsibility toward at least one system of public or civic order and is in fact incompatible with (destructive of) any such system. A system of public or civic order exalts common interest over special interest; violations of the common interest for special advantage are corrupt.[15]

Rogow and Lasswell indicate that corruption can occur without any financial incentive or gain, and that abuse of power for status or political purposes—what Mark Lilla might consider ideological gains[16]—or to subvert accepted political processes and norms is just as corrupt as offering unmarked bills in plain brown envelopes to Maryland State governors.[b] Whatever the excesses of Lieutenant Colonel Oliver North and Rear Admiral John Poindexter during the Iran–Contra affair, their actions were certainly directed to political advantages for the Reagan

---

[b] Spiro Agnew, vice president under Richard Nixon, was able to continue and elevate this venerable tradition of Maryland politics up to the Office of the Vice President of the United States.

administration rather than personal financial gains (excepting a personal security system for North). Indeed, Lowi would argue that this critical amendment addresses Big C, which is much more pernicious than "private-regarding" or Little C, because "Every act of Big Corruption puts the state itself at risk."[17]

Finally, we need to recognize that the level of corruption deserving our attention is an action involving at least two participants. For Lowi's Little C (what we have termed scandal), there is no reason why more than one or two people would be involved in such acts as embezzlement, tax evasions, or special privileges of office. However, for Big C, many participants must be cooperatively involved, if not in the act itself, then in the necessary conspiracies of silence. Bribery, after all, is a crime in which both parties benefit; there is no "victim" in the traditional sense. Thus, political corruption (as opposed to political scandal) requires a certain amount of deliberate, coordinated action among the participants in order to share the benefits and subsequently to hide the activity from regulators, the press, or the parties being disenfranchised.

Reduced to its quintessential meaning, *political corruption is a cooperative form of unsanctioned, usually condemned policy influence for some type of significant personal gain, in which the currency could be economic, social, political, or ideological remuneration.*

Corruption as Part of the Political System

The central assumption of this argument, one I shall attempt to validate during the course of this book, is that political corruption is an ingrained, systemic part of the American political processes. This suggests that political corruptions are much more than episodic, anecdotal events and that "the study of corruption must take broader social and political settings into account."[18] The occasional exposés should not be viewed nor treated as aberrant, unexpected occurrences, but rather as manifestations of an underlying, perhaps self-perpetuating phenomenon. In short, corruption reflects an ongoing, functioning part of the political system. As James Scott observes in his analysis of corruption across a number of different governments:

> The perspective of this book is that corruption, like violence, must be understood as a regular, repetitive, integral part of the operation of most political systems. . . . Recurring acts of violence and corruption are thus

> more successfully analyzed as normal channels of political activity than as cases of deviant pathology requiring incarceration and/or moral instructions for the perpetrator(s). . . .

And

> Far from being pathological, patterns of corruption . . . may actually represent channels of political demands without which formal societal arrangements could scarcely survive. . . . Corruption . . . may [thus] be seen as an informal political system.[19]

Johnston concurs:

> corruption grows out of much more fundamental forces and tensions in the political system than individual behavior, structural deficiencies, or insufficient ethical training.[20]

It should be little surprise, then, that public administration, with its traditional emphasis on the rectitude of the individual administrator and, more recently, bureaucratic structures, has been especially incapable of alleviating administrative corruption. Or that economic analysis, based largely on the principle of individual income maximization, has been similarly ineffective. Or that political scientists, academically concerned with politics as the art of the possible, would choose to leave corruption relatively untouched as long as it could be presented as merely another vector and property of governance.

The general idea that corruption is endemic in the American political system springs primarily from the functional school of corruption, that is, the idea that corruption serves some needed function in a system of government. Therefore, it could be understood as providing social and political benefits to some, either directly (e.g., those "purchasing" a valuable building permit) or indirectly (construction workers employed as a result of the expedited building permit). The idea, partially in reaction to the moralist notion that corrupt acts were due to corrupt people, is commonly credited to the great sociologist Robert Merton with his examination of the American urban political machines.[21] Simcha Werner later observed that "The functionalists came to regard corruption as an inherent aspect of the normal growth–decay life cycle, and challenged the moralist school which deemed corruption to be ultimately pathological and, therefore, destructive."[22]

Merton held that corruption, if viewed from a morally neutral perspective (what he calls "moral innocence")—much as economist Thomas Schelling displays a rather agnostic approach toward the nature of organized crime[23]—could be seen as fulfilling a necessary although "latent societal function." Economists would analogously describe this situation in value-neutral terms such as corruption being a "monopoly rent seeking" behavior, that is, "supply" (response) to a demonstrated "market demand," which would, naturally, "capture" "excess rents."[c] Merton, using a generic corrupt political machine to illustrate his thesis, explains the difficulty in proposing the functional position as well as its alluring persuasiveness:

> Since moral evaluations in a society tend to be largely in terms of the manifest consequences of a practice or code, we should be prepared to find that analysis in terms of latent functions at times runs counter to prevailing moral evaluations. . . . Proceeding from the functional view, therefore, that we should *ordinarily* (not invariably) expect persistent social patterns and social structures [involving political corruption] to perform positive functions *which are at the time not adequately fulfilled by other existing patterns and structures*, the thought occurs that perhaps this publicly maligned organization is, *under present conditions*, satisfying basic latent functions.[24]

The central contribution of Merton's argument is that there may well be a number of desired government functions, typically short-term and self-serving in nature, that are not sufficiently well attended to by authorized, legitimate offices and procedures. In these cases, Merton concludes that *"the functional deficiencies of the official structure generate an alternative (unofficial) structure to fulfill existing needs somewhat more effectively."*[25] If these should fall outside the bounds of generally accepted norms and practices, then they are knowingly sacrificed on the altar of convenience, probably with more *sangfroid* than sorrow.

Couched in public policy terms, this functional interpretation can be

---

[c] In English: "monopoly rent seeking" is when a person has exclusive rights to a specific good or service, which he will "supply" to meet the "demand" for that resource. Because he is the only seller, he can demand (i.e., try to "capture") as much money as the buyer can afford to pay (as opposed to what the buyer would prefer to pay). The difference between "afford" and "prefer" constitutes "excess rents."

translated into what we might call a "bottleneck," or a situation in which the delivery of government goods and services is obstructed by mandated rules and regulations. These rules have commonly (and pejoratively) become known as "red tape." Herbert Kaufman's Cassandrian description of red tape in 1977—"The sheer mass of binding official promulgations and interventions in the marketplace begins to become oppressive" [26]—would seem even more applicable and pressing today in light of the increasing role of government. Attempts to bypass institutional bottlenecks would be cause for functional corruption. How can a beleaguered private sector contractor obtain a rapid transfusion of public sector business if the necessary government approvals require numerous time-consuming reviews? The answer by now is depressingly apparent.

It makes little difference that citizens themselves are ultimately the source of red tape, or that red tape manifests a consensual social value for equal access and due process. The only condition that appears to matter to some people seeking government funding or services is that rules and regulations exist, that they impede what some actors deem essential transactions, and that they need to be circumvented. Corruption, in this sense, clearly indicates a preference for efficiency over equity as the pivotal societal and political values.

Michael Johnston has most cleanly articulated the condition under which functional corruption will (N.B., not "can") occur:

> 1. The fruits of government action are often extremely valuable (or, in the case of penalties and sanction, extremely costly), with demand for benefits frequently exceeding supply.
> 2. These benefits and sanctions often can be gotten or avoided only by dealing with government.
> 3. The routine process through which benefits and sanctions are conferred is time-consuming, expensive, and uncertain in its outcome.[27]

Given the ubiquity of these conditions, Johnston and others logically conclude that

> Corruption is an informal kind of political influence that can break through this bottleneck. . . . It can speed things along, make favorable outcomes much more likely, and cost less than legitimate forms of influence. . . . The basic pressures and tensions that make corruption so advantageous and tempting are products not of the kinds of people to

whom we entrust public power, nor necessarily of flawed institutions, but rather of government's basic relationship to society.[28]

The pressures for companies dealing with the government to succeed, even to survive, can generally be seen as leading to various types of informal, often illegal, means of political power, designed to provide more assured access (and favorable outcome) to otherwise difficult-to-obtain (illegal?) goods and services. In this sense, the Philippine expression *lagay* ("speed money") or the Indian phrase *khilana para* ("feed him")—both meaning corruption—ring true: money or some other means of influence (e.g., free use of a yacht, blackmail, or a cushy job for a relative) is used to expedite an otherwise lethargic regulatory or political decision (or alter a negative decision) to particularly preferred ends.

In many instances, circumventing a governmental bottleneck, even when the stakes are great, is seemingly as innocent as it is understandable. If, for instance, a new business is told that the telephone company will need six months to install a telephone connection, the proprietor might readily decide to bribe a telephone company employee rather than endanger the fledgling business. (In some cases, an analogous form of "bribery" is sanctioned; one can secure faster service in obtaining a U.S. passport or mail delivery if additional fees are paid.) The argument can likewise be extended to liquor licenses, building permits, health inspections, and other government-controlled permits. Less hypothetically but probably more problematic, as we shall see, worried executives of the Wedtech corporation bribed government officials to obtain much-needed procurement contracts; HUD contractors used expensive consultants to overcome the HUD bureaucracy and what public housing contractors considered to be its snail's-pace operating procedures. The latter examples are more nettlesome not simply because they were on a larger scale of bribery (there was more money exchanged) but because they came closer to Wilson's warning of debasing the carefully constructed processes and the authority of the agencies involved, not so ultimately reflecting adversely on the government's very integrity.

Corruption as speed money is not just a one-way channel, exclusively directed from private vendors to public officials under the ruse of enhanced efficiency. It can also flow in the opposite direction and, in rare instances, between government agencies. One motivation behind the highly secret operations of the Iran–Contra affair was the insistent attempt by Lieutenant Colonel North and his odd company of accomplices to circumvent their own government's checks (e.g., congressional legislation as well as State and Defense Departments' oversights) against supplying military aid to the administration-favored Nicaraguan rebels. And an appointed official in the Department of the Navy has pleaded guilty to leaking weapons system development information to potential defense contractors as a means of expediting what seemed to them to be an unwieldy and cumbersome (read: bureaucratic) procurement contracting processes. There are, in such incidents, explanations (however tenuous) for various parts of the government repudiating and short-circuiting governmental regulations in order to "get the job done." In the latter case, Department of the Navy officials were apparently trying to shorten the time necessary to move a weapons system development contract from initial concept to operation, all in the good name of improved national defense.

However, if government officials are prepared to disregard their own codes (procedural and ethical), if a marine lieutenant colonel and a navy rear admiral are willing to set aside their oaths as officers to uphold and defend the U.S. Constitution, then is it scarcely any wonder that corruption can be viewed as just another form of influence within the halls of government? Or be viewed from a functional, morally neutral perspective as simply another part of the political system, somewhat akin to the impersonal economic market forces? Or that an already skeptical public will adopt an even more cynical attitude?

For this reason, I shall explain political corruption as primarily systemic phenomena. This perspective certainly is not intended to absolve the actual perpetrators from responsibility, for after all, it is individuals—not some mechanical, efficiency-maximizing system—that actually engage in corrupt activities. Likewise, institutions can be seen to act in and reinforce a corrupt manner; the big city bosses' political machines come most readily to mind, but Poindexter's National Security Council and HUD Secretary Samuel Pierce's executive office (both under the Reagan administration), as well as President Nixon's White House (and its infamous plumbers) were also corrupt in the execution of a few of their government duties. But, at heart, I shall argue below that for the most part the systemic conditions taken contextually tolerate, at times even encourage, individuals and institutions to seize politically corrupt opportunities toward favored, highly vested ends.[d]

Still, one can legitimately ask, "Possibly all good and true, but so what?" Does political corruption make a whit of difference to the average American citizen, particularly if it can be seen as an integral, indeed a functioning, occasionally benefit-providing part of the American political system? It is to this question that I now turn.

But Is There a Problem?

Although Merton specifically makes the point that a functional view of corruption should not be interpreted as a benediction,[e] his disclaimer has proven difficult for others to dismiss with the necessary amoral aplomb. Hence, we need to join the question directly: Is corruption a problem?

As we have seen, the answer to this question should not be facilely predisposed. Corrupt practices could conceivably enhance governmental processes. This would be particularly true in cases where laws and regulations appear to some to be perverse in the general operations of government and society. Furthermore, some scholars have suggested that certain types of corruption can be considered beneficial in terms of political recruitment, assimilation, and the overall efficient distribution of government goods and services.[29] For the owner of a diner to give a free lunch to a cop on the beat could easily be construed as low-level bribery, but it might just as justifiably be viewed as a form of direct taxation to pay for a retainer, services rendered, or maybe little more than a tip for overtime; similarly, a bribe might be considered a user's fee for overcoming bureaucratic bottlenecks. No harm, no foul.

---

[d] Naturally there are a few human characteristics (e.g., greed and lust) that always manifest themselves in some extreme forms of self-serving activities, regardless of the environment. I will return to this all-too-human condition when I discuss what might be done to reduce political corruption.

[e] Merton explains: "I trust it is superfluous to add that this hypothesis is 'not in support of the political machine.' The question of whether the dysfunctions of the machine outweigh its functions, the question of whether alternative structures are not available that may fulfill its functions without necessarily entailing its social dysfunctions, still remain to be considered at an appropriate point." Robert K. Merton, *Social Theory and Social Structure* (New York: The Free Press, 1968 ed.), p. 126.

To synthesize briefly the functional contention, it has been argued that while political corruption exists, it is either

1. not a problem because corruption is such a trivial sideshow of the American political circus that it hardly warrants attention and correction, or
2. so ingrained in the system that its exorcism would not be worth the expense, even assuming that it could be eliminated.

In each case, the underlying message is that the study (and subsequent correction) of corruption would not be worth the effort. In the first case, if it is no big deal, why bother? In the second case, if there is no solution, there can be no problem, so, again, why bother? Even if we admit the grating contradictions between the two propositions—one camp views the problem as trivial, the other as insurmountable—we need to agree that they hardly justify our ignoring the effects of corruption on the body politic.

The first, or triviality, argument perhaps has some face value in purely financial terms, even though the desired precision—how much?—is problematic in light of the monumental data problems. Nobody has any reliable estimate of the aggregate financial cost of corruption. Even to speculate would be irresponsible in light of the definitional problems and the thousands of governmental units. Payoffs and kickbacks are, by their very nature, hidden exchanges between consenting parties. Unlike more felonious acts (such as robbery or embezzlement), neither party has an incentive to report the crime because both stand to benefit from it. Furthermore, even if one could estimate the amounts (in either incidents or dollars) of the transactions, the costs are ambiguous at best, because it is unclear what the corrupt practices are actually purchasing. While there might be a "market price" (e.g., fifty dollars for an expedited permit, one thousand for union cooperation) for a particular "speed money" transaction, there is little way to determine its true market value—that is, what it is buying priced in terms of opportunity costs—since, after all, one might very well obtain the permit or win union support legitimately anyhow. Likewise, it is uncertain how the price might be affected by the degree of government surveillance and enforcement.

As if this were not enough ambiguity in estimating the relatively straightforward costs of corruption, Benson and his colleagues assert that organized crime's multifaceted profits are a direct function and result of political corruption;[30] therefore, its illicit gains should also be debited to the costs of corruption. Although this is far from a proven indictment, the prospects of assessing these charges are even further beyond the most fanciful accounting. The ledgers of organized crime are notably closed to public audit, so any estimates must be wildly speculative. Nevertheless, we can safely assume that they are immense. Still, the danger of assessing the magnitude of the ill-obtained gains lies in a romantic overestimation of both the extent of organized crime's activities and their profits; surely not all drug sales or prostitution proceeds line *mafioso* wallets.[31]

If we make an absolutely worst case argument and combine the two, the "costs" of corruption writ large might easily run into the tens of billions of dollars, certainly not an insignificant line item in anybody's annual budget. But compared to the trillion dollar plus federal budget and additional state and municipal expenditures totaling close to two trillion, or a gross domestic product of about five trillion, it surely pales in relative significance. Thus, we might agree that the financial costs of corruption are little more than fiscal frictions, the sad but predictable "costs of doing business" that can be as easily tolerated by the public as breakage or spoilage is by the merchant.

While this might be true, a strictly dollar accounting of the costs of corruption is terribly incomplete in assessing its societal effects. The more substantial social and political costs resulting from corruption would be paid in the fragile currency of public confidence accorded its political leaders and the equity of the political process. Public opinion surveys of presidential popularity after Watergate and the Iran–Contra affair[f] indicate just how closely the public's faith in government is tied to the perceptions of its leaders' and institutions' integrity. The immensely popular President Reagan suffered a precipitous decline in his popularity as a direct result of the Iran–Contra affair; only 26 percent of the Americans polled responded that the president was being truthful when he said he had no knowledge of what was going on, even after Admiral Poindexter testified that he never informed the president of the National Security Council's (NSC) actions.[32]

The malaise is more than an impersonal repudiation of distant officials someplace far removed in Washington D.C. Benson quotes from

---

[f]Both of these incidents thankfully mixed political corruption—defined in terms of abuse of power—with political ineptitude.

the *Knapp Commission Report on Police Corruption* in New York City on the immediate vitality of this cause-and-effect relationship:

> But perhaps the most important effect of corruption in the so-called gambling control units is the incredible damage their performance wreaks on public confidence in the law and the police. Youngsters raised in New York ghettos, where gambling abounds, regard the law as a joke when all their lives they have seen police officers coming and going from gambling establishments and taking payments from gamblers. . . . While it is certainly not true that all police officers, or even a majority, get rich on gambling and narcotics graft, the fact that a large number of citizens believe they do has a tremendously damaging effect on police authority.[33]

In a democratic society, these symptoms constitute a witch's brew, a potion for potential disaster. As Edmund Burke cautioned the sheriff of Bristol over 200 years ago, "Among a people generally corrupt, liberty cannot long exist." To violate patently the democratic ethos with corrupt activities produces a serious decline in public support of government, a perilous (albeit inestimable) price to pay. New Yorkers scarcely need the convictions and a suicide emanating from the scandals of the Parking Violations Bureau to rationalize their continued contempt for and disregard of the city's parking and violations;[34] nor does the American voter need the U.S. House of Representatives' lax (nonexistent?) policy on its members' bounced checks to denigrate further an already low opinion of Congress. Nor does the public need to discover that U.S. postal authorities have used their inside information on how the postal system works to manipulate Super Bowl betting contests.[35]

Moreover, perceived corruption can reify, reinforce, and multiply itself. Reports of ethical "lapses" by the Internal Revenue Service will provide ready rationales excusing income tax cheating for people all too willing to latch onto the feeblest illustration that the system is corrupt in order to exercise their own larcenous ways.[36] Those susceptible to corruption will naturally gravitate toward its apparent loci in search of possible spoils, while those repelled by it will locate elsewhere, both geographically and professionally. Nixon White House aide Alexander Butterfield, when asked during his Watergate testimony if idealistic young Americans should seek their futures in Washington, was blunt in his advice: "Stay away." On the attraction side, HUD under secretary, Alfred A. DelliBovi (during the Bush administration) described HUD programs under the Reagan administration as inviting people to steal: "Crooks and thieves flocked to these programs like moths to light."[37] These immigrations and emigrations could thus increase the likelihood of corrupt practices and further undermine the government's ability to operate in a fair and equitable manner, a condition that could ultimately prove debilitating, even lethal, to the body politic.

A corollary to this line of thought is that a certain amount of corruption should be tolerated because it is arguably functional—maybe even beneficial—to the political operations of government and its efficient distribution of services. To summarize this stance, it is seen as a safe release for general frustrations and access that might otherwise be more violently manifested. Although this posture is most often cited in discussions of the emerging nations and their bureaucracies, it is found in much of the contemporary literature on American administrative corruption as a means of informal political influence. This view holds that corrupt activities, such as bribery, expedite the workaday mechanisms of government by reducing the uncertainties of, for instance, personal safety (through an occasional free meal or, more systemically, extorted payoffs to police officers) or the delays inherent in the regulatory process. From this functional perspective, corruption is not viewed as a pernicious circumstance, but rather as just another cost and mode of doing business, a neutral buffer at worst (rather like automobile or theft insurance) and a beneficial one if it permits the affected parties to succeed (or at least operate more efficiently) in their business practices. Robert Klitgaard cogently summarizes this perspective:

> the putative benefits depend upon the assumption that the corruption transgresses a wrong or inefficient economic policy, overcomes limitations in an imperfect political system, or gets around imperfections in organizational rules. In short, *if the prevailing system is bad, then corruption may be good.*[38]

This position has generally been attributed to building contractors or other such crassly motivated entrepreneurs. Nevertheless, it has also surfaced among the highest councils and most well-intentioned personnel of government. The Watergate conspirators, who often showed a certain amount of unfortunate entrepreneurial initiative in their plans and activities, cited national security reasons for their illegal actions and subsequent cover-up. The actions of Reagan administration's NSC during the Iran–Contra imbroglio were certainly meant to avoid congressional involvement or, most dreaded, public exposure. Former National Security adviser Poindexter, in later explaining to the congressional investigating committees his decision to hide the NSC's arms-supplying and money-transferring enterprises from clearly mandated congressional review, was unapologetically candid in his testimony that he considered congressional oversight to be a faulty part of the political system, an unwarranted intrusion. As such, he and North simply moved to "correct" the procedural glitch, hardly an unheard-of moral calculus in which one wrong is used to justify another.

Fundamentally, then, both the Watergate and "Irangate" perpetrators violated legal and expected norms, that is, they were driven to corrupt actions because of what their instigators viewed as potential hindrances upon their particular freedom of action. Expected and established procedures were circumvented or ignored—in other words, corrupt actions were resorted to (and later stoutly defended as necessary)—in order to "grease" the workings of the government and protect the perpetrators from public scrutiny. That these were functional acts should not disguise the fact that they were basically illegal acts, designed to attain personal and institutional gains outside the normal and accepted government practices, and, in doing so, to undermine the very system of government they were nominally protecting; this is Lowi's Big C in action. Reagan's secretary of state George Shultz put Poindexter's actions in perspective during his July 23, 1987, testimony to Congress: "I don't think desirable ends justify the means of lying, deceiving, of doing things outside our Constitutional processes."

The functional argument also encompasses the "victimless crime" issue: prostitution, narcotics, and number games are illegal, yet they flourish and are indeed eagerly sought out by everyday citizens. They are accessible, Benson and his colleagues aver, only because of the corrupt actions (or inaction) of law enforcement agencies. Merton estimates that in 1950 there were more than twice as many prostitutes as physicians. Efforts to eradicate these crimes would violate social norms or personal preferences and would therefore, he argues, be doomed to failure. Prohibition is the historical example most often cited as an illustration of a government regulation virtually unenforced because of popular sentiment against it. The current American hard drug pandemic and its army of illegal users would seemingly fit this mold as billions of dollars in illicit profits from citizens are used to corrupt local law enforcement efforts while federal government reactions are characterized by ideological myopia that covertly compromises stated foreign policy goals.[39] In the latter case, Elaine Sciolino and Stephen Engelberg reported that from Afghanistan to Mexico,

> like its predecessors, the Reagan Administration has repeatedly subordinated the drug issue to other American interests, from support for insurgents fighting leftist regimes to the belief that punishing drug-producing countries might destabilize them.[40]

A corroborating document prepared by a Senate Foreign Relations subcommittee found that the Reagan administration support of the Contra rebels and Panamanian president Manuel Noriega had repeatedly undermined its highly publicized efforts to interdict drug trafficking.[41]

The common, unifying thread to the functional propositions is the allegation that corruption benefits a population well beyond those who actually pocket its immediate profits, producing a populace who therefore blinks at its presence. Not amazingly, there is some evidence that electorates knowingly and willingly chose to support corrupt practices as long as they were seen as, on balance, not harmful. How else can one explain the clear graft and durability of the New York, Chicago, Boston, and Philadelphia political machines? In this view, demonstrated corruption is only one variable in government, a practice whose nominal if uneasy acceptance changes in light of the context.[42] But we also need to recognize that Americans consistently value and vote for equity and the democratic ideals, even if it translates into a loss of efficiency. They tacitly realize, in Rose-Ackerman's words, "the case for corruption often presupposes a strikingly undemocratic standard for government action." [43] And, in point of historical fact, all of these storied machines were voted out of power.

In conclusion, this "beneficial" perspective of corruption—if people want it, it should be and indeed is available—is a difficult one to dispel conclusively but it does appear to be wrongheaded for at least two reasons. In the first place, the resort to kickbacks or other illegal activities to circumvent government bottlenecks or to influence decisions directly undercuts the equity ideals upon which democratic governments are ultimately based. To be sure, a few persons are benefited but a far larger number can be directly harmed. John Gardiner and Theodore Lyman substantiate this point, assessing the costs of corruption in urban development:

> Corruption involves more than a few dollars changing hands between sleazy characters. Corruption is developments where people don't want them or where communities aren't ready for them. It is shoddy construction which must be immediately redone or which becomes rapidly obsolete. It is tax dollars used to fund inflated contracts or to replace skimmed profits. It is old or new buildings which threaten the health and safety of their occupants and neighbors. It is something we all pay for.[44]

Fields of empty, dilapidated condominiums in Texas, the ruinous harvest of the S&L scandals, indicate that Gardiner and Lyman were not dealing in hypothetical losses; Americans will pay over $2,000 apiece to recover those S&L incurred costs. The immense flow of illegal drug money through the American banking system has had adverse effects on people who have no idea what is transpiring but are sorely harmed all the while.[45] Stripped to its essentials, the functional view represents a rejection of democratic ideals and an affirmation of social Darwinism and potential anarchy. While it is impossible to assess accurately what those trends might portend (after all, a government could theoretically function with little more than its citizens' collective acquiescence), few Americans would wish to subscribe to such dangerous risks.

Without serious fear of contradiction, one might suggest that there is a certain daredevil aura surrounding questionable gains, a "beating the system" syndrome that somehow colors corruption better than it realistically is. In point of fact, Klitgaard admonishes that corruption signals that something is wrong with the political system, for "only when corruption circumvents already existing 'distortions' can it be economically, politically, or institutionally useful." Although it might supply a short-term palliative or corrective, the longer-term effects are much more deleterious and widespread; "Whereas an occasional act of corruption may be efficient, corruption once systematized and deeply ingrained never is."[46]

In the case of the Iran–Contra machinations, we will see that the tactics employed by Reagan administration officials grievously violated the traditions of checks and balances within the American system of government and, as such, can be seen as seriously undermining the basis of that system. Similar conclusions can be drawn from the behavior of many bank officers that led to the S&L crisis. These examples indicate another problem with the functional perspective—its self-serving nature. Surely there is no reason why those who abide "by the rules" of the political game should be consistent losers as a result of their adherence, as was the case when well-connected consultants and politicians short-circuited agency regulations to obtain contracts for the Wedtech Corporation, or kept "zombie" S&Ls alive. To permit citizens to be disadvantaged because they chose to play by the rules would effectively destroy the entire game, and with it, the social contract.

The second major problem with the functional treatment of corruption is that it is highly unlikely that society in general or even the specific users (as opposed to small, often criminal interest groups) benefit from the illicit activities facilitated by corruption. The American hard drug epidemic is imposing inestimable social, physical, economic, and psychological havoc, even on national governments, regardless of its insistent consumer demands.[47] The inner cities are hardly more congenial places in which to live because of numbers games, loan sharks, and narcotics.

Public officials and usually the American political system certainly receive body blows when public corruption is uncovered. It is one thing to replace an errant congressman or governor, but when the office itself is indicted, then public alienation is the only recourse. Is the American citizen better off when the democratic symbols and processes predicated upon equal opportunity are so publicly revealed to be inequitable? No wonder that a 1990 *Los Angeles Times* survey of over 3,000 respondents found that "Despite the personal popularity of President Bush, cynicism towards the political system in general is growing as the public in unprecedented numbers associate Republicans with wealth and greed, Democrats with fecklessness and incompetence."[48] Certainly, discovered corruptions are not the only, or even the major reason for this disaffection, but it unquestionably does little to remedy the malady.

The litmus-test question needs to be asked of the functionalist's view: if corruption provides a general benefit, why does its public persona remain socially, politically, and legally outside the openly accepted pale? Naomi Caiden justifiably asks, "If a corrupt practice is truly functional, presumably it would be better to legalize it by incorporating market mechanisms into public transactions, but often to do so would undermine the whole rationale for government actions in the first place, particularly distributional objectives. . . ."[49] Lowi's Big C caution again prevails. It would appear that in politics as well as art and surely life, there is a criterion, an authority beyond efficacy.

One could claim that the villain here is publicity, that the little corruptions leading to efficiencies would be relatively harmless, hence fine, if they were known to only the privileged few. But that would be a covert tenuous reed, a condition none would wish to inculcate into American politics any further than is already the case. The fact is that corruption, however functional, extracts a grievous political price for a little fiscal or institutional efficiency. As such, even though its actual costs might be unimportant in the pecuniary scheme of things, political corruption represents a Faustian agreement in terms of the American social contract for which few would bargain.

In short, the functionalist brief for corruption as a necessary lubricant for government operations turns out to be fatally shortsighted and personalistic. There are very real prices to pay in terms of the normative foundations of the American democratic ethos. These shortcomings render the functional interpretation dysfunctional from a public policy perspective.

If we can agree, then, that corruption's costs are not so trivial that they scarcely merit our attention, let us examine the second horn of the dilemma—the argument that corruption is so much a part of the political system and structure that we could not eradicate it even if we wanted to. (The now familiar strains of the functional brief resonate here as well.) According to this view, there is simply no effective solution to the problem, so we should not break our lance tilting with these windmills. This interpretation is often heard in the context of political campaign financing; Berg and his colleagues contend that personal payoffs and campaign contributions are at the heart and soul of all political corruption.[50] However, as one might expect, the realities of campaign financing are arguably as complex as they are corrupt; current campaign requirements and reforms clash with few resolutions short of the draconian in sight.[51] Johnston, for his part, seconds the insolubility conclusion when he demonstrates the intractability of real political campaign reform; if you close one loophole, another—surely as lucrative and maybe worse—is quickly discovered. And, besides, he makes the excellent point that in a democracy, constituents ought to be able to support candidates of their choice.[52]

In another vein, Gardiner and Lyman quote the 1973 National Advisory Commission on Criminal Justice Standards and Goals as their illustration of the enormity issue:

> The direct costs of corruption are incalculable, but they are believed to be astronomical enough to support the wry observation of one high U.S. Department of Justice official, who stated that "when we finally stop payoffs to public officials at all levels in this country, we will have found the cure to inflation." [53]

The magnitude argument is partially dependent upon what we care to single out as the root causes of corruption. We can identify two bases, the personal and the systemic. First, if one perceives corruption as nothing more nor less than a component in the human condition, specifically avarice or greed, then the notion of completely eliminating it is either unacceptable (e.g., implanting electrodes in millions of crania) or quixotic.

Greed, of course, is hardly irrelevant in any corruption calculus, especially with the Wall Street scandals and the S&L bankruptcies fresh in our memories and checkbooks. Convicted entrepreneur and arbitrager Ivan Boesky, arguably the most visible of the recent crop of Wall Street felons, has been quoted as exhorting a University of California, Berkeley, MBA seminar that "Greed is healthy. You can be greedy and feel good about yourself." [54] Nonetheless, it would be simplistic and misleading to overstate the avarice argument. Money may be the flower, but it is not the root of all evil in a governmental environment. Increased bureaucratic salaries would not necessarily reduce corruption. The convictions of Boesky, Michael Milken, and other "inside traders" indicate that even the fabulously wealthy, rich beyond the dreams of any Croesus, can be seduced into engaging in illegal activities. Nixon's Watergate conspirators were unquestionably corrupt in a Big C manner with their abuses of power, but they were not perforce lusting after monetary gain. Political power and ideological rectitude mint their own very convincing coin. Finally, if greed were as human a condition as its proponents would claim, then we would find much more corruption than is the case; bureaucrats everywhere would indulge their pursuit for greater gains. But they demonstrably do not. Thus, we need to consider personal financial enhancements as often, maybe even usually present, but not always sufficient to explain political corruption.

If the level of attention is, as we have suggested above, systemic—that is, the system itself creates costly bottlenecks and red tape that inevitably provoke corrupt responses as a counter—then there is no solution short of creating a perfect political system based upon unimpeachable standards of conduct and morality. This is, of course, impossible. The standards would sooner or later be derided for their inevitable failures, thereby possibly even exacerbating the very problems they were meant to relieve; again, witness the effects Prohibition had on the nation's law enforcement and the citizens' caustic view of government.

Through both the individual and the systemic perspectives, we might reluctantly agree that the problems manifested by corruption could easily be of such endemic and enormous magnitude that they are indeed beyond our corrective powers. Yet this admission does not mean we have to take the next discouraging step and declare with sad resignation that since there is nothing we can do, why bother? Without prematurely detailing the arguments of the final "What Can We Do?" chapter of this book, it would be useful to set aside this sorry reading, at least momentarily, and examine not the solution per se but what we mean by solutions.

A more realistic reading of what can be done is dependent on what we think should be done. If, as the above contentions suggest, the problems are ingrained and immense, truly beyond our abilities to correct, we would defy Merton's functional injunctions and probably court failure if we were to seek the complete eradication of all the symptoms and maladies.

> [T]he foregoing analysis ... exemplifies a basic theorem: *any attempt to eliminate an existing social structure without providing adequate alternative structures for fulfilling the functions previously fulfilled by the abolished organization is doomed to failure. ... To seek social change, without due recognition of the manifest and latent functions performed by the social organization undergoing change, is to indulge in social ritual rather than social engineering.*[55]

However, the "solution" need not be total in order to be effective and serve a valuable purpose. Major reforms in the federal civil service system in the last century, particularly the Pendleton Civil Service Reform Act of 1883, and the progressive political movement after the turn of the century, have not rooted out all vestiges of corruption, as even a cursory review of post–World War II incidents demonstrates. Yet these and other acts have essentially eliminated the spoils system, greatly improved the federal government's workings, and generally increased the public's faith in the fairness of the bureaucracy. Likewise, the Knapp Commission's 1973 thoughtful findings and recommendations on corruption within the New York City police force did not eliminate all the force's corrupt and bad cops—as the 1986 revelations witness—but they did much to improve the force's professionalism and give New Yorkers greater confidence in the fairness of their police officers; the Knapp Commission signaled that now everybody was accountable to some sort of similar rules. In both these and other instances, the "payoffs" of partial solutions were significant, at least from a symbolic standpoint, a key point since I have argued that a central component of corruption's menace lurks in its symbolism. As such, the second argument for the "untouchable" nature of corruption and its conclusion—that we abandon all reform sacrifices on the twin horns of "nothing can be done" and "all or nothing at all"—fails to persuade.

In review, we can set forth two conclusions. First, that political corruption represents a problem of sufficient size and cost to warrant our attentions. Second, that while we might not be able to arrive at a complete solution to the problem, even partial solutions would have returns at least commensurate with the expended efforts and resources. This is especially true if the public loss of faith in its governmental processes and leaders is calculated as part of the cost of corruption. If we can accept those positions, we can propose a working model for thinking about corruption, a task to which we can now turn.

Thinking about Corruption

Drawing heavily upon the preceding discussions, we can move rapidly through the description of a model of political corruption that explains the phenomenon with more coherence and utility than the typically historical narrative with its idiosyncratic admixture of the moralist's episodic outrage, the functionalist's academic detachment, and the citizen's cynical resignation. The model's objective is to facilitate a better understanding of the conditions that proffer fertile grounds for corruption as well as ideas that render these same grounds somewhat less bountiful.

I have already set out at some length the argument that there are two principal components. First, the decentralized nature of the American political-economic system provides both the incentives and the ambiguities—the rewards and the opportunities—that sustain and, at times, encourage corruption. Second, the individual, with a full set of mixed (occasionally inconsistent) motives, is the actual perpetrator of the questionable actions, the one who physically takes advantage of (sometimes even works to create) these opportunities toward his or her personal unsanctioned reward. These distinctions between the roles of the individual and the system are admittedly more clear cut in the fog of concept than in the honest light of daily application. In practice, individuals operate within a system and, by so doing, affect that system, just as the system dynamics affect individual behaviors. Still, the differentiation serves as a helpful insight for thinking about corruption and implies some powerful policy considerations. It explicitly implicates both the system and individual as culpable, thereby distinguishing the discussion from the traditional public administration view that corruption is the regrettable result of an official's moralistic shortcomings and the economist's view that everything is determined by the amoral efficiency-maximizing market.

The bedrock of this model is that corruption often serves a purpose besides lining a miscreant's personal pockets. As the functionalists would advise us, corruption is viewed as an informal system of allocating government goods and services that expedites or perhaps supplants the otherwise cumbersome although admittedly legitimate activities of public regulation. The logical extreme of this position—that if government interventions imposed no transaction costs, if regulations were "frictionless," there would be no corruption—is attractive but, of course, an impossible condition because citizens demand that governments set protective procedures and regulations intended to create the very frictions that lead to circumvention and corruption. They are not the product of lifeless whimsy. (Similarly, one could argue that there would be no crime in a perfect communist economy in which goods were distributed strictly according to need. Again, a situation so far outside our societal ken as to not warrant examination.) Even if this frictionless government were possible, the corruption-free condition would not necessarily hold since there appears to be some part of human nature that will attempt to maximize personal gains (the "greed" factor) or play "beat the system" for no better reason than the direct challenge. In any case, my thesis here has little concern for logical extremes. The point is that corruption is not entirely lacking in social value or conscience, the product of baseless conspirators, rather, it serves as a sub rosa form of influence within the halls of power, explainable if not exactly excusable.

The model does not include a cultural variable. As explained in the first chapter, virtually all politics and political behaviors are heavily culturally dependent. What violates political norms in, say, India or Italy as opposed to Indiana will largely be a function of their respective and respected cultures. While I am confident I can make analogous arguments for different political systems, I am content at this juncture to keep matters as straightforward as possible and restrict our purview of political corruption to the contemporary American federal system.

In short, we will view corruption as a deliberate, coordinated behavior to which some people resort as a means of manipulating the "system" (in other words, making it work or function) in ways that are preferential to their particularistic goals. By this description, both the individuals and the system are held at fault. However, it is primarily the system and its inherent rewards and choke points that sometimes urges the individual to act in unsanctioned manners. The system might, as a consequence, indeed be more responsible than the immediate perpetrators. Nevertheless, to absolve individuals of their responsibility—to claim that the occurrence of corruption is as deterministic as the collapsing suspension bridge in Thornton Wilder's *Bridge of San Luis Rey*[8]—is nothing more than to ignore the moral responsibility of the citizen and official. The reality is that the functional apologia is twice deficient, that is, beneficial only in the short term and highly partisan to the point of contravening the public welfare.

The present perspective departs from previous examinations of political corruption by emphasizing that its political, economic, and social effects can be of a lasting duration and that citizen tolerance is largely due to the public not realizing its pervasive and pernicious effects. Therefore, public policies need to be devised that will address the long-term reduction of the problem.

Before posing what I think can be done toward these ends, let us

---

[8] "On Friday noon, July the twentieth, 1714, the finest bridge in all Peru broke and precipitated five travelers into the gulf below." Thornton Wilder, *The Bridge of San Luis Rey* (New York: Harper & Row, 1927), p. 1.

pause to explore five recent examples of political corruption in order to add some evidentiary flesh to an otherwise bare conceptual skeleton.

Notes

1. James Q. Wilson, *Thinking about Crime* (New York: Basic Books, 1983), p. xviii.

2. Theodore J. Lowi, "The Intelligent Person's Guide to Political Corruption," *Public Affairs*, Series 81, Bulletin No. 82 (September 1981), p. 2. Logically, Lowi refers to these two types of corruption as Big C and Little C, respectively.

3. Susan Rose-Ackerman, *Corruption: A Study in Political Economy* (New York: Academic Press, 1978), pp. 1, 2, and 9, emphasis in the original.

4. *Ibid.*, p. 216.

5. John G. Peters and Susan Welch, "Political Corruption in America: A Search for Definitions and a Theory, or If Political Corruption Is in the Mainstream of American Politics, Why Is It Not in the Mainstream of American Politics Research?" *American Political Science Review*, Vol. 72, No. 3 (September 1978), p. 974.

6. James Scott, *Comparative Public Corruption* (Englewood Cliffs, NJ: Prentice Hall, 1972).

7. Michael Johnston, *Political Corruption and Public Policy in America* (Monterey, CA: Cole, 1982), chap. 1.

8. George C.S. Benson et al., *Political Corruption in America* (Lexington, MA: Lexington Books, 1978), p. xiii.

9. Peters and Welch, "Political Corruption in America," p. 976.

10. Arnold J. Heidenheimer, "Perspectives on the Perception of Corruption," in Arnold J. Heidenheimer et al., eds., *Political Corruption: A Handbook* (New Brunswick, NJ: Transaction, 1989), p. 161.

11. Michael Johnston, "Right and Wrong in American Politics: Popular Concepts of Corruption," *Polity*, Vol. 18, No. 3 (Spring 1986), p. 379.

12. Lowi, "The Intelligent Person's Guide to Political Corruption," p. 3.

13. Naomi Caiden, "Shortchanging the Public," *Public Administration Review*, Vol. 39, No. 3 (May/June 1979), p. 295; Caiden's emphasis.

14. Joseph S. Nye, Jr., "Corruption and Political Development: A Cost–Benefit Analysis," *American Political Science Review*, Vol. 61, No. 2 (June 1967), pp. 417–427, at p. 419.

15. Arnold A. Rogow and Harold D. Lasswell, *Corruption, Power, and Rectitude* (Englewood Cliffs, NJ: Prentice Hall, 1963); more generally, see Harold D. Lasswell and Abraham Kaplan, *Power and Society* (New Haven, CT: Yale University Press, 1950).

16. Mark T. Lilla, "Ethos, 'Ethics,' and Public Service," *Public Interest*, No. 63 (Spring 1981), pp. 3–17, refers to a "patriotic corruption."

17. Lowi, "The Intelligent Person's Guide to Political Corruption," p. 3.

18. Michael Johnston, "Corruption and Political Culture in America: An Empirical Perspective," *Publius*, Vol. 13, No. 1 (Winter 1983), p. 39.

19. Scott, *Comparative Political Corruption*, pp. viii and 2.

20. Johnston, *Political Corruption and Public Policy in America*, p. 3.

21. Merton originally proposed the idea in 1949. See Robert K. Merton, *Social Theory and Social Structure* (New York: The Free Press, 1968). Johnston, *Political Corruption and Public Policy in America*, chap. 3, typically reflects Merton's contribution.

22. Simcha B. Werner, "New Directions in the Study of Administrative Corruption," *Public Administration Review*, Vol. 43, No. 2 (March/April 1983), p. 146.

23. Thomas C. Schelling, *Choice and Consequences* (Cambridge, MA: Harvard University Press, 1984), chaps. 7 and 8.

24. Merton, *Social Theory and Social Structure*, pp. 125–126, emphasis in original.

25. *Ibid.*, p. 127, emphasis in original.

26. Herbert Kaufman, *Red Tape: Its Origins, Uses, and Abuses (Washington D.C.: The Brookings Institution, 1977)*.

27. Johnston, *Political Corruption and Public Policy in America*, p. 20.

28. *Ibid.*, p. 23. Also see Scott, *Comparative Political Corruption*.

29. Admittedly, these arguments are thought to be most germane to developing nations and their bureaucracies; see Nye, "Corruption and Political Development;" Samuel P. Huntington, *Political Order in Changing Societies* (New Haven, CT: Yale University Press, 1968); and Fred W. Riggs, *Administration in Developing Countries* (Boston: Houghton Mifflin, 1964). Not surprisingly, many officials from the developing nations have taken great umbrage at this assertion; see Werner, "New Directions in the Study of Administrative Corruption."

30. Benson et al., *Political Corruption in America*.

31. Peter Reuter, *Disorganized Crime: Illegal Markets and the Mafia* (Cambridge, MA: The MIT Press, 1983), is one of the few books to examine this topic dispassionately.

32. From a *New York Times*/CBS News Poll; Richard J. Meislin, "A Majority in New Poll Still Find Reagan Lied on the Iran–Contra Issue," *New York Times*, July 18, 1987, pp. 1, 6. Fifty-six percent responded that they thought the president was lying while the remaining 17 percent had no opinion.

33. Benson et al., *Political Corruption in America*, p. 190.

34. Andy Logan, "Around City Hall: A Fine Mess," *The New Yorker*, Vol. 62, No. 46 (January 6, 1987), pp. 74–82. The PVB scandal almost surely contributed to the defeat of Mayor Ed Koch by David Dinkins a few years later.

35. Leonard Buder, "Giants 39, Broncos 20 and Cheaters $85,000," *New York Times*, April 20, 1988, pp. A1, A17.

36. Compare Nathaniel C. Nash, "Officials of I.R.S. Accused by Panel of Ethical Lapses," *New York Times*, July 21, 1989, pp. A1, C2, with Daniel Goleman, "The Tax Cheats: Selfish to the Bottom Line," *New York Times*, April 1, 1988, pp. 1, 28.

37. Quoted by Carol F. Steinbach, "Programmed for Plunder," *National Journal*, Vol. 21, No. 37 (September 16, 1989), p. 2261.

38. Robert Klitgaard, *Controlling Corruption* (Berkeley: University of California Press, 1988), p. 33; Klitgaard's emphasis.

39. Philip Sheldon, "Enemy Within: Drug Money is Corrupting the Enforcers," *New York Times*, April 11, 1988, pp. 1, 8; the pernicious effect of the cocaine

trade on a supplying nation is detailed by Bruce M. Bagley, "Columbia and Its War on Drugs," *Foreign Affairs*, Vol. 76, No. 1 (September 1988), pp. 70–92.

40. Elaine Sciolino with Stephen Engelberg, "Narcotics Effort Foiled by U.S. Security Goals," *New York Times*, April 10, 1988, pp. 1, 10, at p. 1.

41. Richard L. Berke, "Foreign Policy Said to Hinder Drug War," *New York Times*, April 14, 1989, p. A7.

42. Barry S. Rundquist, Gerald S. Strom, and John G. Peters, "Corrupt Politicians and Their Electoral Support: Some Experimental Observations," *American Political Science Review*, Vol. 71, No. 3 (September 1977), pp. 954–963.

43. Rose-Ackerman, *Political Corruption*, p. 10.

44. John Gardiner and Theodore Lyman, *Decisions for Sale: Corruption and Reform in Land-Use and Building Regulations* (New York: Praeger, 1978), p. 202.

45. Jeff Gerth, "Vast Flow of [Drug] Cash Threatens Currency, Banks, and Economies," *New York Times*, April 11, 1988, p. A8.

46. Both quotations from Klitgaard, *Controlling Corruption*, pp. 35 and 42, respectively.

47. Philip M. Boffey, "Drug Users, Not Sellers, Termed Key Problem," *New York Times*, April 12, 1988, pp. A1, A5.

48. The *Los Angeles Times* poll is quoted by Michael Oreskes, "Alienation from Government Grows," *New York Times*, September 19, 1990, p. A17.

49. Caiden, "Shortchanging the Public," p. 295.

50. Larry L. Berg, Harlan Hahn, and John R. Schmidhauser, *Corruption in the American Political System* (Morristown, NJ: General Learning Press, 1976).

51. See the special report on "Campaign Grease" in *National Journal*, Vol. 22, No. 24 (June 16, 1990), pp. 1448–1485.

52. Johnston, *Political Corruption and Public Policy in America*, chap. 6.

53. National Advisory Commission on Criminal Justice Standards and Goals, *Community Crime Prevention* (Washington, D.C.: Government Printing Office, 1973), p. 206; quoted in Gardiner and Lyman, *Decisions for Sale*, p. 5.

54. Quoted by Andy Logan, "Around City Hall: Stormy Weather," *New Yorker*, Vol. 62, No. 51 (February 9, 1987), pp. 81–91, at p. 84. A minor cottage publications industry has been created over the current Wall Street troubles; see, inter alia, Michael Lewis, *Liar's Poker* (New York: Norton, 1989); and James B. Steward, *Den of Thieves* (New York: Simon & Schuster, 1991).

55. Merton, *Social Theory and Social Structure*, p. 135, emphasis in original.

Part II
FIVE CASES OF CORRUPTION

3

"WE HAD NO IDEA . . ."

There is no obvious structural reason why the Department of Housing and Urban Development (HUD) should have been singled out ahead of time for particular scandal. Yet beginning in April 1989 with the publication of a report by Paul Adams, HUD's inspector general, criticizing HUD's Moderate Rehabilitation Program (MRP or Mod Rehab), the department became the most complete bureaucratic standard-bearer for political corruption during the eight-year Reagan administration.

While petty scandals had pretty much harassed HUD since its inception in 1965—for instance, real estate speculators during the 1970s, failure to correct possible conflicts of interest, and President Jimmy Carter's apparently funneling of urban development funds to many of his Massachusetts campaign contributors[1]—the magnitude of the HUD improprieties under Reagan's secretary of HUD, Samuel R. Pierce, seemed unprecedented. *Time* magazine's cover story was headlined, "Sam Pierce's 'Turkey Farm.'"[2] Under the banner, "The HUD Ripoff," *Newsweek* magazine emphasized: "For sheer hypocrisy and cynicism, few scandals can match the fraud and mismanagement at Housing and Urban Development. It's emerged as a rampant case of influence peddling, favoritism and lust for power."[3] The Wall Street Journal titled a front-page story "Favoring Friends," and characterized HUD's Mod Rehab "as a pot of gold for fat-cat Republican contributions, well-connected developers, and powerful Washington consultants."[4] The usually more reserved *National Journal* was similarly inclined toward sensationalism when it entitled its article "Programmed for Plunder" and headed it thus: "Congress, digging deeply into the scandals at the Housing and Urban Development Department, is uncovering wide-spread fraud in programs that were ripe for plunder."[5] Even President George Bush's Office of Management and Budget seemed to join the blame game, as Director Richard Darman ordered all federal agencies to review their management practices, so as to avoid "another HUD." Little surprise, then, in 1990, upon the instigation of the House Judiciary Committee and the request of Attorney General Richard Thornburg, former federal Third Court of Appeals Judge Arlin Adams was appointed independent counsel to investigate the various allegations directed at HUD personnel, including perjury.

To be certain, there were clear-cut grounds for such heated allegations, in terms of both scope and magnitude. The House of Representatives Subcommittee on Employment and Housing (of the Committee on Government Operations), with only minor party politicking, in a bipartisan decision condemned Pierce's HUD during 150 hours of hearings held over fourteen months. After the 1988 change of administrations and the appointment of former representative Jack Kemp as the new HUD secretary by newly elected President Bush, "HUD officials .. . confirmed that waste, fraud, and mismanagement plagued at least half of HUD's 48 programs during the Reagan years. . . ."[6] Kemp himself referred to his department as a "swamp" and immediately suspended suspect programs. The cost estimates for the scandal ranged from Secretary Kemp's estimate of $2 billion to Senate Majority Leader George Mitchell's (D-ME) price tag of $6 billion–$8 billion. Mitchell put these losses into perspective: "It is obvious that HUD was used as a political slush fund. . . . It is astonishing that losses to the agency over the last several years could amount to more than Congress actually appropriates [to HUD] in a single year today."[7] (It should be remembered that both Kemp and Mitchell each certainly had their own political agendas underlying their rhetoric and estimates.)

Still, in spite of this seeming consensus, we need to examine the circumstances that resulted in the tawdry revelations at HUD before we can determine, first, if such vitriol is warranted and, second, its roots. For instance, Suzanne Garment, while marginally conceding the seriousness of the charges, suggests that much of the rancor was more due to members of Congress lusting after publicity—zealously if not entirely responsibly—than the inherent nature of the alleged HUD corruptions themselves.[8]

Pierce's Hud

Ronald Reagan's appointee to be secretary of HUD, Samuel Pierce, was a candidate of public service distinction by many measures. Trained as a lawyer, he had been a congressional staff member, an official in the Treasury, and a criminal court judge before assuming the leadership of the department. During his 1981 confirmation hearings, Senator Daniel Patrick Moynihan (D-NY) praised Pierce, saying that "There are few men in our time who have served with such distinction as Judge Pierce has in such a broad range of response [sic] positions in public and private life."[9] However, Pierce had two profound shortcomings as he entered HUD: he knew little about managing an organization the size and complexity of HUD and even less about public housing. The first rendered him managerially indifferent, a cabinet secretary by delegation; the second rendered him ignorant of the formidable HUD technical regulations and procedures happening all around him. Moreover, Pierce's attitude toward the department itself reflected and in many ways executed President Reagan's well-known philosophical lack of sympathy—indeed, virtual antipathy—for the HUD mission. In a 1976 campaign speech, Reagan had claimed that "For more than 20 years, the Federal Government has been building low-cost housing for the poor. And they're constantly building new programs, as each one fails." A 1982 HUD report indicated that the trappings of power had not tempered that perspective:

> [I]n the past, the federal government has too often mandated unassailable social objectives and left it to others to pay the bill. . . . State and local governments have amply demonstrated that, properly unfettered, they will make better decisions than the federal government acting for them.[10]

Secretary Pierce indicated to a congressional subcommittee shortly after he left office precisely where his sentiments lay during his tenure, especially regarding the Moderate Rehabilitation Program (MRP), which was proven to be the wellspring of HUD's alleged improprieties:

> I, along with others, considered the MRP to be an economically inefficient and ineffective program, and during my last six years as Secretary . . . , we tried to terminate it. However, each year that MRP was left out of HUD's budget request, Congress appropriated funding for it anyway.[11]

Perhaps as a result of these attitudes, the Reagan administration treated HUD as a "dumping ground," larding it with political appointments, some appointees so unqualified as to draw protests from Secretary Pierce himself. The good news is that few of them stayed very long; the assistant secretary for Housing position had seven incumbents in eight years. The bad news is that many of them returned to HUD corridors as well-wired, high-priced consultants able to short-circuit HUD regulations to their clients' benefits. And the worst news is that they all viewed HUD as a politicized agency.

Finally, as if these portents were not sufficiently potent, this combustible situation was compounded by the Reagan administration's bedrock belief in "privatization," the idea that government services should be turned over to the private sector whenever and as much as possible. One of Pierce's early appointments as assistant secretary for Policy Development and Research, E.S. Savas, was probably the most outspoken privatization proponent in academic circles.[a] In short, HUD Secretary Pierce was a hands-off manager with little interest in the workings of his department, except to cut back on its congressionally mandated responsibilities.

And cut back the Reagan administration did. The HUD budget plummeted from $36 billion in 1980 to $15 billion eight years later, with the staff being reduced from 16,000 to 13,000. The budget for the Moderate Rehabilitation Program, later revealed to be the genesis of much of the controversy, was cut by close to 75 percent (from $1.8 billion to $496 million). Less apparent was the manner in which Pierce's executive office doled out federal funds, inserting political palatability as a principal criterion. DuBois Gilliam (deputy assistant secretary for Program Policy Development and Evaluation from April 1984 to September 1987), one of Pierce's closest associates at HUD,[b] testified to the House Subcom-

---

[a]While at HUD, Savas published *Privatizing the Public Sector: How to Shrink Government* (Chatham, NJ: Chatham House, 1982); in 1983, he resigned following allegations that he had used HUD staff to edit and proofread the manuscript during their working hours.

[b]When considering Mr. Gilliam's testimony, it should be remembered that he was convicted in 1988 of two counts of accepting gratitudes and one count of conspiring to defraud the U.S. government; he was sentenced to 18 months in the federal prison at Lompoc. His testimony to the House Subcommittee on Employment and Banking was under an order of immunity such that his testimony could not be used against him in a subsequent criminal trial.

mittee that "during that period. . . , [HUD] was the best political machine I have ever seen, and we dealt strictly politics. . . ."[12] Secretary Pierce's executive assistant during the same period, Deborah Gore Dean, described the MRP to the *Wall Street Journal* as "set up and designed to be a political program. . . . I would have to say we ran it in a political manner."[13] To be fair, Pierce has denied these allegations, saying that "When I saw [Dean's statement], I almost went through the roof. It was not run as a political program. . . . My decisions were based on facts, law and logic, not on political party."[14] However, the overwhelming amount of contradictory testimony to date renders these disavowals suspicious.

The pervasive scope of the HUD problems was disclosed during 1989 and 1990 in a number of different programmatic areas. Under Foreclosed Property Sales, HUD agents would sell properties whose home owners had defaulted on their FHA-insured mortgages; HUD would then receive the proceeds. HUD housing agent Marilyn Louise Harrell, realizing that HUD's monitoring of the problem was less than lax, admitted that she diverted $5.5 million to give to the poor as an act of Christian charity.[c] Although hers was not the only instance, Harrell later received press notoriety as "Robin HUD." Under the co-insurance program, HUD and private mortgage lenders would agree to co-insure apartment properties being renovated. In exchange for assuming 20 percent of the risk, the private lenders would collect fees based on the size of the mortgage. To claim larger fees, property values were often greatly exaggerated. When the projects subsequently defaulted, HUD was left holding over a billion-dollar debt. There were also repeated instances of FHA improprieties; as of 1989, the *National Journal* estimated that "over 340 real estate agents, brokers, appraisers, speculators, and lenders nationwide have already been convicted of illegal activities. . . ."[15] However, for present purposes, the discussion of HUD corruption will focus on Mod Rehab, with a few exceptions, to argue that the HUD corruptions were at least as systemically based as the congressional indictments of the laid-back management style and the political proclivities of its secretary would explain by themselves.

---

[c]In her June 16, 1989, testimony to the investigating House Subcommittee on Employment and Housing, Ms. Harrell referred to the scripture, in the Books of John, Peter, and James, to explain her actions.

The Moderate Rehabilitation Program

Mod Rehab was the most visible and understandable of HUD's menu of scandals, and, apparently, the most politically motivated. Independent Counsel Adams has gained guilty pleas or convictions for eight defendants to date. However, the following account is drawn from the extensive public record of hearings before the House of Representatives' Subcommittee on Employment and Housing. The five volumes of subcommittee hearings into the various alleged HUD improprieties (plus a summary report by the parent Committee on Government Operations) total close to 4,000 pages of transcripts and documents, with the largest proportion concerning MRP. While these hearings by themselves do not prove anybody guilty of anything, they do represent an under-oath record of the actions of most of the participants[d] and can serve as an interim basis for detailing the questionable operations within Pierce's HUD.

The Moderate Rehabilitation Program was created by Congress as part of the Section 8 Existing Program (hence the MRP is also referred to as Section 8), under the Housing and Community Development Act of 1978, amending the original U.S. Housing Act of 1937. The MRP's purpose is to distribute federal funds to private development groups for the repair and renovation of substandard rental housing and then to provide rental subsidies for lower-income families who might not be able to afford the new going rate. The low-income tenants would pay 30 percent of their monthly income for rent; HUD would then pay the landlord the difference between that amount and a HUD-determined fair market value. To encourage participation, developers are assured of these rental incomes for fifteen years. In addition, federal tax credits are available to the builders; under the 1986 tax act, a developer may receive an annual tax credit of 9 percent for ten years. Typically, the tax credits are syndicated by the developer and sold off at the beginning of the renovation project as a means of generating capital.

HUD's Mod Rehab proposal mechanism was well known, both in terms of its legal requirements and its time-consuming, often frustrating

---

[d]Six persons, including Secretary Pierce and his executive assistants Lance Wilson and Deborah Gore Dean, exercised their constitutional prerogatives under the Fifth Amendment against self-incrimination and refused to testify before the investigation House Subcommittee.

ways. Basically, a local Public Housing Authority (PHA) would apply to HUD for MRP funds, documenting the availability of apartment units suitable for rehabilitation and demonstrating a need for low-income housing in its area. After lengthy review and final approval by HUD staff, the PHA would publicly advertise the availability of funds to solicit competitive bids, and then choose among the various developers who responded. Numerous HUD regulations monitored the quality of the redevelopment and helped determine the rent structure. During the early 1980s, HUD eliminated its New Construction and Substantial Rehabilitation programs, thus leaving the Mod Rehab program as the only funding source in town for housing developers. When MRP, in turn, suffered its own severe budget cuts, the competition for these funds became even more intense.

Until 1984, Congress had mandated that HUD allocate the MRP money on a "fair share" basis, that is, geographically distributed in a relatively equitable manner throughout the nation, depending on varying income levels. However, as the Reagan administration's budget cuts began to reduce the amount of available Section 8 funds, Congress waived the fair share criterion. This waiver was approved because it was thought that with the smaller amounts of funds, a fair share criterion would spread the money so thinly as to be of little good to any particular project. In retrospect, this reasonable concern opened the HUD sluice gates to political corruption, gates that were already well worn.

In an exemplary display of pass-the-bureaucratic-buck, Secretary Pierce testified on May 25, 1989, that HUD's general counsel, John Knapp, rendered a legal interpretation of this waiver as meaning that *all* Section 8 criteria were now lifted and that therefore MRP funds were totally discretionary—that is, Pierce's to dispense. This reading was seconded in Knapp's testimony later the same day, only amended by Knapp's explanation that his was a "verbal" opinion reached after consultation with his associate General Counsel Robert Kenison, thus confirming Pierce's statement that the legal opinion had "trickled down to me."[16] Then, on June 9, Knapp wrote Subcommittee Chair Tom Lantos (D-CA) that his testimony on this point was "historically inaccurate." Shortly after Knapp's appearance before the subcommittee, Kenison telephoned him and made it clear that no such conversation between the two of them on the issue of the waiver had taken place, that is, no such opinion had been given. Knapp "fully" accepted Kenison's correction and continued:

[I]f I did not discuss the question of applicability of the regulatory selection criteria with Mr. Kenison, then I did not state an opinion on the subject to anyone else, either. . . . It appears reasonably certain, therefore, that in fact I did not give the "opinion," oral or otherwise, . . . to which I admitted and testified last week.[17]

Whatever the case, it made little difference, because Secretary Pierce now viewed the congressional waiver of the fair share criterion as effectively making Section 8 program funds completely discretionary, an opportunity soon utilized. By the time HUD Inspector General Adams reported in April 1989, ten states had been allocated 51.6 percent of the Mod Rehab funds between 1984 and 1988, whereas their collective share under the fair share criterion would have been 16.2 percent, a 350 percent increase; conversely, six states, including California and New York, declined from an aggregate 39.4 percent to only 11.34, a 28 percent decrease. Adams also reported a "perception" that former HUD employees were particularly successful in obtaining Section 8 funding; one such group was awarded funds for six out of the seven projects it proposed, a phenomenal success record given the scarcity of funds.[18]

Underlying these changes was the reiterated charge that HUD and specifically the Office of the Secretary were making MRP funding decisions based on highly politicized and often personalized criteria. We will examine four such cases here: Seabrook, New Jersey; Essex, Maryland; Arlington, Texas; and Durham, North Carolina.

Seabrook, New Jersey

One of the most flagrant cases of MRP abuse occurred over the Seabrook Apartments in Upper Deerfield, New Jersey. In September 1986, CFM Development Corporation, led by Black, Manafort, Stone & Kelly, a Washington political consulting group, became interested in rehabilitating the Seabrook Apartments, 326 units originally constructed as temporary housing for persons of Japanese ancestry relocated from the West Coast during the Second World War. A representative of the investment group met with Pierce's executive assistant, Deborah Gore Dean, on November 14 to inform her of the its interest in Seabrook and inquire as to the possibility of obtaining MRP funding for the project. Paul Manafort, a major Republican operator and one-third partner in CFM, later testified that after the meeting with Dean, "we had expectations it would be funded."[19]

Five days later, another CFM partner and a Black Manafort employee contacted and convinced the New Jersey PHA that it should apply with the utmost urgency for Section 8 monies to rehabilitate the Seabrook units. PHA officials testified that they were told that if they hurried, "there were HUD Secretary's discretionary funds available for the project at Seabrook." When asked if they understood the urgency, they said that Black Manafort representatives "did not explain. . . . They indicated these funds were presently available and we had to apply quickly if we were going to draw them down."[20] The investors further specified that the application should not be processed through the HUD's New Jersey regional office in Newark, but rather through New York's HUD office with an unacknowledged (i.e., "blind") copy directed to secretary's office care of Deborah Gore Dean. On November 20, the application was filed through the New York HUD office without any knowledge of the New Jersey office or even the local authorities in Upper Deerfield, with Dean receiving her blind copy.

On January 9, 1987, Assistant Secretary for Housing Thomas Demery met with Dean, approved the request, and notified the New York HUD administrator of the grant. In February, CFM signed an option to buy Seabrook, and on April 8 exercised the option. On April 24, the HUD New York office formally notified the New Jersey PHA that it had been awarded monies to redevelop 326 units, the first such award in New Jersey since 1984. On May 18, the advertisement required to invite bidding for a housing project, technically anywhere in New Jersey, appeared in a rather obscure local newspaper, the *Millville Daily* (circulation 7,000), stating that "All projects must contain at least one hundred (100) units and must be located in the city of Seabrook." These were important details because there is no city of Seabrook (although it is a recognized suburb) in New Jersey, nor any other rehabilitation sites meeting the specified size. William Connolly, New Jersey's director of Housing, later testified:

> those ads ... were really honoring the letter rather than the spirit of HUD's own rules because we were under no illusions at this point that we had no authority to move those units to some other project, that that commitment had come all the way from the Secretary for that project.

> *Representative Tom Lantos.* Would it be fair to characterize the public notice as a sham?
>
> *Mr. Connolly.* Oh, absolutely.[21]

Seabrook Associates (owned by CFM) was the only applicant and was awarded the contract for all 326 units on June 1.

The New Jersey PHA did not inform the local authorities of the project until August 12. Connolly told the House Subcommittee that even though HUD regulations did not mandate the local community be informed of a Mod Rehab project, this was the only instance he knew of in which local involvement was precluded. The testimony of Mr. Bruce Peterson, the mayor of Upper Deerfield, is revealing:

> Township officials, myself included, were under the definite impression that this project was a "fait accompli" and that the municipality had very little say in the matter. . . .
>
> The township was never consulted by HUD about this project. No one from HUD has ever come to the township to talk to the governing body about the project or the community's concerns. To this date, I am not clear, nor have I ever had the program fully and adequately explained to me. . . .
>
> I think we would have preferred to see the majority of the units torn down, they were in such terrible shape.[22]

The cost to taxpayers for Seabrook was approximately $42.2 million, including $31.2 million in rent subsidies to be paid out over the fifteen-year lifespan of the project, plus another $11 million in tax credits over a ten-year period. Black Manafort received a fee of $1,000 per unit, or a total of $326,000 (which, according to Paul Manafort's testimony, bills out at roughly $1,000 per hour), as well as Manafort's personal profits from his partial ownership of CFM.[23] This for a renovation project that was later charged with slip-shod construction, forced evictions of lower-income tenants, and rents above the local market value.

The irregularities surrounding Seabrook document the charge that the entire transaction—alpha to omega—was fraudulent. The application was seemingly initiated with HUD by private consultants, not the local PHA as specified in HUD's MRP regulations. The application was not routed through the cognizant HUD regional office, but through the New York office, one identified by later testimony as much more compliant to the political considerations within the secretary's office. The funding decision was apparently made in Pierce's office despite the secretary's sworn statements that he never intervened in these decisions. And, lastly, the required public announcement was an admitted sham, one surely designed to solicit the solitary bid by CFM.

Essex, Maryland

The Essex project was a low-income housing project in Baltimore County, Maryland, with 312 dilapidated units originally built in the 1940s. In 1984, the Maryland Community Development Administration, which was the local PHA, selected the project for rehabilitation when it was submitted by a developer in response to a notice of funding availability, thus nominating Essex as a candidate for HUD MRP support. The state PHA allocated one million dollars of its own funds but, from 1984 to 1986, Essex received no HUD funds.

The Landex Corporation purchased Essex in 1986. Judith Siegel, president of Landex, testified to the House Subcommittee of her early recognition of the need for HUD funding and the stalled state of affairs within the department regarding the Essex proposal. Landex therefore invited former Secretary of the Interior James Watt to join the firm as a consultant, even though all parties agreed that he had no experience in real estate or development; indeed, Siegel testified that "Mr. Watt never represented that he had any experience." The reasoning was straightforward:

> *Ms. Siegel.* [James Watt] was attempting to get HUD to pay attention to this application, an ability I didn't possess. Mr. Watt can get phone calls returned at HUD. I can't.
>
> . . .
>
> Mr. Watt was a Cabinet Secretary and I am a million miles from that.

Landex retained Watt's services on a contingency basis, offering him $1,000 for every MRP unit his services might deliver. For this particular project, Watt testified that he made about a half-dozen telephone calls and met once with Secretary Pierce, a total of no more than two hours. When Landex was awarded the Essex project 312 units, he received $300,000. The nature of these services was transparent; Watt would be utilized for nothing more than what Chairman Lantos referred to as "influence peddling," as Siegel's exchange with Congressman Barney Frank (D-MA) indicated:

> *Mr. Frank.* Did he give you any advice about how to go about the construction business?
>
> *Ms. Siegel.* Absolutely not.
>
> *Mr. Frank.* Did he give you any advice about how to syndicate?
>
> *Ms. Siegel.* No.
>
> *Mr. Frank.* Did he give you any advice about how to structure the deal legally?
>
> *Ms. Siegel.* No.
>
> *Mr. Frank.* So the only thing Mr. Watt did then, . . . was to intervene on your behalf with HUD?
>
> *Ms. Siegel.* Correct.
>
> *Mr. Frank.* Did he ever intervene [at HUD meetings]? In other words, was he an advocate as to any specific aspect that was in dispute?
>
> *Ms. Siegel.* No.
>
> *Mr. Frank.* No. So all he did was . . . get phone calls returned and he—for the $300,000 you gave Mr. Watt, you bought not just access but—well, you bought access to HUD officials. Do you think that the fact that you paid him $300,000 influenced the decision that HUD made? . . . If you hadn't paid James Watt $300,000 to make those phone calls and do whatever else he did, would you have gotten this project in your judgment?
>
> *Ms. Siegel.* I don't know.[24]

Another developer, Joseph Strauss (former special assistant to Secretary Pierce from May 1981 to May 1983), likewise employed Watt as a consultant to HUD for his Phoenix Associates, and for similar reasons:

> I make no bones, Congressmen, about the fact that the reason James Watt was hired ... was not because of his housing knowledge or his technical knowledge or his legal skills, which may in fact be there. The reason was because of his access and his influence.[25]

The explanation for resorting to Watt has that the HUD system was simply not working as it should. Ms. Siegel explained that neither the developers nor the PHAs had much idea as to how funding requests worked their frustrating way through the HUD bureaucracy:

> It's a trickle-down theory. It's been a mess at the agency. The programs start at headquarters and, as a result, the local agencies, the States and counties don't really know—have a sense of what's going on. Sometimes they get money, sometimes they don't get money. . . . The funding of the public housing authorities is arbitrary and unpredictable.

Siegel agreed with Dean's *Wall Street Journal* characterization of the department as "political." As a result, "My strategy was to always have an application that had a lot of political support. They could not be funded without a lot of political support."

She encapsulated the obstacles facing the "unconnected" bidder:

> During the 15-month development period, having Mr. Watt on our team served to reduce our risk. If we needed to get the agency's attention, if we needed a phone call returned or a letter reviewed, he would be the best person to get it done for us or he would advise us on how to move things along and get them going.
>
> Mr. Chairman, I am sure you recognize that HUD is not an easy agency to work with. It is an agency in disarray, with confused and conflicting policies, and we needed someone who could get it to respond. Mr. Watt played that important role, one that was, unfortunately, a necessity.
>
> In summary, do I think this selection process was good public policy? No. Do I think a more competitive process would have made better public policy? Of course, but the system was there. I follow the rules and I developed high-quality low-income housing. Developers must not be blamed for the system they neither created nor administered.[26]

When Secretary Watt appeared to testify before the subcommittee, his demeanor could best be characterized as truculent, even combative. His opening statement sounded many recurrent themes. Watt first insisted that

> I have never received for my involvement in the project one nickel of Federal funds. Let me repeat. I have never received any HUD funds, any Federal money funds, or government funds—not U.S. Government money or State government money or city or country tax dollars.

His second chord was the legality of his interventions.

> I have received no Federal funds. The Department of Housing and Urban Development has spelled out with great clarity that the fees such as were paid to me are not part of the housing project costs, nor do they serve to increase tenant rents. These fees are not subject to HUD review or jurisdiction because they are paid by the developer, not the Government. They are not Federal funds.

His third was the reasoning behind his actions, castigating both the HUD bureaucracy and its political appointees.

> My objective was to get the career bureaucracy to review the application submitted to HUD by the State of Maryland's housing authority. . . . The problem was that the HUD bureaucracy was not processing the public housing authority application.
>
> . . .
>
> I came to the conclusion that the political appointees at HUD were immobilized with the fear of doing something wrong, and, therefore, applications were not even being reviewed. Fear paralyzed an agency. . . . Near paralysis was the result. I determined it was a waste of time to go to anyone other than Secretary Pierce.

Finally, Watt aggressively and repeatedly defended his actions as "legal, moral, ethical, and effective. And I'm proud of my participation."[27]

The exchanges were often acerbic. When Watt was castigated by Chairman Lantos, who asked if his were a case of "influence peddling," Watt responded,

> I avoid the use of the term influence peddling because I think it is a harsh partisan term used by Republicans and Democrats to describe someone of the other party carrying out an activity.
>
> . . .
>
> If I were a Democrat, I would say that Jim Watt engaged in influence peddling ... [but if I] were an objective Republican, ... I would say there is a skilled talented man who used his credibility to accomplish an objective.[28]

On the crucial matter under investigation—did James Watt illegally persuade Secretary Pierce to award the Maryland PHA the Mod Rehab funds that were later given to Landex—the record is ambiguous. Both Pierce and Watt testified that the discussion was low-key, with Pierce explaining in "great detail that he did not ever select a project or a developer ... and that he never gave approval to any particular application." Watt "countered" that all he was asking Pierce to do "was to get the career bureaucracy to process and review the Maryland PHA application," which the secretary agreed to.[29] Pierce testified that he did not think "Mr. Watt got any special choice, because of any special attention." When asked if Watt helped the proposal, Pierce replied, "I don't think so."[30] Still, on June 6, after HUD decided to fund the Essex project, Watt wrote Pierce, "Thanks! You are a man of your word."[31]

By most semantic conventions, it was obvious that Landex hired Watt for his "influence peddling" skills. The fact that Essex was funded shortly after Watt met with Pierce when its application had languished for two previous years indicates that these skills were effective. Although Watt's interventions might have been, strictly speaking, legal, their ethical nature was debated at length. And Secretary Kemp, during his testimony, spoke directly to Watt's protestations that his fees had no tinge of government money:

> In the case of mod rehab, ... HUD paid from 20–44 percent more money than the rental value of the apartments. That extra money goes for excess profits for the developer and, clearly, to cover consultant fees. We give the developer a reason to hire a consultant, and we give the successful bidder the money to pay consultant's fees.[32]

Thus, it is safe to assume that Watt was hired to circumvent a balky HUD bureaucracy and did precisely that. However, by at least expediting the Essex decision through questionable practices, he gave rise to a perception of gross political favoritism for large personal benefit. While his actions may have been strictly legal, their appearance and implications were far from appropriate.

Pebble Creek Apartments, Arlington, Texas

Gerald Carmen was the chief of the Reagan HUD transition team in 1980 and was appointed as administrator of the General Services Administration (GSA), a position he held from 1981 to 1984. He was then named the American Ambassador to the United Nations agencies in Geneva, Switzerland, until 1986, at which time he left government service. Working with Joshua Muss (formerly with the Property Review Board at the GSA) and J. Michael Queenan (a former HUD official in HUD's Denver office), Carmen identified a possible rehabilitation project in Arlington, Texas (later named the Pebble Creek Apartments), sometime toward the end of 1986. According to his sworn testimony before the House Subcommittee, Carmen met with Secretary Pierce regarding the proposed project sometime during "the first quarter" of 1987, talking with him "closer to fifteen minutes than to half an hour." Carmen stated that Pierce made no promises:

> Mr. Lantos. What did Secretary Pierce respond to you when you made the pitch for your project?
>
> Mr. Carmen. There was no response. He neither said yes or no.[33]

On March 2, the MRP selection committee met. On March 4, the results of those deliberations were recorded in a memorandum from Assistant Secretary for Housing Tom Demery to Deborah Dean. Handwritten in the margins of the awards was the notation, "Plus 316 units for Arlington, TX." On April 1, an attorney for the investment group wrote the Arlington PHA urging it to apply for Section 8 funds, even including sample letters and forms. On April 7, Dean wrote a memorandum to Pierce, in which she noted under Mod Rehab, "[former Republican U.S. Senator from Massachusetts Edward] Brooks and Carmen are set." On April 8, the Arlington PHA formally applied to HUD for moderate rehabilitation money.[34] And on April 15, Demery signed off on the allocation, with the Regional Office being notified nine days later.

These were the first and only Section 8 funds that the Arlington PHA administered, and it took less than a month from initial application to final approval, this in a bureaucracy famed for its glacial ways.

The required advertisements inviting competitive bids were published in the *Arlington Daily News* (circulation around 6,000) on July 5 and 12, even though a later HUD inspector general's report noted that there were three major metropolitan newspapers in the area (circulation about 250,000). On July 15, Carmen and Muss submitted a proposal, along with a bid from another developer. On August 10, the Arlington PHA awarded the Pebble Creek rehab project to Carmen and Muss.

The property was subsequently mortgaged under HUD's co-insurance program with Benton Mortgage Company for $8.1 million, $4.1 million as the purchase price and $4 million for the renovation costs. The HUD inspector general later claimed that the property had been overvalued by more than $2 million, thus allowing for Carmen and Muss to request higher tax credits and rent subsidies. Benton Mortgage was suspended by HUD in November 1989 from participation in the co-insurance program for its questionable business activities.

Two parts of Carmen's testimony sparked particular congressional fire during the Pebble Creek hearings. The first was when Carmen admitted that he stood to profit around $1.2 million from the project without having to put any of his own personal money into the project: "We didn't put very much cash into it. We incorporated it and the thing flowed off of its own cash flow."[35] The second was Carmen's insistence that it was his privilege as an American citizen to importune Secretary Pierce personally:

> *Mr. Carmen.* I think I had every right in the world to be there.... I think that the program was designed to have Arlington compete, but was not intended to exclude people who are interested in getting into those projects from going anywhere they want. We have access to our own government. I have access to the Secretary of HUD. I have access to anyone I want. Every American has.

> *Mr. Lantos.* Yes. The problem is that not every American citizen can call up the Secretary of HUD and get an instantaneous appointment.... The whole point is people like you and Jim Watt who took advantage of your influence and your personal knowledge of these people that perverted and undermined this program [sic]. So, if I were in your position, I would be a lot less self-righteous than you seem to be.[36]

As was the case with the Seabrook apartments, the Pebble Creek MRP certainly appears to have bypassed the published, required channels, with the developer appealing directly to Secretary Pierce, who, in turn, seems to have ordered the funding with none of the mandated documentation in hand. Indeed, Carmen seemingly was awarded the MRP funds before the Arlington PHA even submitted an application, with the apparent intention that Carmen would win the local competition. (When shown the HUD memoranda during his appearance before the subcommitte, Carmen said that this was the first time he had seen or heard of them.)

Durham Hosiery Mill Project, Durham, North Carolina

The final illustration was over the Durham Hosiery Mill Project. In the early 1980s, John Allen, a Boston-based developer, submitted a plan with the local PHA to renovate about 150 units of housing converted from an old hosiery mill originally built in 1902—at the time, the largest such mill in the world. In 1982, the HUD staff recommended against its funding, noting that the mill was located on a hazardous waste site, sitting on top of 100 fifty-gallon drums, some containing sulfuric acid and others cyanide. An operating railroad freight line ran less than forty feet from the site. One HUD staffer wrote in a February 16, 1982, memorandum that "[This proposal] is in fact not reasonable if we are cognizant of waste and abuse in government."[37] Nevertheless, for reasons never officially explained, on February 18, 1982, HUD selected the Hosiery Mills for $17 million in substantial rehabilitation funds. However, on September 27, the monies were "suddenly and inexplicably withdrawn," according to Allen.

The reasons, unknown to Allen at the time, were much less than "inexplicable." On September 17, Secretary Pierce was notified that President Reagan was flying to New Jersey to give a campaign speech for Republican senatorial candidate Millicent Fenwick. A local news report the following day documents the president's speech and indicates where the money may have "suddenly" gone.

> A $6 million senior citizens' housing project here that has been delayed by funding problems for four years got the green light yesterday—from none other than the President of the United States.
> And the project's developer didn't know about it until he saw a

videotape of the presidential announcement on the CBS Evening News.

President Reagan, speaking ... on behalf of Rep. Millicent Fenwick's U.S. Senate candidacy, interrupted his prepared remarks to say he had "an announcement that will surprise all of you."

"In spite of our cutting back," the president said, "the Department of Housing and Urban Development has agreed to supply public funds for 125 units of elderly housing at Park Place in Ewing, New Jersey."

Then, turning toward Mrs. Fenwick, he quipped: "If you don't elect her as senator we'll take it away."[38]

Still, with the support of Durham officials, Allen persevered in his proposal, hiring three "political" consultants to access HUD. They apparently had the intended effect. By the mid-1980s, the Hosiery Mills again was an issue within HUD. However, based on the strongest advice from the HUD career staff, Maurice Barksdale turned the project down three times while he was the assistant secretary for Housing.

On February 19, 1985, Allen met with Deborah Dean regarding his proposed project. In that meeting, he described the difficulty he had encountered in getting the HUD staff to approve the Mod Rehab funds and, in addition, an Urban Development Action Grant (UDAG).[e] Sometime in mid-March, according to Allen, Dean telephoned to say "you can put your UDAG application in. . . ." Since the UDAG was the key to his MRP, he considered this a favorable indication.[39]

Shirley Wiseman, who was the acting assistant secretary for Housing following the departure of Barksdale, was given the Durham Hosiery Mills file by Dean in the spring of 1985 and asked for her approval. She had the file reviewed by the HUD staff, and testified that "There were subsidy upon subsidy, there were waivers that would be required, there were excessive costs that made the project, in their opinion, prohibitive and they would recommend to me that I not fund the project." When Dean called to ask if she had approved the project, Wiseman told her that she could not. Dean told her that the secretary wanted it funded, to which Wiseman responded, "I am sorry, I can't fund it." Three or four days later, Pierce himself telephoned Wiseman.

---

[e] UDAG required funds supplied by the developer. In the case of the Durham Hosiery Mills, Allen proposed to use MRP funds as his contribution, a highly unusual suggestion the HUD staff found unacceptable; Durham was the first time it happened.

She recalled the conversation for the House Subcommittee on Employment and Housing:

> It was a very short conversation. He asked me if I had received the Durham packet and had Deborah spoken with me, and I said yes, I had received it, and yes, Deborah had spoken with me, and he said—the Secretary said I want the project funded, . . . I said I can't fund it, Mr. Secretary, and he said, well, I want it funded, and I said, well, I am sorry, I can't fund it, but I will send it upstairs to you, and that was the end of the conversation.[40]

Wiseman left HUD at the end of April to return to the private housing sector community.

Janet Hale succeed Wiseman as the acting assistant secretary for Housing. On Hale's first day on the job, Dean gave her the Durham package and asked that she sign the papers because, according to Hale's testimony, the "Secretary wanted the project funded."[41] Hale was given a "Rapid Reply" authorization form that already had been signed by Pierce. The formal authorization papers notifying Durham of an $11 million award were dated May 13, 1989.

The reservations of the HUD staff were subsequently realized. Special waivers were later required because of the proximity to the Mills to the railroad, because the rents were 132 percent above the market rate, and because of problematic occupancy levels; however, the hazardous waste site was successfully cleaned up. The developers of Durham Hosiery Mills complex received $11.3 million in Mod Rehab funds, a $2.3 million UDAG grant, and $3 million in rent subsidies for 151 units. According to local press accounts, the apartment complex has been well accepted in the Durham community.

The Durham Hosiery example strongly suggests that Pierce's testimony that he did not involve himself in the selection of particular projects is at direct odds with Wiseman's testimony. In fact, Wiseman related that this was the only incident in which Pierce had talked with her about a specific project. When Pierce later appeared before the investigating House Subcommittee on September 26 and October 27, 1989, and was given the opportunity to explain his actions regarding the Durham application and their rationale, he invoked the Fifth Amendment's privilege against self-incrimination and refused to testify.

Conclusions

There is no compelling need to restrict our corruption purview of Secretary Pierce's HUD to Mod Rehab projects. Apparent improprieties abound. The secretary's Special Projects and Technical Assistance (TA) funds, which were legally at his discretion, financed projects that even Pierce's close associates questioned; DuBois Gilliam, when asked about a TA grant in May 1985 for $321,099 to the Center for Resource Development (CRD) in East Orange, New Jersey, told the Subcommittee staff that "nobody in their right mind would have given them a grant."[42] Pierce probably wanted CRD funded because one of its principals was an old acquaintance, in fact, his campaign manager when Pierce had earlier run for public office. Secretary Pierce persisted in the TA application even after his friend was indicted for grand larceny. Another highly problematic TA grant of $267,933 was awarded to Bush and Company, whose president, Frederick M. Bush (no relation) had served as deputy chief of staff to Vice President George Bush until December 1983.[43]

UDAG grants were also subjected to extremely personalized measures, both pro and con. Pierce's former executive assistant, Lance Wilson, who had already profited handsomely from HUD contracts after he left HUD in June 1984, requested UDAG funding for a project in Florida in association with Leonard Briscoe. Pierce had twice named Briscoe the minority contractor of the year. In March 1987, when their Belle Glade proposal was ranked too low on the priority list to be funded, Gilliam contacted Wilson and told him "you would have to call the Secretary to encourage him or ask him to reach your project." Gilliam recounted Secretary Pierce's decision to the subcommittee:

> I went and met with the Secretary, prior to us going to the conference room to meet with other staff members, who went over the final list of UDAG projects. I indicated to him, have you received a call from Lance? He said, yes. I said, this is Lance's project right here, the Belle Glade project. He indicated to me, well, I don't like Leonard Briscoe. He said, Leonard Briscoe is a crook and he was greedy. [f] He said you

---

[f]One might justifiably wonder how Pierce could have twice named Leonard Briscoe minority contractor of the year. Briscoe was convicted in January 1993 for offering gratuities to federal housing officials.

tell Lance this is it; no more. And the Secretary agreed at that point to make the cut-off Belle Glade, Florida.

On the less supportive side, when Texas Congressman Henry Gonzalez, chairman of the House Subcommittee on Housing and Community Development, telephoned Gilliam to voice his support of a UDAG in San Antonio (a common congressional action), Pierce's reaction was completely different, although just as blatantly subjective. Gilliam testified: "The Secretary says, does Gonzalez want the project? I say, yes, Mr. Secretary. The Secretary's response was, well, 'Gonzalez don't got the project.' "[44]

However many programs were affected by Pierce's questionable actions, there are ample grounds within the MRP for our discussion of the HUD corruptions. Despite the lack of testimony by many of the central participants, including Secretary Pierce, Deborah Gore Dean, and Lance Wilson, three observations can be safely gleaned from the subcommittee transcripts. First, Pierce's testimony to the contrary, Deborah Dean was a major actor. Many personal, "Dear Debbie" notes from developers and consultants were introduced into the House hearings. Moreover, numerous witnesses testified that she was Pierce's designated spokesperson. When Thomas Demery became the assistant secretary for Housing in late 1986, he asked to meet with the secretary to discuss the direction and management of the Mod Rehab program.[g] In his testimony, Demery related how he had been given little direction:

> During the first two months as Assistant Secretary for Housing, documentation for mod rehab funding decisions consisted of scraps of paper listing various PHAs which Ms. Dean would hand me and tell me, the Secretary wants these requests funded. ... When I challenged her directives, Ms. Dean would question my loyalty to the Secretary.

On January 13, Demery met with Pierce and Dean, asking what his program authority was. According to Demery, Pierce's reply, inter alia,

---

[g]It should be recognized that Demery was apparently not a model of bureaucratic probity. On June 8, 1992, he was charged with conspiracy and conflict of interest by Independent Counsel Adams. See Jeff Gerth, "Former Top H.U.D. Official Is Charged with Conspiracy," *New York Times*, June 9, 1992, p. A8. In December, additional indictments were filed by Adams; Kelly Richmond, "Winn Condo Leads to Charges," *Denver Post*, December 5, 1992, pp. 1A, 14A. Demery has denied all accusations.

centered on the following: (1) the mod rehab program was his to run as he wanted; ... (2) program authority had not been delegated to me as Assistant Secretary for Housing; (3) a selection committee ... would meet to review future mod rehab requests; (4) Secretary Pierce would speak through Ms. Dean to this committee....

Dean substantiated Pierce's orders in a memorandum she prepared for Pierce on the same day.

You have all the power authorized to the Department, and even when you delegate authority you still have concurrent authority. ... In other words, it is so much yours, you can't even give it away. OGC [Office of the General Counsel] can find no document that says you have ever delegated authority over mod rehab to anyone. You have sole responsibility for that program.[45]

This testimony supports a second observation, that Secretary Pierce was a deliberate, major participant in deciding who received what funds. In his May 25 testimony and his interview in *Time* magazine, he firmly avowed that while he was the secretary he never interfered with specific funding decisions, steadfastly denying the allegation to the contrary. In his own words, "[HUD] was not run as a political program. ... My decisions were based on facts, law and logic, not on political party." [46] Yet there is testimony from many of Pierce's HUD associates that indirectly and directly contradicts his statements of noninterference. This is corroborated by circumstantial evidence of projects funded after meetings with the secretary.

The third observation deals with the political nature of HUD. Pierce's executive assistant made it clear in her *Wall Street Journal* interview that her office and activities were patently political. Federal Housing Commissioner Silvio DeBartolomeis described his sense of the MRP selections: "I felt uncomfortable because I felt it would be viewed that they were being done in a political manner."[47] DeBartolomeis was correct. One MRP consultant, William Taylor, who was also a member of the Republican National Committee (RNC), petitioned Dean using his RNC stationery on numerous occasions "because I'd like for Mr. Pierce to know that Bill Taylor is the National Committeeman from Florida."[48] Deputy Assistant Secretary (Policy Program Development) Gilliam could not have been more to-the-point: "The policies during the years when I was at the Department of Housing and

Urban Development dealt explicitly with political favoritism."[49] Even if we were to set aside the Dean and Gilliam statements, the sworn statements of a succession of assistant secretaries for housing and the MRP funding record would loudly contradict Pierce.

Probably the most consistent illustration of political cronyism favored the so-called "Winn group." Although never incorporated as a legal entity, the Winn group gained some fame (or notoriety) during the subcommittee hearings as a loosely aligned group of HUD alumni who were exceptionally successful in obtaining Section 8 funding.[50] The principal participants included Philip Winn (former assistant secretary of Housing from April 1981 to March 1982), Philip Abrams (who began at HUD in March 1981 as general deputy assistant secretary for Housing and left in November 1984 after serving as under secretary for a year), Lance Wilson (executive assistant to Secretary Pierce from January 1981 until June 1984), and J. Michael Queenan (former director of Housing in HUD's Denver office). In 1986, they were joined by Silvio DeBartolomeis (whose last HUD post was acting assistant secretary with Section 8 responsibilities).

Because of their past associations within HUD, Winn group members had ready access within the department. The General Services Administration reviewed a sample of 20 percent of all telephone calls placed from the office of the assistant secretary of Housing between August 1987 and February 1988 and found that the Winn group had received forty-two, extrapolated to an average of 400 calls per year from Demery's office. During the testimony of Phil Abrams, two handwritten notes from Abrams were introduced, the first dated May 10, 1986:

Dear Debbie:

Just a short note about one of the Housing Authorities that has a great need for mod rehab Section 8 funds that you and I spoke about. . . . The bottom line is they need *160 units*. . . .

I would appreciate it if you could accomodate [*sic*] their request. Thanks.

Sincerely,

Phil

The second is dated September 15, 1986:

> Dear Debbie:
>
>> Enclosed is the request from Oklahoma for 170 mod rehab units.
>> The energy crisis makes this a very pressing matter.
>
>> Sincerely,
>>
>> Phil[51]

Both of these applications were funded. Indeed, in 1987, the Winn group received over 1,300 Mod Rehab units worth about $135 million in subsidies and $29 million in tax credits; these awards—to six out of the seven applications submitted by the group—represented one-sixth of the Mod Rehab units awarded in the nation that year. In the no-nonsense summation of Michael Queenan, "We were winners."[52] In retrospect, for good reason.[h]

The final example of favoritism is possibly the most glaring. According to the sworn testimony of DuBois Gilliam, in July 1987, he told Secretary Pierce that he would probably be indicted on bribery charges and that consequently he should leave the Department.

> *Mr. Gilliam.* And so therefore I told the Secretary, I'm going to leave but I may need some help. He indicated to me that he would help me in any way that he could and he thought it would be better for me to go ahead and leave. That may slow down the investigation some.
>
> . . .
>
> *Mr. Lantos.* And what did he do?
>
> *Mr. Gilliam.* I left his office and then I had a conversation with Deborah Dean. I told Deborah about my conversation with the Secretary and that as a part of my leaving I needed to get 400 units of Section 8 mod rehab, and I wanted to have that arrangement before I left. I told her I wanted her to talk to the Secretary about it because I did not want to have a direct conversation with him about those units because I thought there might be some legal problems.
>
> So Deborah went and spoke to the Secretary, the way she explained

---

[h]Small wonder, indeed, as subsequent criminal charges revealed. Philip Winn pleaded guilty to criminal conspiracy for giving illegal gifts to two senior HUD officials. Lance Wilson was convicted of offering gratuities to federal officials. Silvio DeBartolomeis pleaded guilty to conspiring to mislead Congress.

> to me. She came back and told me I had 250 units. I couldn't have the 400 units because I was being greedy. And I told her I would take the 250 units.

Gilliam testified that these units, including tax credits, would have amounted to a severance package of about one-and-a-half million dollars.[53]

We can safely argue, then, that Secretary Pierce's HUD was pervasively infected with "abuse, favoritism, and mismanagement." But the more interesting issue is, of course, why. Why HUD at this time? Why not any other government agency with millions of dollars in grants and awards? Was there something besides Pierce's partisan management style? Stuart Butler of the conservative Heritage Foundation suggests that the fundamental causes lie within the defined HUD mission of funding "the supply [i.e., developer] side of the housing market. . . . The basic systemic problem is that you have loads of cash in HUD to bribe construction companies to do something that is against their economic interests."[54] Naturally, then, builders might be inclined to gain whatever and however they could, legally or otherwise.

The answer, however, is more complex than supply-side doctrine would have it. First, the drastic reduction in the availability of HUD funds made the MRP award competition all but lethal to the excluded firms; in other words, the stakes and financial risks were higher than before with little reason to think that the condition was temporary. Second, Secretary Pierce's office was known in the housing community to be open to selection considerations outside those mandated by published HUD regulations. This was especially the case for MRP after Congress waived the fair share criterion, which Pierce conveniently interpreted as making Section 8 awards totally at his discretion. And, third, there really was something "wrong" within HUD and particularly the Section 8 competitions. Virtually every witness testified to the frustrations, the unanswered letters, the perception that once a proposal was submitted, it disappeared into the HUD bureaucratic netherworld with hardly a trace. PHAs naturally became disappointed and disillusioned, and even more so when the Section 8 funds were cut back. Developers were reluctant to work through disheartened PHAs and formidable HUD regulations. Rather than be stymied by the seemingly intractable procedural bottlenecks, and with their institutional existences at stake, developers understandably devised ways to reduce the risk and expedite the process.

The fact that Pierce was willing to play the role of facilitator does not make him any less culpable, but it is more complete to point out that it was the conditions around him in addition to Pierce himself that led to the corruptions at HUD. In other words, Pierce, Dean, Gilliam, and others were certainly necessary, but their mere presence was not sufficient to explain all of what happened during their watch. Times were tough in the MRP world, and the HUD bureaucracy—the pro-scribed system—was seen to be unresponsive.[i] In that environment, Pierce was willing to compromise HUD regulations to expedite MRP funds. This by itself would not constitute wrongdoing; but it was Pierce's and Dean's consistent favoritism toward Republican applicants that turned his compromise into corruption, or, in Welfeld's phrase, a "tribal potlatch."

> The shame of HUD was that it had become a law unto itself. The fact that those in power in HUD didn't like the law didn't give them the authority to shift its focus from the welfare of the poorly housed to lavishly housing the . . . Manaforts and Wattses [sic] of the world.[55]

Perhaps of equal interest is how the HUD scandals do not fit into the conventional corruption scenario. Samuel Pierce would probably have gone back to his old law firm not much richer—possibly poorer—than when he left. While he surely would not have been financially impov-erished, there is no indication that he received any financial remunera-tion from the grants he apparently directed to various developers. Indeed, DuBois Gilliam, whose testimony, even as a convicted felon, is the most damaging to Pierce's defense, claimed, "I do not believe, in the bottom of my heart—I never believed that Secretary Pierce ever took any sort of gratuity or kickback while at HUD."[56] Deborah Dean has been indicted for accepting $4,000, hardly the financial return on

---

[i]The systemic nature of HUD's malaise was again shown in a confidential report by President Clinton's transition team review of the department. Drawing upon GAO and HUD inspector general reports, the transition team concluded that HUD was so badly managed that even after four years of HUD Secretary Kemp's reform efforts, "another HUD scandal is a distinct possibility." The report found that HUD mismanagement was so "clear and devastating" that it "opens the door to the systematic plunder of many millions of taxpayer dollars," leaving the "de-partment with an uncertain grasp of more than $1 trillion in financial commit-ments." See Jason DeParle, "Housing Dept. Is Called Vulnerable to New Scandals," New York Times, March 11, 1993, p. A13.

which one would expect a person to wager her professional life. Her motivating reason appeared to be to reward members of the Republican Party and assorted friends, including former Attorney General John Mitchell.[57] Whatever the financial gains to be made would have been made after leaving the administration, always a dicey bet. If so, their personal rewards would be exactly that, personal and ideological rather than monetary. Hardly grist for the traditional corruption mill.

Perhaps it was for these reasons—the apparent lack of kickbacks to the principals, or the active support of the favored developers under a partisan banner, or the general knowledge of HUD's bottlenecks among developers—that the HUD corruptions went virtually undetected throughout Secretary Pierce's tenure. Even though HUD had an active Inspectors General Office (whose reports were admittedly widely neglected) and an Ethics in Government Office (which had legal purview but little clout), there were hardly more than unsubstantiated "street" rumors of "abuses, favoritism, and mismanagement" within HUD until the final days of Pierce's secretariat. Former Senator William Proxmire (D-WI)—surely one of the Senate's most noted watchdogs, the keeper of the "Golden Fleece Award"—was invited to testify before the House Subcommittee on Housing and Employment; when was asked why he, as chairman of HUD's cognizant subcommittee in the Senate, did not "act to prevent this waste and fraud," he replied: "The answer is simple. We had no idea it was going on." [58]

Notes

1. For a more detailed—albeit occasionally irresponsible—account, see Irving Welfeld, *HUD Scandals: Howling Headlines and Silent Fiascoes* (New Brunswick, NJ: Transaction Publishers, 1992), Part I.

2. Nancy Traver, "Sam Pierce's 'Turkey Farm,' " *Time*, September 18, 1989, pp. 20–23.

3. Steve Waldman et al., "The HUD Ripoff," *Newsweek*, August 7, 1989, pp. 16–22.

4. Edward T. Pound and Kenneth H. Bacon, "Favored Friends: Housing Subsidy Plan for the Poor Helped Contributors to the GOP," *Wall Street Journal*, May 25, 1989, p. A1.

5. Carol F. Steinbach, "Programmed for Plunder," *National Journal*, Vol. 21, No. 37 (September 16, 1989), pp. 2259–2262.

6. Ibid., p. 2259.

7. Ibid., p. 2260.

8. Suzanne Garment, *Scandal* (New York: Random House, 1991), chap. 6.

9. Senate Hearings, quoted in Welfeld, *HUD Scandals*, p. 71.

10. Lee May, "U.S. Softens Urban Policy after Criticism," *Los Angeles Times*, July 10, 1982, p. 6.

11. United States House of Representatives, (Hearings before the) Employment and Housing Subcommittee of the Committee on Government Operations, *Abuses, Favoritism, and Mismanagement in HUD Programs*, 101st Congress, Vol. 1 (Washington D.C.: Government Printing Office, 1991), May 25, 1989, p. 187. Subsequent references to these hearings will be cited by title, volume number, date, and page number. Volumes 1 and 2 were published in 1990; volumes 3, 4, and 5 were published in 1991.

12. *Abuses, Favoritism, and Mismanagement in HUD Programs*, Vol. 5, April 30, 1990, pp. 94–95.

13. Pound and Bacon, "Favored Friends," p. A1.

14. Interview with Nancy Traver, " 'Silent Sam' Speaks Up," *Time*, September 18, 1989, pp. 23–24.

15. Steinbach, "Programmed for Plunder," p. 2260.

16. Testimonies of Samuel R. Pierce and John J. Knapp, *Abuses, Favoritism, and Mismanagement in HUD Programs*, Vol. 1, May 25, 1989, pp. 252 and 299, respectively.

17. Letter to Subcommittee Chair Tom Lantos from John J. Knapp, June 9, 1989; reprinted in *Abuses, Favoritism, and Mismanagement in HUD Programs*, Vol. 3, pp. 809.

18. Testimony of Inspector General Paul Adams, *Abuses, Favoritism, and Mismanagement in HUD Programs*, Vol. 1, May 8, 1989, pp. 12–13.

19. Testimony of Paul Manafort, *Abuses, Favoritism, and Mismanagement in HUD Programs*, Vol. 2, June 20, 1989, p. 79.

20. Testimonies of Roy Ziegler and William Connolly, respectively, of the New Jersey Department of Community Affairs, *Abuses, Favoritism, and Mismanagement in HUD Programs*, Vol. 2, June 29, 1989, p. 453.

21. Testimony in *Abuses, Favoritism, and Mismanagement in HUD Programs*, Vol. 2, p. 471.

22. Bruce Petersen, in *Abuses, Favoritism, and Mismanagement in HUD Programs*, Vol. 1, pp. 10, 11, and 50, respectively.

23. These estimates are from the U.S. House of Representatives, Committee on Government Operations, *Abuse and Mismanagement at HUD*, 24th Report (Washington, D.C.: Government Printing Office, November 1, 1990), p. 17.

24. Testimony of Judith Siegel, *Abuses, Favoritism, and Mismanagement in HUD Programs*, Vol. 1, May 25, 1989, pp. 153, 141, and 167, respectively. The exchange with Congressman Frank is on p. 162.

25. Testimony of Joseph Strauss, *Abuses, Favoritism, and Mismanagement in HUD Programs*, Vol. 2, June 22, 1989, p. 170.

26. Siegel testimony in *Abuses, Favoritism, and Mismanagement in HUD Programs*, Vol. 1, pp. 157, 164, and 142, respectively.

27. All of the James Watt quotations are from his testimony in *Abuses, Favoritism, and Mismanagement in HUD Programs*, Vol. 1, June 9, 1989, pp. 351–352, 352, 353 and 355, and 379, respectively.

28. Ibid., pp. 377 and 388.

29. Ibid., p. 353. Cf. Secretary Pierce's earlier testimony in Vol. 1, May 25, 1989, pp. 212–213.

30. Samuel Pierce, in *Abuses, Favoritism, and Mismanagement in HUD Programs*, Vol. 1, May 25, 1989, pp. 219–220.

31. Quoted in *Abuse and Mismanagement at HUD*, p. 23.

32. HUD Secretary Jack Kemp, *Abuses, Favoritism, and Mismanagement in HUD Programs*, Vol. 2, July 11, 1989, p. 746.

33. Testimony of Gerald Carmen, *Abuses, Favoritism, and Mismanagement in HUD Programs*, Vol. 4, October 13, 1989, p. 614.

34. The memoranda and correspondence are reprinted in *Abuses, Favoritism, and Mismanagement in HUD Programs*, Vol. 4, October 13, 1989, pp. 618, 628–629, 631–632, and 621, respectively.

35. Testimony of Gerald Carmen, *Abuses, Favoritism, and Mismanagement in HUD Programs*, Vol. 4, October 13, 1989, p. 647.

36. *Abuses, Favoritism, and Mismanagement in HUD Programs*, Vol. 4, October 13, 1989, p. 611.

37. The memorandum is from a list compiled by the House Subcommittee on Employment and Housing, *Abuses, Favoritism, and Mismanagement in HUD Programs*, Vol. 3, p. 12.

38. The memorandum to Pierce, and Anonymous, "Reagan OKs Funds for Seniors in Ewing," *Trenton Times*, September 18, 1982, both reprinted in *Abuse and Mismanagement at HUD*, pp. 28–29.

39. Testimony of John Allen, *Abuses, Favoritism, and Mismanagement in HUD Programs*, Vol. 3, July 17, 1989, p. 288.

40. Testimony of Shirley Wiseman, *Abuses, Favoritism, and Mismanagement in HUD Programs*, Vol. 3, July 14, 1989, pp. 13, 14, and 14–15, respectively.

41. Testimony of Janet Hale, *Abuses, Favoritism, and Mismanagement in HUD Programs*, Vol. 3, July 14, 1989, pp. 18–19.

42. Interview with DuBois Gilliam by the subcommittee staff; quoted in *Abuse and Mismanagement at HUD*, p. 63.

43. See the testimony of Frederick M. Bush, *Abuses, Favoritism, and Mismanagement in HUD Programs*, Vol. 2, June 29, 1989, pp. 347–448.

44. Testimony of DuBois Gilliam, *Abuses, Favoritism, and Mismanagement in HUD Programs*, Vol. 5, April 30, 1990, pp. 75 and 70, respectively.

45. Testimony of Thomas T. Demery, *Abuses, Favoritism, and Mismanagement in HUD Programs*, Vol. 5, May 23, 1990, pp. 324–325, respectively.

46. Interview with Traver, " 'Silent Sam' Speaks Up," pp. 23–24.

47. Testimony of Silvio DeBartolomeis, *Abuses, Favoritism, and Mismanagement in HUD Programs*, Vol. 1, June 9, 1989, p. 417.

48. William Taylor, *Abuses, Favoritism, and Mismanagement in HUD Programs*, Vol. 3, July 24, 1989, p. 325.

49. DuBois Gilliam, *Abuses, Favoritism, and Mismanagement in HUD Programs*, Vol. 5, April 30, 1990, p. 66.

50. David Johnston, "H.U.D. Grants under Reagan: A Case Study in Connections," *New York Times*, July 14, 1989, pp. A1, A9.

51. Testimony of Philip Abrams, *Abuses, Favoritism, and Mismanagement in HUD Programs*, Vol. 2, June 22, 1989, pp. 234-235. Emphasis in original.

52. J. Michael Queenan, *Abuses, Favoritism, and Mismanagement in HUD Programs*, Vol. 4, October 13, 1989, p. 591.

53. DuBois Gilliam, *Abuses, Favoritism, and Mismanagement in HUD Programs*, Vol. 5, April 30, 1990, pp. 160–161.

54. Quoted in Steinbach, "Programmed for Plunder," p. 2261.

55. Welfeld, *HUD Scandals*, p. 106.

56. *Abuses, Favoritism, and Mismanagement in HUD Programs*, April 30, 1990, p. 123.

57. Martin Tolchin, "Grand Jury Indicts Ex-Aide to Reagan's Housing Chief," *New York Times*, April 29, 1992, p. A8. Dean was re-indicted on July 6, 1992, for directing awards to favored developers; Mitchell, strongly presumed to be the unnamed, unindicted co-conspirator, was very close to Dean. See David Johnston, "Aide to Reagan Housing Secretary Is Indicted on Favoritism Charges," *New York Times*, July 8, 1992, pp. A1, A7.

58. Testimony of former Senator William Proxmire, *Abuses, Favoritism, and Mismanagement in HUD Programs*, Vol. 3, July 13, 1989, p. 710.

4

WEDTECH AT LARGE

The Wedtech scandals have drawn the heated fire of three books whose titles—*Too Good to Be True,*[1] *Feeding the Beast,*[2] and *Feeding Frenzy*[3]—provide some journalist indication of the flamboyant nature of the scandals. Basically, these books chronicle how the laudable idea of procurement contract "set asides" for minority contractors, when carried just a bit further to a position of institutional advocacy, resulted in widening circles of political corruption, rising from the South Bronx up to Congress, through federal agencies to the Department of Justice and even into the Reagan White House. Rather than a heartening story of a ghetto entrepreneur making good, Wedtech became the disheartening story of a minority contractor going bad in a big-time way.

On January 21, 1982, John Mariotta, the founder and co-owner of the Welbilt Electronic Die Company (renamed Wedtech in 1983) was invited to the White House for a publicity function, one emphasizing the administration's urban enterprise zone initiative. The meeting had been convened by the president and was attended by Vice President Bush and a few cabinet officers, as well as some real-life illustrations of ghetto entrepreneurs, for instance, Welbilt's John Mariotta. To everybody's surprise, Mariotta rhetorically made himself the center of attention. After claiming that drugs and welfare reliance were killing the nation, he continued to explain how he had been told that it took $25,000 in welfare payments annually to support a family of four; thus, a company like his that could hire a thousand welfare recipients would save the government $25 million and generate, in his case, $100 million in new business. The Bronx alone could support ten such companies. "Mr. President," he concluded, "spread this penicillin to a hundred cities, and you will save one hundred billion dollars." Afterwards, at lunch, President Reagan personally commended Mariotta for his comments.[4]

On March 6, 1984, President Reagan came to New York to address a $1,000-a-plate campaign banquet at the Waldorf Astoria hotel. Wedtech had purchased two tables, as befitting a growing company that had prospered thanks to government defense contracts during Reagan's first administration and gave every indication of continuing to do so during his second. The president's speech was replete with politics, criticizing Democrats and praising local Republicans. As was his preference (and unbeknownst to Mariotta), Reagan closed his speech with one of his trademark personalized anecdotes:

> Real progress in this country can be traced to the work of conscientious and hardworking individuals. . . . One such person is John Mariotta, who's providing jobs and training for the hardcore unemployed of the South Bronx.
>
> Born of Puerto Rican immigrants and having served in the United States Army, Mr. Mariotta has had all the ups and downs associated with entrepreneurship. And today, through Wedtech, he not only has built a successful corporation, he's helping hundreds of people who would otherwise be condemned to menial jobs or a life on the dole.
>
> And what gave Mr. Mariotta the courage to keep going when others quit? He tells us it was his faith in God. Now, his faith has moved mountains, helping hundreds of people who'd almost given up hope.
>
> People like John Mariotta are heroes for the eighties.[5]

President Reagan's accolades were seemingly well deserved. Wedtech was to garner hundreds of millions of dollars in government contracts during the 1980s, and train, then employ hundreds of underskilled workers, many of them as illiterate as John Mariotta himself.

But it really was too good to be true. A few years later, Mariotta and his Wedtech associates were indicted and pleaded guilty to bribery, tax evasion, racketeering, and other crimes that had contributed to their business successes. In addition, many of their supporters in and out of government, including two congressman and a close associate of President Reagan, were also convicted; others, including Attorney General of the United States Edwin Meese III, were tarred by their association with Wedtech. The *New York Times* summarized the Wedtech roller coaster:

> Once billed as a symbol of hope for the depressed inner city, Wedtech has
> become an emblem of white-collar greed, entering the nation's vocabulary
> as a synonym for corruption, bribery, and unethical conduct.[6]

However, as in the case of the HUD scandals, we need to step aside
from the emotion and criminal charges of Wedtech to ask if the corruption was as insidious and pervasive as the newspaper coverage and
convictions would have us believe. Again, Suzanne Garment offers an
alternative thesis, that while the Wedtech owners themselves were assuredly guilty of serious crimes, the criminal indictments of the people
with whom they worked were highly questionable, their charges often
consisting of little more than shady but nevertheless legitimate lobbying. Garment claims the prosecutors were politically motivated, either
out of professional pique at being unable to charge Attorney General
Meese himself, or by political ambition, as in the case of Ruldolph W.
Giuliani (then U.S. attorney in the Southern District, New York, the
nation's largest federal attorney's office), who was preparing to run for
mayor of New York City.[7] Garment's accusations are given some credence by the fact that many Wedtech convictions of the more notable
participants (excepting Wedtech management itself) were later overturned by the U.S. appellate courts for a variety of technical reasons.
Similarly, we need to ask if the Wedtech scandals were the result of
personal avarice on the part of a few or a manifestation of a more
systemic malaise encompassing the many.

Therefore, before we decide to join either the chorus of condemna-
tion or the choir of acquittal, we should carefully examine the particulars surrounding Wedtech to ascertain if indeed they constitute a case of
systemic political corruption or merely a localized incident of a small
minority-owned company trying too hard to go too far too fast, caught
in a political context where the process was more culpable than the
admitted criminals themselves.

Wedtech: A Humble Beginning

John Mariotta, born in Spanish Harlem of Puerto Rican immigrants,
barely finished junior high school and dropped out of vocational
school. He had, however, a genuine aptitude for mechanics and worked
as a tool and die maker. In 1965, he was brought in as a partner to
Welbilt Electronic Die Company, a small, constantly struggling ma-

chine shop in the Bronx. When his partner retired in 1971, he persuaded Fred Neuberger to become his new partner and half-owner of
Welbilt. Neuberger was born in Rumania, escaped Nazi persecution as
a teenager, and emigrated to the United States through Israel. In 1971,
urban renewal forced them to relocate their facility to 164th and
Washington, the "Fort Apache" area of the Bronx, which Mariotta
later described as being located "between a dope pusher and a car
thief." In 1973, Welbilt's sales totaled $200,000.

In 1975, Mariotta decided to bid on a defense contract, a Bell
helicopter fuel filter assembly for the U.S. Army. On one of his
regular scouting trips to the New York office of the Defense Contract Administration, he had found a Request for Proposal for the
fuel filter. The request's blueprints were so poorly drawn that
Mariotta could scarcely read them. Still, Welbilt was able to prepare the low bid and was awarded the army contract, thus beginning its involvement in the defense procurement contracting
business.

Around the same time, Neuberger convinced Mariotta that they
should apply to the Small Business Administration (SBA) for minority-
owned business status, thus making Welbilt eligible for minority set-
asides, so-called Section 8(a) contracts. Section 8(a), an outgrowth of
President Lyndon Johnson's War on Poverty, specified that designated
government contracts could be awarded on a noncompetitive basis to
legitimate minority-owned businesses. "In theory," Sternberg and Harrison later commented, "this program would help revitalize the urban
ghettos by providing upward mobility and jobs. In reality, it was a
recipe for scandal."[8] A 1978 congressional report was even blunter:
"For a lucky, mainly non-disadvantaged few, the 8(a) program is a
gravy train of impressive proportions."[9]

To secure a minority status for Welbilt, Neuberger agreed to surrender his 50 percent ownership, accepting one-third to Mariotta's
two-thirds. To lend greater credibility, they back-dated the arrangement to 1972. However, both later admitted that they secretly understood that the 50–50 partnership they had originally formed
would remain de facto in place. On September 25, 1975, Welbilt was
assigned a minority business status by the SBA, opening it to a trove
of opportunities unfettered by competitive market forces. More important, the SBA now became a crucial institutional booster within
the government for Welbilt, frequently willing to extend itself well

beyond administrative propriety as a means of supporting its 8(a) program.

In early 1976, Mariotta was referred by Bankers Trust to the Urban Business Assistance Corporation, which had been established by New York University to help minority businesses. Mariotta took classes there and was able to persuade his instructor, Mario Moreno, an émigré from Columbia, to join Welbilt in 1978, first as a part-time employee, later as full-time treasurer. Moreno, who secured Welbilt's first major bank loan, was to provide the political acumen that held the company together.

In 1976, Welbilt was awarded an 8(a) contract for a bit over $800,000 and then, in the following year, an air force contract for $115,000 to build a part of the GE jet engines that powered the F-4 jet fighter; the engine component contract was renewed and ultimately proved worth $2.5 million. In the fall of 1979, Welbilt landed its largest 8(a) contract, a $4 million agreement to build suspension units (and later refrigeration units for cooling the engines) of the army's M-113 armored personnel carrier. This latter contract also included an option for an addition $4 million for the following year, should the parties agree.

On January 13, 1978, the New York *Tribune*'s Mort Young wrote an article on the urban decay of the Bronx, in which he made passing reference to Welbilt as a "ray of hope."[10] Shortly after this welcomed recognition, Mariotta and Neuberger were contacted by Representative Mario Biaggi, a five-term Democratic congressman from New York, who in turn introduced the firm to his law firm, Biaggi, Ehrlich & Lang.[a] Even though Welbilt was not located in his district, Biaggi took a distinct interest in the fledgling firm, indicating that he would be able to assist it in obtaining government contracts. His interest was soon reciprocated. In April, Welbilt retained Biaggi's law firm for $20,000 annually. Similar but less formal understandings were reached with Representative Robert Garcia, a Democrat who did represent Welbilt's congressional district. In 1978, Welbilt management contributed $3,000 to his election campaign, and another $5,000 the

---

[a]Biaggi, Ehrlich & Lang became Biaggi & Ehrlich a short time later. In 1979, Ehrlich purchased Biaggi's half of the firm for $320,000. However, the firm's name was unchanged, reflecting its new partner, Congressman Biaggi's son, Richard, as well as the congressman's continued presence.

following year. Both congressmen were to prove extremely useful in the very near future.

To finance its new contracts, Welbilt had to make major alterations in its new facilities as well as purchase machinery and hire personnel. So in late 1979, Moreno applied to the Economic Development Administration (EDA) for a $2 million loan, plus another $2 million in loan guarantees. The request was a long shot, at best. Welbilt was already on tenuous financial footing, and, moreover, the EDA rarely gave two awards to a single company. However, Welbilt was desperate for the funds so Mariotta and Moreno decided to test their Washington connections. Congressman Garcia agreed to send his administrative aide to accompany Mariotta and Neuberger to the Philadelphia EDA regional office and then up to Citibank. Garcia's aide was able to convince both of Welbilt's merits, and the following February EDA gave the firm its requested $2 million grant and Citibank extended it another $2.2 million, with EDA guaranteeing 90 percent of the note. This was an enlightening experience for Welbilt, for it demonstrated to its owners that political influence, one, was available for a few thousand dollars and, two, could be brought to bear for the company's immediate benefit.

By that fall, Welbilt was again in dire financial straits. It had used up the loan money and was facing imminent bankruptcy. About this time, an employee in its accounting section informed Moreno that the Defense Contract Audit Agency was not keeping close tabs on the bills Welbilt was submitting for the army contract. Viewing this lapse as an opportunity, Moreno proposed to the partners that they could get an "interest-free loan" from the army by submitting bills for goods yet to be delivered. They rationalized that Welbilt was only getting what was due, just a great deal earlier. More critically, the "pre-payments" would keep the company afloat, albeit illegally. With this purpose in mind, Welbilt decided to engage in fraud, using doctored invoices from suppliers to document its requests for payment. (Shortly thereafter, Moreno demanded to become a partner and was given 9 percent of the firm, although the stock transfer was kept hidden from the SBA.)

A final episode from Welbilt's early years was occurring at the same time. The army had decided to purchase up to 100,000 small, portable engines and, as the technology was relatively straightforward, set the contract aside under Section 8(a). Mariotta was able to persuade the SBA to nominate Welbilt for what appeared to be a heretofore unimaginably lucrative contract. However, the army was an extremely sophisticated purchaser. It estimated that the engines should cost around $1,500 a piece for 13,100 engines, with a fair market contract value of $19 million. But these estimates were for a proven machine company with the necessary machinery already in place. Welbilt was far from fitting this description, so its original bid was $99.9 million, about $7,600 per engine. Although Welbilt later lowered its bid to just under $39 million, the army, after visiting the Welbilt facility and judging it technically inadequate to the task, rejected the bid on April 13, 1981, and petitioned the SBA to remove the engine contract from the set-aside program.

For unknown reasons, Mariotta and Neuberger personalized the army's decisions, thinking that their rejection was the individual fault of the army procurement officer. Focusing their disappointment on him personally, they went so far as to consider hiring a private investigator to see if the problematic army procurement officer could somehow be blackmailed or his professional credibility undermined. They contacted a private investigator in San Francisco who told them that their idea was unlikely to succeed. He did, however, lead them to what was to be the final piece in the Wedtech mosaic. He suggested that they would be better served by the proverbial "friends in high places," and recommended them to E. Robert Wallach, a very successful and liberal personal injury San Francisco lawyer and a long-standing personal friend of Edwin Meese, who, at the time, had just been appointed White House counselor to the newly elected President Ronald Reagan.

In late April 1981, Mariotta and Neuberger invited Wallach to visit their Bronx facility and he accepted. He was immediately taken by the management, the facility, its apparent mission, and its ghetto location. Somehow, Welbilt struck a responsive chord in Wallach's liberal perception of himself as social activist. He quickly offered to help represent the foundling company in Washington and, in particular, to Meese.

Welbilt mobilized all its available forces to convince the army to reconsider its offer—in procedural terms, to conduct an audit that they were hopeful would substantiate Welbilt's bid as both legitimate and fair. The president of the Latin American Manufacturer's Association (LAMA), who was secretly subsidized by Welbilt, wrote letters introducing Mariotta to Hispanic members of Congress and to White House aides such as Lyn Nofziger, Elizabeth Dole, Michael Deaver, and James Baker. The SBA, prompted by White House admonitions to support one of its promising Section 8(a) firms, refused the army's request to delete the small engine contract from its set-aside status. Representative Biaggi recruited Representative Joseph P. Addabbo (D-NY, Chair of the Small Business Committee, and a member of the House Military Appropriations Subcommittee) to the cause and then called upon the newly elected Republican senator from New York, Alfonse D'Amato. Senator D'Amato, never one to neglect his New York constituents, wrote to Secretary of the Army John Marsh, asking that "a competent, growing firm like Welbilt [be given] a fair opportunity to meet the army's needs."[11] And Wallach, who wrote literally hundreds of memoranda to Meese, repeatedly brought Welbilt to his friend's personal attention, even indicating in one memorandum that Meese should urge Secretary of Defense Caspar Weinberger to intervene with Secretary Marsh on Welbilt's behalf. Meese, for his part, passed the Welbilt file on to some of his White House aides for action, who, in turn, proselytized the army procurement hierarchy on Welbilt's behalf.

The army contracting officers soon realized that they had little choice but to surrender their procurement prerogatives to higher authorities. In August 1981, after meeting with a White House staff member, the army succumbed to Welbilt's political pressure and agreed to audit its decision, that is, to examine again if Welbilt's price and capabilities were suitable for the portable engine contract. Welbilt considered the re-audit as a major reprieve, a result of its political full-court press.

In November, the army announced that $6.2 million of projected expenditures in Welbilt's last $38.9 bid were not valid, while it had raised its own best estimate from $19 to $23.7 million, largely because of inflation. Mariotta and Neuberger were encouraged; they now calculated that only the difference between $32.7 and $23.7 million—a mere $9 million—lay between the army and their winning the contract. On January 15, 1982, a meeting was convened by the White House staff to argue for Welbilt, but it was hardly propitious; the SBA refused to ante up the difference, the army refused to raise its estimate to meet Welbilt's, and, once more, there was talk of removing the engine from the set-aside list. Partially because of SBA's refusal to bridge the $9 million gap, its administrator was removed by the White House shortly thereafter, and a more amenable administrator put into his stead.[12]

A new player now entered the lists. Long-time conservative Republican operator Lyn Nofziger had joined the White House staff as director of the Office of Political Affairs when Reagan took office. In late January 1982, Nofziger resigned his position and became a partner in Nofziger and Bragg, a Washington public relations firm. Nofziger retained his political sensitivities as to what would enhance Republican political fortunes and, even more valuable, his well-recognized ties to the White House. One of Nofziger and Bragg's first clients was LAMA (in essence, Welbilt), which Nofziger viewed as a Republican inroad into the potentially valuable Hispanic vote. In March, the SBA again refused to permit the army to withdraw its engine contract from the 8(a), but it likewise refused to allocate the necessary funds to subsidize the contract. Now officially a lobbyist and private citizen, Nofziger telephoned Secretary of the Army Marsh and made it clear that the Reagan administration was interested in the Hispanic-owned Welbilt.

On April 5, Nofziger met with Ed Meese to discuss the situation and three days later sent Meese a memorandum indicating that awarding the engine contract to Welbilt would "be a major first step in the president's commitment to revitalize the South Bronx," and suggesting that Marsh "would listen carefully to [Deputy Secretary of Defense Frank] Carlucci or Weinberger or even Reagan." He concluded,

> Ed, I really think it would be a blunder not to award that contract to Welbilt. The symbolism either way is very great here.[13]

Nofziger's memorandum to Meese clearly violated the Ethics in Government Act, which forbade former government employees from contacting their agencies concerning business opportunities for a year after their resignations. Nofziger had been specifically briefed on compliance with the act by White House Counsel Frank Fielding prior to his departure from the White House, apparently to little avail.[b]

Meese, who had also received extensive entreaties from Wallach on Welbilt, asked his aide, Jim Jenkins, to pursue the matter. Money concerns were again pressing Welbilt. On April 16, Secretary Marsh yet again decided against Welbilt and asked that the engine contract be released from Section 8(a) and put out for competitive bid. Also on April 16, in response to an inquiry from Jenkins as to the propriety of

---

[b]Nofziger was convicted of violating the Ethics in Government Act as a result of this memorandum, but his conviction was subsequently set aside on appeal due to a technicality arising from the ambiguous wording of the legislation.

intervening on Welbilt's behalf, Craig Fuller, a cabinet officer, cautioned Jenkins of the ethics of the issue by stating, "I strongly suggest no White House action be taken." As Jenkins himself scribbled in the margins to Fuller's letter, "Too late." Later he told Senate investigators, "[Fuller] wasn't my boss, so he couldn't tell me not to."[14] Indeed, on April 22, Jenkins wrote James Sanders, the new SBA administrator, informing him of Meese's continued interest in Welbilt and requesting a briefing on the matter. Sanders later explained that this was the only time during his four-year tenure at SBA that he had ever been called to the White House, except for the time the White House tried to eliminate the SBA. Fuller had sent a copy of Jenkins' April 22 letter to the White House Counsel Fielding, whose aide wrote back advising that "the White House should not get involved." Marching order seemingly in hand, Jenkins again refused to be deterred by counsel's advice.

On May 19, Jenkins convened a White House meeting of Welbilt management and representatives from the army, HUD, the EDA, and SBA. Jenkins' very political intention and message were made absolutely clear to all in attendance; as he later recounted the meeting,

> I was not going to stand for any bullshit . . . [nor] for any foot dragging or fogging the issue. . . . I wanted them to know that besides my knowing that I would be able to tell immediately if they were pulling this stunt, I wanted them to know that I wouldn't stand for it and that I would be talking to them directly, or their bosses about it, if I ran into evidence of such foot dragging.[15]

The parties understood the charge and acted accordingly. The army raised its estimate by about $4 million, citing inflation; the SBA gave Welbilt a $3 million Business Development Expense grant (almost half of the BDE funds for that year) and a $2 million loan. SBA's commitment to Welbilt was made on June 18, a minor embarrassment since Welbilt did not formally request the funds until ten days later. On September 13, the army and Welbilt agreed to a $27.2 million bid. On September 28, the contract for over 13,000 engines was finally announced with great political fanfare at Welbilt's Bronx facility. Jenkins sent Meese a copy of the press release, scribbling "Though you cannot tell from reading any of this, your personal go-ahead to me saved this project."[16]

Mariotta, Neuberger, and Moreno had managed, with more than a little help from their friends, to engineer a procurement coup of the first magnitude—one seemingly well beyond their technical competence—against a determined and knowledgeable procurement officer. As was the case with the EDA grant, it became very clear to them that in dealings with the government, technical capabilities were secondary to political skills; it paid to purchase assistance in all the right places; and, most important, this strategy had few constraints or nay-sayers.

Wedtech Goes Public

Flushed by its success in winning the army contract, Welbilt found to its dismay that it was once again anything but flush with funds. Given its immediate financial condition, banks would no longer lend it bridge money. The BDE grant from the SBA could only be spent on machines and tool dies, not the necessary machinists. Moreover, Welbilt's many "supporters" began to call in their tickets. The local teamsters union representative, already receiving $3,000 a month to ensure labor acquiescence, upped his entitlement (i.e., extortion) to $5,000 a month. Representative Biaggi raised Welbilt's retainer to his "former" law firm to $55,000 per year and also extracted a promise of 5 percent of Welbilt when it went public. Wallach presented his statement for $150,000 plus his demand for stock and a percentage of any business he brought the firm. Facing certain bankruptcy, Mariotta and Neuberger even agreed in their desperation to a $500,000 personal loan from an unnamed "private investor"; the money, literally delivered in a cash-stuffed briefcase, had to be repaid entirely in three months along with $150,000 interest. Much to the consternation of the principals, Welbilt was unable to meet the repayment schedule but was able to negotiate a three-month extension for an additional $150,000. Finally, when they could not meet the new deadline and at wit's end, the partners asked Representative Biaggi to intercede and reach an agreement under which they would repay the loan (with yet another set of usury charges) after the firm went public.

Issuing public stock had many advantages, not the least of which was that Mariotta and Neuberger would become instant millionaires. It would also provide imperative capital to prepare to meet the army's delivery contract as well as Welbilt's outstanding loans. Furthermore, a public issue would provide instant respectability to Welbilt's desperately upwardly mobile owners. However, there were several obstacles involved with going public, the most dangerous being that Welbilt's books would have to undergo a financial audit. The Big Eight accounting firm of Main Hurdman was dutifully engaged and almost immediately uncovered Welbilt's fraudulent army pre-billing on the M-113 contract. The head of the audit team, Richard Bluestine, informed Welbilt management that his firm would have to consider withdrawing from the audit (to "disengage" is a serious reprimand in the accounting community) unless Welbilt immediately notified the government of its billing practice. The situation became even more perilous when the auditors discovered that Mariotta and Neuberger had been supplementing their salaries by covertly diverting company funds into a private account.

By now, however, Mariotta and Neuberger were well practiced in handling such situations. They quietly offered to make Bluestine a partner in the firm (effective as soon as the firm when public), giving him 9 percent of the stock, and then hired the audit's chief accountant, Anthony Guariglia, with a lucrative salary and a promised 1.5 percent of the stock. Both accepted; Guariglia immediately, Bluestine to join later. To meet Main Hurdman's disclosure requirement, Bernard Ehrlich (of Biaggi & Ehrlich) reported to Peter Neglia, the regional SBA administrator, that Welbilt was having some minor troubles with the Defense [Department] Contract Audit Agency but that they were being taken care of. This casual conversation permitted Biaggi & Ehrlich to notify Main Hurdman that

> Mr. Ehrlich has discussed the matter extensively with the SBA and that matter has been resolved. The SBA has indicated that they will be satisfied so long as significant inventory and shipments exist to cover the advance payments and progress payments,[17]

thus satisfying the accounting firm that Welbilt had carried out its obligation to inform the "government" of its accounting shortcomings. Neuberger, on his part, assured Main Hurdman that his diversion of $185,000 was, in reality, only a personal loan that he would repay with part of his proceeds from the upcoming public stock sale. With Bluestine's reassurances, Main Hurdman gave Welbilt the clean bill of financial health necessary for its registration statement—in other words, the documentation necessary for the Security and Exchange Commission to approve a public offering.

Following Wallach's repeated urgings, Welbilt began searching for a respected law firm to prepare the legal papers required for certification. Overriding the parochial protests of Biaggi & Ehrlich, Welbilt retained the firm of Squadron, Ellenoff, Pleasant & Lehrer as corporate counsel, with specific responsibilities in taking the firm public. Not incidentally, Welbilt also retained Squadron Ellenoff's cachet to support its shaky legitimacy. Although Squadron Ellenoff's lawyers, in preparing the offering's registration papers, uncovered much of the same material as Main Hurdman's auditors, they were equally willing to accept Welbilt's explanations and exclude the highly questionable arrangements from the public documentation. On May 5, the firm of Moseley, Hallgarten, Estabrook & Weeden agreed to prepare the prospectus and underwrite the offering, estimating the firm's value at $100 million (much to Mariotta and Neuberger's delighted surprise). In July, Mariotta and Moreno began to make sales presentations to prospective investors.

Two minor details required last-minute attention. First, the Welbilt Corporation, a New York–based firm, filed suit to enjoin Welbilt against using the name, so Welbilt, for purposes of the public offering, was forced to become Wedtech in early 1983. More critically, before its bank would agree to approve a loan package of $5.1 million, Wedtech needed to convince the EDA that it should "subordinate" its loan, that is, give the bank first rights to Wedtech's assets in case of bankruptcy. All the subordination required was the simple approval of Carlos Campbell, the assistant secretary of Commerce (for EDA), but obtaining Campbell's approval turned out to be anything but simple, and soon required Wedtech to turn out its complete complement of New York and Washington lobbyists.

Campbell viewed his "mission" at EDA "to clean up the agency's horrendous loan portfolio—42 percent of the loans were delinquent—and protect the taxpayers' money."[18] Initial efforts by Representative Biaggi and Senator D'Amato to persuade him to compromise that mission and subordinate Welbilt's loan failed, so Moreno enlisted Nofziger, Bragg, Wallach, and, through Wallach, Edwin Meese himself. SBA's Neglia was able to secure the regional EDA approval, but on July 11, Campbell told the inquiring Bragg that he had decided to refer the request to EDA's legal counsel. Despairing for funds, Wedtech decided it was time to play the "White House card."

On July 15, Moreno met Wallach in Washington very early in the morning to discuss how critical Campbell's approval was to Wedtech's future. Wallach then met with Meese in the White House for a 7:15 breakfast, whereupon Meese called Secretary of Commerce Malcolm Baldrige (one report had Baldrige—plausibly—in the shower) and asked if the secretary could sign off for his obstructionist assistant secretary. Baldrige called back late that afternoon to report that Campbell still had the responsibility for the case and that a conference had been arranged for Wedtech and its lawyers to meet with him on July 19. Campbell, swayed by Howard Squadron's argument that the safest way to recoup EDA's money was to expedite the new bank loan, thus paving the way for the cash influx promised by the stock sales, finally agreed to subordinate the loan. Wedtech had assembled an inordinate amount of political firepower for what Campbell later described as a minor bureaucratic decision; indeed, he claimed that Wedtech's tactics extended rather than expedited his decision.[19] However, once again, Wedtech perceived its road to success as paved with political leverage.[c]

On August 25, 1.5 million Wedtech shares (at $16 per share) were publicly offered on the NASDAQ exchange. Pyramiding upon the 1983 bull market fever and its seductive high-tech image, investors in Wedtech were willing to overlook questionable items in its prospectus (e.g., 153,000 shares set aside for "additional senior management personnel," the partners' subterfuge for the yet-to-be-announced Richard Bluestine) and, of course, knew nothing of the firm's financial skullduggery. The subscription was sold out by September 2. Mariotta and Neuberger had each sold $2.7 million worth of stock. The Wedtech officers celebrated by leasing six Mercedes-Benz automobiles that very afternoon.

But the celebration was premature, for Wedtech soon discovered that there was one overwhelming reason for not going public—it endangered the firm's 8(a) status. At first, this was thought to be inconsequential; the prospectus had even mentioned that the firm "may" no longer be eligible for its protected status. Almost immediately after the stock offering, SBA regulations began to dictate the transition out of the set-aside shelter. All of the 8(a) rationale and criteria were seemingly inapplicable: Wedtech was no longer a minority-owned firm (Mariotta's ownership was listed in the prospectus as 26.7 percent); it was no longer "economically disadvantaged," having just garnered $30

---

[c] For his efforts to "protect the taxpayer's money," Campbell was fired by the Reagan administration six months later.

million from its public offering. Moreover, the guiding philosophy behind the set-aside program was that it would incubate struggling minority firms until they were ready to enter the competitive marketplace; Wedtech's success in winning military contracts and its stock sale were evidence that it had passed the stand-alone market test. All of these arguments were brought to a head when the SBA notified Wedtech in September that its 8(a) status would expire in October 1983. The transition worries might have been little more than bothersome had not Wedtech learned that the navy was planning to award a huge construction contract for pontoon causeways, potentially worth well over $100 million, and that the procurement might possibly be awarded on a set-aside contract basis.

Wedtech had as much experience in building pontoons for the navy as it did engines for the army, that is to say, none. Nevertheless, the partners decided to pursue the contract with their characteristic fervor. They realized that their only chance was to convince the navy brass to set aside the contract for 8(a) firms. But first they had to protect their now-challenged certification and persuade the SBA that Wedtech was still a bona fide minority contractor.

Getting an extension to mid-October and a second one to January 16 was easily accomplished with the assistance of the SBA's Peter Neglia. The Squadron Ellenoff lawyers, working quietly in conjunction with Neglia, proposed a number of ways in which Wedtech could again list John Mariotta as the firm's majority owner. They ultimately decided on the other partners transferring enough shares (SBA's lawyers advised that stock options alone would not be sufficient) to Mariotta so that he would again have the minimum 50 percent; he, in turn, promised he would pay for them after two years, and if he should die or default on his payments, the shares would revert to their owners. Naturally Mariotta gave his word that he would default (thus legally voiding the "transfer"); with great trepidation, the other major shareholders (two notable exceptions: Squadron Ellenoff and Wallach) agreed to the stock transfer plan on December 27.

On January 4, Wedtech's appeal for continued 8(a) status was delivered to Neglia by Biaggi & Ehrlich, featuring the duplicitous stock transfer proposal and the ingenious argument that Wedtech was, in fact, still economically disadvantaged compared to such giant military contractors as General Dynamics. Neglia sprinted it through the SBA regional bureaucracy so that on January 5, he was able to recommend to

Washington that Wedtech's set-aside status be granted a three-year extension. The file was reviewed by the SBA general counsel and its administrator, James Sanders. On January 25, Wedtech was formally notified of a three-year extension. Sanders' recollection reflects the possible thinking at the time that would have persuaded the SBA bureaucracy to ratify such a transparent subterfuge claiming minority ownership:

> I think that there was by that time a kind of inertia or a momentum by the firm and by those that were involved with them . . . almost as a bank does when someone gets deeply in debt to them—we've got to see those people succeed.[20]

While fighting the 8(a) battle, Wedtech was concurrently engaged in active political combat for the navy's pontoon procurement on two fronts. The first entailed making sure that the navy would place the contract under a minority set-aside status, the second, that Wedtech would be awarded the contract. Neither was particularly easy, especially since the responsible navy civilian official (Acting Assistant Secretary Everett Pyatt) and his navy officers had made it clear that they strongly favored a competitive bidding procedure; moreover, experienced contractors had already begun preparing their bids. By now, the partners had a time-tested battle plan. As their opening gambit, in October 1983, Moreno paid $60,000 to Richard Ramirez, who directed the navy office responsible for identifying small and minority contractors; in exchange, Ramirez kept Wedtech informed as to what was transpiring within navy councils as well as promoting Wedtech's cause whenever possible. Next, they activated their Washington political allies.

On November 8, Sanders, promoting the SBA set-aside program, wrote to Secretary of the Navy John Lehman requesting that he reconsider his assistant secretary's pending decision and place the pontoon contract under 8(a). Nofziger spoke directly with Pyatt regarding Wedtech. On December 8, Pyatt agreed to set aside a relatively straightforward part of the pontoon contract, about a quarter of the total work. The Wedtech principals viewed this as a temporizing negotiating ploy on the road to complete capitulation. They were sure they could do better and, in the end, they did. With Nofziger leading the charge (it is suspected that he was able to capitalize on Pyatt's desire for the political appointment that would remove the "Acting" modifier from his title), Pyatt reversed himself entirely. On January 6, he announced that he would "entertain" placing the entire pontoon contract under a set-aside program and, despite facing the unified opposition of his uniformed officers, did precisely that on January 19.

The rest of the contest consisted of little more than mopping up. Other minority firms' bids (some with much better experience for pontoon contracts) were either withdrawn or denied (usually under unexplained circumstances). In spite of a report from the navy's site visit team of Wedtech's facilities stating that the contractor "cannot meet the schedule," negotiations with the firm continued. Wedtech submitted a bid of $36 million, a full $12 million over the navy's estimate. The SBA refused to make up the difference. Facing a March bond offering and realizing the bonds would be significantly more attractive with a signed contract in hand, Moreno reluctantly agreed to a $24.5 million contract on March 28, with the first causeway to be delivered in October. Although the price was unquestionably far too low for Wedtech to realize anything but a disastrous financial loss, the company hoped to recoup its losses and make its profit with the follow-on contracts. Thus, at an April 23 press conference attended by its political allies, Wedtech was able to announce that it had captured yet another military construction contract.

Wedtech had, of course, no possibility of meeting the navy's delivery schedule. It did not even own a construction facility when it signed the contract, let alone have the personnel with experience in marine engineering. However, by this stage in its life, little daunted the firm. When the navy program contract officer gave Wedtech a scathing evaluation, the new navy officer with 8(a) responsibilities, Wayne Arny, requested an independent review, which agreed with Wedtech that it would make its first pontoon delivery by the promised October 15 date. On October 9, Moreno admitted to the navy that Wedtech could not deliver its first causeway until November, or the tenth unit before January, a full month behind schedule.

These delays portended serious contractual problems and worse, especially since the navy had agreed to negotiate the 1985 option by October 15. Recognizing that their success lay not with the contract officer (although Wallach did write a memorandum proposing that he be coerced, in Wallach's words, that he be made "aware of Wedtech's general ally structure . . . [and] thus conclude this agreement and fulfill the navy's responsibilities to the public"[21]) but with lucrative follow-on contracts, Wedtech asked Bragg to pressure the navy for an extension. Bragg agreed, asking for $200,000, with another $200,000 if the navy agreed to the option at Wedtech's price. (Wallach, upon hearing of Bragg's arrangement, demanded and received $150,000 of his own if Wedtech received the extension.) On November 18, the program officer wrote Arny that Wedtech would be unable to meet the delivery schedule and, by clear implication, argued against awarding the contract option to Wedtech. On November 19, Arny inexplicably recommended that Wedtech receive the extension by December 5 and that the contract be written on a "cost plus" basis—that is, to reimburse Wedtech for its total costs (whatever they might be) plus a specified profit. The program officer—who, like the army M-113 contract officer, Wedtech began to view as a personal enemy—and his superior were able to derail this recommendation and were forced to reinitiate negotiations with Wedtech.

In late December, Wedtech delivered its first pontoon causeway. The product was blatantly jerry-rigged, having apparently been literally sledge-hammered into meeting the navy's specifications. Still, Wedtech management was not overly concerned. It was much more worried about its cash flow; the company needed the contract renewal funds in order to meet its immediate payroll demands and to purchase the materials for producing both the pontoons *and* the army's engines. Ironically, the navy now needed Wedtech almost as much as Wedtech needed the navy; it was already falling so far behind schedule that to leave Wedtech for a second supplier would have been impractical. The navy offered $42 million; Wedtech demanded $68 million. With the assistance of Representative Biaggi and Senator D'Amato's offices, the navy agreed to the first extension on March 15, 1985, for $51.5 million. "Wedtech now had navy contracts worth $75.7 million. It had yet to produce a single acceptable pontoon." [22]

Wedtech and the navy were not yet finished in their *danse macabre*. During 1985, Wedtech finally began to deliver pontoons, but the navy procurement officers began planning to make the 1986 option competitive. Assistant Secretary Pyatt vetoed the recommendation. For his vigilance (and, in part, responding to letters from Senator D'Amato's office), the navy's project officer who had proven so irritating to Wedtech was forced to accept early retirement; a new, more compliant project officer took his place. Then, due to budget constraints, the navy had to halve its 1986 option; rather than initiate a time-consuming search for a new contractor, the navy, acting upon the March 28 recommendation of the project officer, awarded the second (although smaller than anticipated) option to Wedtech. Before the contract was signed, however, a Defense Department review of the firm's financial records revealed that Wedtech had a negative cash balance (hence, its tremendous motivation for the second renewal), thus making it ineligible for the follow-on contract. Wedtech indignantly demanded a re-audit and, when that also found a negative (although better) cash flow, yet another re-audit, claiming that the audit officer was prejudiced against them, even threatening the Defense Contract Administration Service with a $10 million law suit. Wedtech was at last able to convince the auditors that it was solvent and on May 21, 1986, it received a $48.6 million option. Financially, it was just as ruinous to the company as the original contract.[d] Wedtech could not have survived without the extension, and it could not survive with the renewal.

The Public Finds Out

For all intents and purposes, Wedtech's contracts with the navy were its high-water marks. From mid-1985, even while it was acquiring the trappings of legitimacy with the addition of retired army generals and a former secretary of the air force to its board of directors, the company began to self-destruct in a variety of ways. Its record of questionable contract awards bred resentment among other minority contractors and various government audit agencies. Wedtech's consultant bills became truly outrageous. For instance, in February 1984, Wallach asked for $150,000 in advance so that he could afford to serve as personal counsel for his friend, Ed Meese, who had been nominated as U.S. attorney general by President Reagan. In October, after a protracted confirmation hearing and Meese's final approval by the Senate, Wallach asked Wedtech that his prospective 1985 and 1986 retainer fees, a total of $300,000, be prepaid. He explained that once Meese gave him a government appointment—as he surely would—he could no longer be on the Wedtech payroll. In exchange, he promised Mariotta and Neuberger privileged access to high government circles. New consultants such as

---

[d] Wedtech had already claimed this option on its financial statement, thus permitting it to show a tidy profit in 1986. Unfortunately, the firm had "booked" the extension at $68 million, thus deceiving prospective investors.

Stanley Simon (Bronx Borough President), Jim Jenkins (former White House staff member), Jim Aspin (Congressman Les Aspin's brother), and assorted, much less respectable attendants began to cut deeply into the firm's profits. SBA's Peter Neglia was offered a position with Biaggi & Ehrlich, with Wedtech agreeing to pay half his salary as well as giving Neglia's designated accomplice 20,000 Wedtech stock options (since Neglia could not receive the options as a government official). Representative Garcia not only benefited from increased campaign contributions from the partners, he also demanded a job for his wife, Jane Lee Garcia; Wedtech retained a Puerto Rican lawyer for $86,000 who, in turn and for only a $10,000 consideration, hired Mrs. Garcia as a "public relations" consultant. A more serious drain, however, was that the partners began their pervasive diversions of company funds, engaging in kickbacks, embezzlements, and other ways to luxuriate themselves at the expense of the firm and even each other.

For these reasons, it was not long before Wedtech found itself gravely threatened by more than just the usual crowd of creditors and customers. In 1984, Representative Parren Mitchell (D-MD), chairman of the House Small Business Committee, probably acting upon a tip from a disgruntled minority contractor who had lost out on the navy contract, asked his committee staff to investigate Wedtech. Although the investigation turned up a large number of serious discrepancies in Wedtech's public filings and numerous cases of questionable support by the SBA, the investigation petered out when Mitchell realized that it would take a full-blown committee investigation to explore the issues his staff had uncovered. Rather than devote his committee's time to this detective work whose payoff was uncertain, Mitchell asked the SBA in a letter dated September 25 to answer twelve relatively specific and embarrassing questions. The chore fell into receptive hands. Peter Neglia, whose actions were clearly implicated in SBA's Wedtech files, had become Sanders' principal deputy. In that capacity, he was able to leave the questions unanswered until April 1985 (by which time he had already agreed to join Biaggi & Ehrlich and accepted Wedtech stock options), and then, when they were finally addressed, the SBA investigation exonerated the agency completely. Facing the challenge, Wedtech had acted in its now thoroughly lubricated fashion. Neglia had kept the partners well-informed, even showing them the confidential letter Mitchell had sent to the SBA. LAMA orchestrated a vocal protest in Mitchell's office against his "persecution" of a Hispanic firm, while representatives Biaggi and Garcia weighed in. Almost predictably, Wedtech identified some new "consultants"—especially two Baltimore attorneys who happened to be cousins of Chairman Mitchell—who they thought could terminate the investigation; the Mitchell cousins were paid $50,000 for their efforts.[e]

By 1986, the company was becoming terminally fissiparous. The partners viewed John Mariotta as increasingly unreliable, with Neuberger even broaching the possibility (twice!) of having him murdered. In February 1986, as soon as Mariotta had honored the December 1982 stock "transfer" agreement by rescinding the stocks to their original owners, the board voted to remove him from his chairmanship of the company. Faced with a subsequent "show cause" letter from the SBA asking why the company should still qualify as a minority contractor, Wedtech at first protested but then adopted a virtue out of necessity stance by notifying the SBA of its resignation on March 27:

> WEDTECH CORP. is proud to report that it is prepared to accelerate its graduation from the SBA's 8(a) program. This premature departure is based upon two factors: (1) ... the Company will have substantially achieved the goals of its business plan; (2) the Company believes it has attained the ability to compete in the market place.[23]

Interestingly, Wedtech did not make its 8(a) exit decision public information until April 17. The partners' (including the now-ousted Mariotta) main preoccupation seemed to be their attempt to sell off company stock. Even with the third navy pontoon option and a new $2.9 million contract from the Postal Service (for which Wedtech had bribed a postal employee $20,000, as well as benefiting from the assistance of Representative Garcia, who sat on the House Post Office Committee), the partners knew that the company was collapsing faster than it could attract new capital, and were selling off their stock while it still had value. When brokers noticed the peculiar sell-off, the partners blithely blamed it completely on the disgruntled Mariotta's unloading his vast wealth of Wedtech stock.

---

[e] There was no evidence that Mitchell's cousins ever attempted to influence the chairman. It would seem that they were willing to swindle Wedtech, both in this case and a follow-on case for another $50,000 retainer, and a third for $10,000. They were later fined and sentenced to two-and-a-half years in prison for tax evasion.

But much more was up than the financial scam and the minority contractor chicanery. In the spring of 1986, federal and local district attorney offices in Baltimore (keying in on the Mitchell cousins), Manhattan, and the Bronx all began to discover—usually as a tagline to other investigations—that Wedtech was operating in a highly unusual manner with very suspicious people, finding traces of fraud, payoffs to a wide range of politicians, kickbacks, and embezzlement. The traces, in the particular vein of Robert Wallach, probably ran directly to Attorney General Meese, that is, to the Reagan White House. Although there was a certain amount of competitive friction among the simultaneous investigations as they jockeyed for the prosecutorial lead, it soon became clear as the press learned of the subpoenas that Wedtech's skein was expiring. In October, Marilyn Thompson of the *New York Daily News* began publishing such a devastating series of articles on Wedtech's alleged improprieties that the firm threatened the *News* with a $400 million law suit; the *News* refused to capitulate and was joined by the *New York Times* and the other metropolitan papers in revealing Wedtech's alleged improprieties.

Not surprisingly, given all the public charges flying about, the financial community was unwilling to extend credit to shore up Wedtech's dwindling resources. The imminent soon became reality: on December 14, 1986, after close to $500 million in federal contracts and $160 million in public securities, Wedtech filed for bankruptcy. The petition, showing a little over $67 million net, was as well-cooked as the Wedtech books; "the assets were to prove to be largely illusory, the liabilities grossly understated." [24] The 1,400 employees Wedtech had so proudly displayed—the very heart of Wedtech's ghetto enterprise— were almost the last to learn that they would not be receiving their Christmas paychecks.

The next day, federal prosecutors discovered incriminating evidence in Meese's White House files, a touchy investigation since, as attorney general, Meese was the federal attorney's boss, and he was proving remarkably recalcitrant in reclusing himself from the investigation. Nevertheless, since the Wedtech officers were admitting to only the lesser charges while successfully concealing their more serious criminal acts, the prosecution's cumulative evidence was incomplete, more damning than convicting. The lead federal prosecutor, acting upon a hunch, told the attorney representing Wedtech that she had uncovered the bank account the principals had used to pay off

Garcia, Biaggi, Simon, and numerous others; the same account had doubled as the principals' personal slush fund and repository for illegal kickbacks. Although she had only an inkling of the slush account—her evidence was fragmentary—her ploy was designed to bluff down the stone wall tactic Wedtech had taken. She succeeded. Guessing that the prosecution's evidence was better than was actually the case, first Moreno and then the others agreed to plead guilty and testify.

On January 24, the individual lawyers representing the different Wedtech principals began their plea bargaining with the New York federal attorney's office, which represented the different district attorney offices. Their main currency was their willingness to become state witnesses and identify the individuals to whom Wedtech had made illegal payments, in exchange for reduced indictments and being able to enter their pleas before more lenient sentencing judges. Mariotta chose not to involve himself in these negotiations.

Numerous convictions were forthcoming over the next few years. The Wedtech principals were fined and handed down sentences ranging from eight years (Mariotta) to eighteen months (Moreno). Representative Biaggi, who had already resigned from Congress after being convicted on similar charges, was convicted on fifteen counts, including extortion, bribery, and racketeering, and was sentenced to eight years, plus a $245,000 fine; his son, Richard, was found guilty of tax fraud and sentenced to two years. SBA's Peter Neglia was convicted of racketeering, bribery, and obstruction of justice; he was fined and sentenced to three years in prison. Other convictions were obtained for persons who were involved in various plots of the Wedtech scandal but who were less central.

Edwin Meese's role regarding Wedtech was the subject of a federal independent counsel's investigation. Although James McKay found that Meese had been "instrumental" in Wedtech's pursuit of the army engine contract and "insensitive in the appearance of impropriety," he concluded in his report that "currently available evidences does not show any criminal wrongdoing" on Meese's part. Claiming he had been vindicated, Meese resigned as attorney general on July 5, 1988.[25] In January 1989, the Justice Department's Office of Professional Responsibility published its own investigation, stating that there was at least an appearance of impropriety and that Meese's behavior should not be tolerated of any government employee, especially not the attorney general of the United States. Were he still serving as attorney general, we would recommend ... that the president take disciplinary action.[26]

Representative Garcia, his wife, and their conduit attorney were tried and convicted of conspiracy, extortion, and receiving illegal payments. Robert Wallach was convicted on fraud and racketeering charges and sentenced to six years in prison by a judge who chastised him for selling "your influence on the back stairs of the White House." [27]

In June 1990, the convictions of the Garcias were reversed by the court of appeals because of an ambiguity with the extortion charge. The court found that while Representative Garcia had engaged in a "disgraceful request for money," he was not guilty of extortion because he was "in effect, offering to sell his Congressional power but he was not using that power in a way to intimidate Wedtech."[28] Robert Wallach, represented by Robert Bork, appealed his conviction, and in June 1991 it was overturned on the grounds of tainted testimony[f] and Wallach was released without having spent any time in prison.[29] As James Traub summarized the denouement, "the moral drama of the Wedtech trials has dissipated on appeal."[30]

Conclusions

In a very real sense, the story of Wedtech represents the conventional interpretation of corruption, one motivated by simple monetary greed evinced by a circus of partakers rather than a political event. Even in Welbilt's early, heady days, Mariotta and Neuberger had their own agenda centered almost exclusively on their personal enrichment. As a matter of convenience, it was easier for them to be successful under the guise of a minority contractor operating in the world of government set-aside contracts than in the open competitive market. That they were located in a ghetto made their charade more acceptable, but their entrepreneurship was primarily fixated on their wallets rather than any elevated

---

[f]Anthony Guariglia, as part of his cooperation agreement with the prosecution, was barred from gambling. When he was confronted with evidence of his gambling during his testimony against Wallach, he denied it, thus committing perjury.

sense of social behavior. To achieve their rags-to-riches ends, they lied to attain their 8(a) status and then, seeing there was little perceptible downside to their prevarications, continued to cheat their way to financial success and certainly to their fifteen minutes of national acclaim, lying to various the federal government agencies, to financial auditors, to their attorneys, to their investors, and even, in the end, to one another. They seemingly had no reservations as to whom they deceived—being equal opportunity liars, as it were—as long as the deceits proved profitable. Wedtech was, in short, the essence of personal greed, which, when practiced in a public setting, becomes political corruption.[31]

We should not suppose that Wedtech management was the only culpable party, the solitary bad apple that rotted the barrel. The company was leaned upon by union leaders, local politicians, eminent lawyers, and congressmen to dabble in and later rely upon payoffs. At the first whiff of success, Congressman Mario Biaggi approached Welbilt and convinced the firm that he could use his congressional position laundered through his law practice to help the firm succeed, an agreement in open violation of the Ethics in Government Act. Congressman Robert Garcia did not lag far behind, differing only in how be accepted payment (at first, via campaign contributions, later more directly). Subsequently, as Wedtech prospered, Biaggi became more insistent, not only reminding Wedtech how helpful he had been in the past, but also how harmful he could be in the future if Biaggi & Ehrlich did not received Wedtech stock. Extortion, pure and simple. Congressman Garcia suggested that his wife be placed on retainer (a suggestion the appeals courts ruled "disgraceful" but not extortion).

However, in many other ways, the Wedtech history more readily fits the concept argued here that political corruption is another form of "doing business" in a government contract–dominated business environment. As Traub argues, perhaps only somewhat disingenuously, Mariotta and Neuberger

> set out to promote their little company, not to corrupt the world; once embarked on their crusade, they discovered that the world was willing to be corrupted. . . . They knew they wanted to get ahead, but they didn't know the rules. So they listened and learned; they adapted; they became what they beheld.[32]

The Wedtech principals discovered early on that the world of government contracting depended at least as much on a firm's political connections as its technical capabilities. There is no other explanation why, even in the set-aside world, Welbilt should have been able to win procurement contracts that it had only the feeblest capability to fulfill on schedule. (To its credit, when its M-113 components were delivered, they were highly rated.) It would have been fiscal folly for the partners to realize what the "rules" of the game were and then to ignore them. Others who did so fell bankrupt before the Wedtech juggernaut. Rather than invest in physical facilities to win government contracts, Wedtech justifiably invested in political connections—legal and otherwise, scarcely recognizing the difference between the two—in pursuit of its goals. And, to be honest, in a world in which contracts are *the* standard of success (and, conversely, lack of contracts the criterion of failure), who could affix the blame solely upon them without apportioning an important part of the onus for their actions upon the system in which they chose to operate?

To be sure, this observation is not arguing that the illegal activities of Wedtech and its gang of supporters were "right" or justified; unarguably, they were both wrong (especially in consideration of other, more honest companies they beat out) and criminal (as witnessed by the multiple convictions). But to be understood, to be recognized as something more far-reaching than simple personal aggrandizement, their actions should be viewed in the context of the system in which they occurred.

If the system is also to be placed in the docket, then we need to examine the system failures. They were numerous, ranging from the craven professional counseling by Wedtech's lawyers and accountants, to sleazy New York City politicos, to the armed forces, to the SBA, to the Congress, and, ultimately, to the White House door. Utilizing this more systemic perspective, we can see that while Wedtech management acted in a corrupt manner, it could not have done so without the active connivance, participation, even encouragement of many other nominally "honest," involved parties who knew better. More telling for our conception of corruption—many participants were acting in concert with Wedtech completely convinced that even though what they were doing might be questionable, it was all for a good and maybe honorable purpose. In the classic rationale, the ends justified the means. Rudolph W. Giuliani, the United States attorney whose office prosecuted the case, viewed the baneful condition in this more balanced perspective:

> If Wedtech was the proverbial American success story, these charges raise serious questions about the way we practice politics and conduct business in this city, state, and nation.[33]

We can ask, for instance, why the highly esteemed accounting firm of Main Hurdman approved the Wedtech books after discovering the fraudulent army billings and slush fund, and continued to certify its financial stability to investors even though it was apparent that Guariglia was only able to balance the books by folding in (averaging) contracts that were not yet signed, or what Sternberg and Harrison refer to as continuously "feeding the beast"? Or why did the reputable law firm of Squadron Ellenoff condone what it must have suspected and prepare what it must have known were dubious explanations to continue Wedtech's 8(a) status? The answer is that while Wedtech was "finessing" its fiduciary and legal requirements, it was seen as merely a small player in a business community where everybody was involved in something akin to its hanky-panky. In their willingness to look the other way, Wedtech's legal and financial advisers contributed to its successes by sanctioning the means used to achieve them; by the same token, they were partially responsible for its ultimate downfall. Whatever the case, Wedtech's highly respectable lawyers and accountants were operating under the system's informal rules; Wedtech was certainly not the only firm for whom the spirit (a usefully subjective view) of the law took precedence over its letter.

There were criminal acts committed by Wedtech's supporters for financial gains. Lyn Nofziger was thoroughly informed by White House legal counsel before he left that he could not lobby his former White House colleagues for a year after his departure; still, he accepted a retainer to that effect and met with Meese to discuss his client. However, let us look at some of the other actors whose decisions were highly questionable but whose motives were far from financial. Edwin Meese, whose conduct was barely tolerated by an independent counsel and roundly castigated by the Justice Department's Office of Professional Responsibility, was arguably motivated by what we have termed ideological corruption. In other words, Meese's patronage of Wedtech was likely seen as a means of enhancing the support by the coveted

Hispanic community for President Reagan and, more generally, the Republican Party. His shortcomings were largely outgrowths of his personal insensitivity (e.g., his reluctance to recluse himself from the federal investigation of Wedtech and his continued championing of Wallach when he knew his friend was under investigation by federal attorneys). As a Justice Department spokesperson observed of the attorney general: "He left his shirttail hanging out at such length that it was easy for those who wished him ill to try and pull him down."[34] Nobody has ever claimed that Meese's Wedtech advocacy made him a rich man.[35]

Jim Jenkins, Meese's White House aide, knocked heads to Wedtech's benefit, but he did so on his boss's, not Wedtech's, direction.[g] Similarly, James Sanders, the SBA administrator throughout much of the Wedtech era, realized no questionable financial gain from his stalwart support. His overt and strong endorsements of Wedtech's bids for defense contracts and, more worrisome, his self-serving acceptance of Wedtech's specious bid to remain with 8(a) status after it had successfully gone public were due to his desire to protect and validate the SBA's star minority contractor in the entire 8(a) program. He was safekeeping his agency's mission during a period when it was under extreme pressures from Reagan's Office of Management and Budget to cease operations. Thus, his concern was more for his agency rather than for Wedtech or any promised money. The same argument could have been posed for Peter Neglia if he had not gone further and recruited Wedtech money and stock options to feather his post-government nest. Even Nofziger, whose public relations firm did receive direct financial payment, found receptive audiences when he couched his arguments to Meese and others in terms of Wedtech's value to the Republican Party.

Suzanne Garment plausibly contends that some of the Wedtech indictments were more a function of a contemporary prosecutorial feeding frenzy than of serious felonies having been committed.[h] The charges against Wallach were particularly weak, fueled, she claims, by

---

[g]Although Jenkins later became a well-paid Wedtech consultant, it is safe to assume that his 1982 actions were not performed on a quid pro quo basis.

[h]Garment may be less than evenhanded in her argument here. Her husband, Leonard Garment, was co-counsel with Robert Wallach in preparing Edwin Meese for his Senate confirmation hearings.

the concurrent New York City scandals and Giuliani's desire to publicize his expected New York mayoral candidacy. Giuliani's political fires, her case reads, would have been stoked had he been able to convict a close friend of the attorney general. "The result, at the end of the line, was an outcome palpably disproportionate to any facts that had been established."[36] But this is a biased reading, predicated on Garment's argument that the scales of justice have been weighted too heavily in favor of virtual head hunting by overly aggressive government investigators. While some of the indictments were less than patent and have been overturned on judicial appeal (part of the system Garment castigates), surely we can agree that "the result, at the end of the line" has been demonstrably discerning in punishing those culprits most deserving.

We should not belabor the argument that Wedtech was an isolated, relatively trivial conspiracy. Even if we set aside the primary felons here—the Wedtech management—and a few of their more guileful operators within the government (e.g., New York City's Stanley Simon, Representative Biaggi, and Richard Ramirez), plenty of public officials were tarred by the Wedtech pitch. Examples include SBA, EDA, army, and navy officials who overrode their staff's advice in order to fund a company that had little technical capability but ample political clout. Their support was not financially motivated; rather, they were responding to political pressures to facilitate normal government procedures and outcomes. And this, of course, is precisely what we have been discussing—political corruption as an alternative form of governmental process. We can therefore view the Wedtech case less as a unique set of circumstances and more as illustrative of systemic political corruption.[i]

If this is true, then the conventional reading of the Wedtech scandal as the avaricious behavior of a small group of individuals lining their wallets at the taxpayer's expense is not the complete or most interesting story. There were many participants who were involved for no monetary gain, whose corruption was for political and bureaucratic purposes, whose actions were well intended. The Wedtech principals themselves, while surely greedy, were engaged in corrupting people—but only as they represented apparently typical procedures—as a way of moving a

---

[i]The next chapter will demonstrate that Wedtech, although one of the most egregious offenders, was not the only firm engaged in shady procurement bids.

bureaucracy perceived as impersonal, unresponsive, and unfair. So while we can easily identify aspects of personal corruption in the Wedtech story, we can equally easily find interpretations of political corruption directed toward some version of implementing the public good. As such, whatever its avarice index, Wedtech can be seen as a case of corruption for political ends, in equal parts personal and systemic.

Notes

1. James Traub, *Too Good to Be True: The Outlandish Story of Wedtech* (New York: Doubleday, 1990).

2. Marilyn W. Thompson, *Feeding the Beast: How Wedtech Became the Most Corrupt Little Company in America* (New York: Charles Scribner's Sons, 1990); Ms. Thompson, while a reporter for the *New York Daily News*, wrote many of the exposés that contributed to the criminal prosecutions of Wedtech.

3. William Sternberg and Matthew C. Harrison, Jr., *Feeding Frenzy* (New York: Henry Holt, 1988).

4. The incident and quotation are from Traub, *Too Good to Be True*, pp. xiii–xiv. The same event is described in Sternberg and Harrison, *Feeding Frenzy*, pp. 53–56.

5. Sternberg and Harrison, *Feeding Frenzy*, pp. 4–5.

6. Mark A. Uhlig, "Wedtech: From Symbol of Hope to Sign of Greed," *New York Times*, August 5, 1988, p. A11.

7. Suzanne Garment, *Scandal* (New York: Random House, 1991), chapter 5.

8. Sternberg and Harrison, *Feeding Frenzy*, p. 15.

9. Quoted in Traub, *Too Good to Be True*, p. 15.

10. Quoted in Sternberg and Harrison, *Feeding Frenzy*, p. 18.

11. Quoted in ibid., p. 34.

12. *Ibid.*, p. 51.

13. Lyn Nofziger's April 8 memorandum to Ed Meese is printed in Sternberg and Harrison, *Feeding Frenzy*, p. 58, and Traub, *Too Good to Be True*, p. 74.

14. Quoted in Thompson, *Feeding the Beast*, p. 69.

15. The May 19 meeting is described by Traub, *Too Good to Be True*, pp. 78–80, and Sternberg and Harrison, *Feeding Frenzy*, pp. 59–60.

16. The memorandum was uncovered by federal independent counsel James McKay examining Meese's involvement in Wedtech; quoted in Thompson, *Feeding the Beast*, p. 73.

17. The Ehrlich letter is quoted in Sternberg and Harrison, *Feeding Frenzy*, p. 95.

18. Sternberg and Harrison, *Feeding Frenzy*, p. 94.

19. Campbell is quoted to this effect in Traub, *Too Good to Be True*.

20. Sanders is quoted by Traub, *Too Good to Be True*, p. 173. A similar quotation is attributed to Sanders in Sternberg and Harrison, *Feeding Frenzy*, p. 114.

21. Wallach's memorandum is quoted in Sternberg and Harrison, *Feeding Frenzy*, p. 144. Traub, *Too Good to Be True*, p. 202, reports that Wallach had

such a conversation with the project officer, who was not impressed.

22. Sternberg and Harrison, *Feeding Frenzy*, p. 146.

23. Cited *ibid.*, p. 250.

24. *Ibid.*, p. 285.

25. Philip Shenon, "Meese Says He'll Step Down, Contending He Is Vindicated by the Special Prosecutor," *New York Times*, July 6, 1988, pp. A1, D21; Linda Greenhouse, "A Tarnished Symbol," *New York Times*, July 6, 1988, p. D20; Jeff Gerth and Philip Shenon, "Prosecutor's Report Shedding New Light on Meese," *New York Times*, July 9, 1988, pp. 1, 8, indicate that many of Meese's problems were accountable to Robert Wallach.

26. The Meese materials are quoted in Sternberg and Harrison, *Feeding Frenzy*, p. 303.

27. James Barron, "Wallach Is Sentenced to 6 Years for His Role in the Wedtech Case," *New York Times*, October 16, 1989, p. A12.

28. William Glaberson, "Garcias' Extortion Convictions Reversed by Appeals Panel," *New York Times*, June 30, 1990, pp. 1, 16.

29. For details, see Constance L. Hays, "Court Overturns Convictions of 3 in Wedtech Case," *New York Times*, June 1, 1991, pp. 1, 26; also Josh Barband, "Robert Wallach at the Heart of Wedtech Scandal," *New York Times*, June 1, 1991, p. 26.

30. James Traub, "The Wedtech 6: A Morality Tale," *New York Times*, June 7, 1991, p. A17.

31. Guthrie Burkhead argues that the Wedtech scandal could have been logically classified as either public or private corruption. See W. John Moore, "Grass-Roots Graft," National Journal, Vol. 17, No. 21 (August 1, 1987), pp. 1962–1967, at 1966.

32. Traub, *Too Good to Be True*, p. xvi.

33. Giuliani is quoted by Uhlig, "Wedtech: From Symbol of Hope to Sign of Greed," p. A11.

34. Terry Eastland is quoted in Lou Cannon, *President Reagan: A Role of a Lifetime* (New York: Simon & Schuster, 1991), p. 795.

35. Gerth and Shenon, "Prosecutor's Report Shedding New Light on Meese," write, "Nor was evidence discovered that Mr. Meese, at any time, knowingly received any money or thing of value from anyone in return for or on account of any official act he performed which benefitted the company [Wedtech]" (p. 8).

36. Garment, *Scandal*, p. 126.

5

IT'S AN ILL WIND THAT BLOWS

Defense procurement scandals appear to be recurring phenomena, almost as regular as the disappointments of new administrations. It should therefore be little surprise that the American public views its defense industry as thoroughly populated with greedy contractors and ready succumbers. It should be even less of a surprise when, after a history of convicting a few individuals, penalizing mildly a few companies, and adding another layer of regulations and oversight officials, analogous cases of abuse and corruption in the Pentagon and its contractors are discovered anew.

In mid-summer 1988, the Justice Department announced what must have seemed like yet another in an endless stream of investigations of corruption in the Department of Defense (DoD). To be more specific, numerous indictments were handed up regarding the way in which weapons contractors developed and delivered weapons and their supporting systems to the three armed services within the Department of Defense. Code-named "Operation Ill Wind," the Justice Department investigation resulted in convictions or guilty pleas of fifty defense officials, executives, and consultants, as well as seven major defense contractors. In the wake of 400-dollar hammers and the infamous 700-dollar toilet seats, revived charges of governmental "waste, fraud, and abuse" reverberated in the press and Congress.[1]

By now we can see that the predictable failure of the conventional remedies is due to the fact that they are largely addressing the obvious manifestations as practiced by a very few people and corporations, acting in an undeniably corrupt manner, who pocket public moneys for

their personal aggrandizement. The continued stream of defense contracting fraud in the face of continued reform and tighter regulation
indicates, however, that there is something more fundamental, more
basic at play than mere avarice. Failing to identify what those forces
might be, we are destined for continued abuses. For instance, a scant
few years after outcry over the seemingly platinum-plated hammer, the
National Journal reported that Senator William Roth (R-DE) was asking the Pentagon to explain the alleged prices of a 117-dollar soap dish,
a 120-dollar cup dispenser, and—yes—a 1,868-dollar "toilet cover assembly."[2] (One immediate result was Senate Bill 1958, which specified
the maximum allowable price of a plastic toilet seat cover.) If systemic
forces are possibly at work, then we had best examine them if we hope
to alleviate the causes—rather than simply the symptoms—of corruption. Operation Ill Wind is amply illustrative of this syndrome of systemic corruption.

To be sure, the Ill Wind allegations, even when we generously estimate the amounts of money involved, were little more than insignificant ants pestering the Defense Department's weapons development
and procurement picnic. Early news reports, almost surely inflated,
guessed that the contracts affected might total a few billion dollars.
This amount represents a tremendous debt in virtually any agency's
budget except Defense's. Every year prior to the demise of the Cold
War, DoD spent approximately $150 billion and innumerable person-
hours to develop and acquire new weapons. Kenneth Mayer puts this
comparison in perspective: "the relatively small number of individuals
and contracts involved must be seen in the context of the millions of
contract actions and thousands of high level personnel involved in the
acquisition process."[3] In short, the relativity argument would have one
believe that the Ill Wind crimes were hardly heinous, little more than a
naughty gust. Such an innocuous assessment would be a mistake. We
might be able to excuse the Ill Wind indictments as aberrations if they
reflected isolated, once-in-a-blue-moon incidents. They do not. Furthermore, as David Rosenbaum points out, the contractors who admitted to violating DoD regulations were some of the most prestigious
defense contractors in the nation.[4] Although the stakes might have been
comparatively slight on the national scale (yet certainly not to individual firms and program managers), the players and potential precedents
assuredly were not.

Similarly, Suzanne Garment seeks to downplay the importance of the Ill Wind procurement scandals and other charges against the DoD abuses by explaining that

> The rising number of defense firms under criminal investigation was not surprising in light of increasingly aggressive behavior by the Pentagon's investigative services. More contractors were suspended beginning in the mid-eighties in no small part because the Pentagon now had special new offices dedicated to suspending them.

On the chance that Garment has not made herself clear, she inverts the issue of ethics: "Often offensive behavior in government tell us less about the ethics of the perpetrators than about the system in which they operate." However, the contention that many of the charges were due to DoD inspectors general industriously making work for themselves rings callow. Even if it were true, it would only suggest that Pentagon employees and defense weapons contractors were finally being called to task, in other words, that previously their corruptions had gone unreported and were tacitly approved. Moreover, since these "special new offices" were in place by the mid-1980s, the fact that the Ill Wind indictments were subsequent to those dates suggests that the entrenched nature of the Pentagon maladministrations transcends the public administration textbook solutions. Even Garment, who primarily castigates the enforcers rather than the conspirators, admits that in the Defense Department, "The practice was more a sign of systemic problems than of moral weakness."[5]

I will examine the Ill Wind investigations to provide evidence of the systemic components that create very real incentives within the defense procurement processes to violate these very processes, that is, to act in corrupt manners. But to do this, I must first discuss the weapons acquisition process in the context of the American political system.

Weapons Development in the United States

Almost since the War for Independence and certainly since the advent of the mass production of weapons in the United States,[a] there have been procurement scandals because of the large amounts of money

---

[a] Eli Whitney, famed as the inventor of the cotton gin, was granted a patent for a system to assemble a musket with interchangeable parts, the first production line.

involved, the presence of the political spoils system, and the lack of public accountability. Faulty rifles, stale provisions, and ragtag uniforms are not a twentieth-century invention.

After the Second World War, however, the defense industry was radically altered by five conditions. First and foremost was the perception of an enormous military threat posed by the Soviet Union. American defense planners (with complete congressional concurrence) demanded better weapons to face, initially, the massive Soviet army and, later, Soviet nuclear forces. In military jargon, these design qualities were referred to as "weapons requirements." Second, weapons became increasingly complex; hence, their design and development required greater technical (i.e., costly) skills and longer time frames (in most cases, in excess of a decade) than had earlier been the case. Third, because of their taxing requirements and complexities, such weapons became very expensive and, perhaps worse, rarely were as good and affordable as promised; moreover, costs and performance were always at odds with one another. Fourth, the weapons industry became very competitive because, given the long development times and high costs, it was seen that the government could not afford to fund enough contracts to support too many companies; the drastic reduction in the number of American aircraft manufacturers since 1945 is a prime example. Finally, for all these reasons but especially the last, weapons development became highly politicized, a matter for intensive industry lobbying and congressional debate.[6]

In attempts to reduce costs without sacrificing weapons requirements, the DoD went through a wrenching series of reforms during the 1960s and 1970s. Succeeding administrations grappled with the contradictory problem of reducing development time and costs while maintaining high performance levels. New forms of contracting and development were tried; all were shown to relieve some problems while increasing others. None was generally effective in reducing overall costs. Secretaries of Defense made repeated attempts to improve the research and acquisition system but were stymied, sometimes for technical reasons (at times, aircraft and missiles could simply not do what was demanded of them), but often for institutional and political reasons.[7] Navy admirals would not share an aircraft development with air force generals,[8] or, more often the case, members of Congress, ever mindful of constituent pressures, wanted acquisition budgets to be spent in their home districts.[9] Finally, congressional "micromanagement" of the defense budget added another level of uncertainty. The result was a jerky cycle of starts and stops, good years and lean, resulting in a great deal of uncertainty within the defense industry. These bouts with uncertainty were heightened by a series of reforms in managerial philosophies, vacillating between centralized developments tightly monitored by the Office of the Secretary of Defense and decentralized developments controlled by the individual services.

By the late 1970s, as defense budgets began to rise, a controversy arose once again over how best to manage the DoD acquisition budget. The skyrocketing cost of weapons (particularly electronics) outstripping the defense budget and the lengthy development times were the driving issues. The problem had two distinct perspectives. From the government's side, the question was how to get affordable but high-performance weapons into operation more quickly. The government's perspective was internally divided by disputes among the services as they fought over their share of the budgetary pie. From the industry's side, the armed services could no longer purchase a large variety of weapons. If a firm were not awarded a development contract that would lead to a large government purchase, the firm's financial future would be endangered. Hence, the competition within the defense industry bordered upon the desperate. A third perspective was that of Congress, which was schizophrenic; in one voice, it would rail against what it viewed as the military spending too much on weapons (the "gold-plating" syndrome) while, in another voice, preventing the military from cutting back on developments and productions that would adversely affect constituents. But always, Congress was deeply involved; in 1983, DoD officials testified before Congress 1,306 times for over 2,100 hours of testimony; in 1985, Congress made over 3,100 program adjustments in the DoD budget.[10] The Defense Department, the military, and defense firms lobbied the Congress extensively, producing, as a result, a patische of a weapons development policy.

A number of less formal rules evolved outside the arcane of government regulations. John Cushman, writing in the *New York Times*, commented on some of these easy-to-understand practices. First, for example, the Pentagon, wishing to draw upon industrial expertise, would recruit its executives from the defense industry; they would serve two or three years in DoD, then return to their original companies and continue to do business with the Pentagon, often with the colleagues and offices they had just left. Privileged access was all but guaranteed, thus making a low-wage tour of government service a valuable investment. Second, in order to reduce personnel costs, DoD decreased its own staff, thereby making itself very dependent upon part-time consultants for "work in drafting specifications for military hardware and in assessing the military requirements for weapons done under contract to the military." And third, the constantly changing rules and dynamic technologies led to the development of a process whereby contractors' representatives met "informally on a daily basis with their counterparts in the Government, often exchanging information with the people they have known for years."[11] These practices had the effect of creating very intimate circles of defense procurement experts completely dependent upon one another and the defense budgets, perhaps working for individual ends but in a highly cooperative manner. They were, in their special area of concern, essentially a shadow weapons procurement bureaucracy, much more integrated than the typical political interest group.

President Reagan, in his fight against the Soviet "evil empire," made the accelerated buildup of the armed forces one of the central themes of his administration. While this largess applied to all of the services, it was particularly true for the navy. John F. Lehman, who had formerly served on the National Security Council under Henry Kissinger, was appointed secretary of the navy with the mission to create a 600-ship navy, the biggest peace-time fleet in the navy's history. To honcho the necessary development and acquisition efforts, Lehman hired his former associate at the Boeing Corporation, Melvin R. Paisley, as the assistant secretary for research, engineering, and systems.

Mandated to build up the navy, Lehman came to his position with impressive credentials as a master of bureaucratic procedures and warfare, but he soon found himself thoroughly frustrated by the navy's procurement bureaucracy, which he called "an incredible and unwieldy monster."[12] In 1985, Lehman

> Simply abolished the Navy's Materiel Command, which had been coordinating the purchase of everything from torpedoes to aircraft carriers since 1960. [This] consolidated Lehman's hold on the Navy's multibillion-dollar acquisition process by removing a layer of analysts and others who had stood between Lehman and the Navy's purchasing commands.[13]

In addition, Lehman instituted a number of policy changes, the most important of which was that weapons development contracts would be awarded on a competitive basis rather than given to a single, familiar contractor (called sole-source contracting). Moreover, the competitors were now required to sink large amounts of their own capital in the developments, thus lowering the costs to the government.[b]

These reforms had been widely recommended by many weapons development experts for years[14] but they failed to anticipate the likely structural and financial consequences for the industry. The military would no longer cover all the research and development (R&D) costs to the firm, which was therefore compelled to assume greater risks in bidding on a contract. As a result, competition among firms for defense contracts, already costly, now became so expensive that winning was paramount and losing prohibitive, occasionally fatal. Any questions of corporate ethics were relegated by DoD to industry self-governance, scarcely sound footing when one foot was thought to be in the fiscal grave.

Lehman handed Paisley the responsibility for the navy's weapons development budget, with the clear understanding that the development and acquisition processes be expedited. Paisley later outlined his duties to Congress just before he left the navy to become a private consultant:

> We have brought the entire range of R&D functions within the direct management of the Navy Secretariat. . . . My immediate staff and I will continue to develop appropriate policy and oversee its implementation. More specifically, I will exercise policy control over R&D requirements, implement the overall Navy and Marine Corp R&D plan, manage the acquisition process through which we conduct R&D and oversee the transition to production.[15]

In short, Lehman and Paisley, abetted by the decentralized hands-off management style emanating from Secretary of Defense Caspar Weinberger's office, had established a streamlined system designed to expedite the weapons processes centralized under Lehman's immediate direction. Unfortunately, by reducing the role of the professional bureaucracy, Lehman, in the words of a consultant generally sympathetic to the secretary's efforts, "created an environment in which it's easy to stray from the straight and narrow."[16] That is, with good intentions toward greater efficiency, Lehman and Paisley had removed most of the bureaucratic checks that delayed weapon developments,

---

[b]Both of these reforms were reflections of the Reagan Administration's philosophical reliance on free market forces.

but in doing so, they also removed the bureaucratic checks on potential abuse and corruption. In an environment already characterized by cutthroat competition, they instituted a system largely vulnerable, even conducive, to corruption.

Operation Ill Wind

In 1986, according to federal investigators, a former navy employee working for a military contractor received a telephone call from a military consultant offering to sell some "inside" information from the Pentagon. The employee notified the Naval Investigative Service, which, with the employee's assistance, wiretapped further incriminating conversations. Using that evidence, the service was able to obtain the consultant's cooperation to wiretap his conversations with his sources within the Pentagon, which, in turn, expanded the investigation to other suspicious networks.

In June 1988, the existence and a few particulars of those investigations became public knowledge. The substance of the charges was that military consultants obtained confidential, even classified information from Pentagon sources and sold it to defense contractors. This information dealt with how the Pentagon would evaluate industry bids on weapons contracts as well as proprietary data on bids prepared by competing firms; these materials would give contractors

> Extraordinary access to closely held information involving competitors' bids on multibillion-dollar military contracts.... The information, if disclosed at a critical moment in contact bargaining, could allow a company to reshape its offer or otherwise influence the outcome of the competition.

In some cases, Pentagon officials were thought to have agreed to rigging the bidding process to favor certain companies, in exchange for either a position after they left government service or just as a personal favor.

The consultants named included Melvin Paisley (who had left the Navy Secretariat in March 1987) and William Galvin. Within the government, officials like Victor Cohen (a deputy assistant secretary of the air force with procurement responsibilities) and George Stone (a civilian with the Naval Space Warfare Systems Command) were said to have sold proprietary information to middlemen, who would then pass it along to defense contractors. The consultants were linked to some of the defense industry's most important companies, such as McDonnell Douglas Aircraft, Litton Industries, Emerson Electronics, Martin Marietta, Teledyne, United Technology, and Unisys.[17]

The disclosures presented a number of problems. Much of the information had been obtained through wiretaps, which, although authorized, would require significant additional investigation before their evidence could be presented in court. It would take the prosecutors some time to assemble this supporting evidence. The Pentagon, on its own behalf, wanted to accelerate the process so as to minimize the disruption the investigations would cause. At the same time, DoD would have difficulty explaining to Congress why firms under suspicion of cheating on contracts were allowed to continue being supported by defense contracts or bid on new ones. Contradicting these pressures was the fear that suspending major defense contractors while the possible indictments slowly worked their way through the courts would eventually affect national security and cause layoffs in the suspected firms.

On July 1, Secretary of Defense Frank Carlucci[c] announced that he was suspending payment to all contractors involved in nine military programs valued at about $1.7 billion. He based his actions on court affidavits suggesting that the contracts might have been tainted by illegal access to inside information. The Pentagon possesses the legal authority to "suspend companies, their subsidiaries, or their offices from doing business with the Government on the basis of suspected improprieties." Indeed, Carlucci commented that "I shouldn't think it would be necessary to have convictions before we act. . . ." When Carlucci was asked about the effect of his actions on the weapon production lines, his response revealed the ambiguity in his position:

> clearly, anything that slows down the process of producing defense equipment, or requires us to reopen contracts, has an impact on our ability to get equipment in the field. If you're talking about grave or serious impact on readiness or modernization programs, I would not yet put what we've done today in that category. But, clearly, it has an impact.

Ten days later, the Pentagon restored all contract payments that Carlucci had blocked. There was some worry within DoD counsel that

---

[c] Caspar Weinberger had resigned as secretary of defense shortly before the Ill Wind investigations became public.

Carlucci might have moved precipitously, but there was even greater concern as to how the suspensions would affect the companies' production lines and the delivery of weapons to the armed forces.[18]

The details of many of the cases are similar, so let us examine two representative cases. On January 6, 1989, the first Ill Wind charges were filed and the first guilty plea entered. Indictments were handed up naming Teledyne Industries. Two military consultants, William Parkin and Fred Lackner, were charged with obtaining information for Hazeltine and Teledyne from Stuart Berlin, a civilian government employee with the Naval Air System Command.

In the Hazeltine and Teledyne incidents, Teledyne paid Parkin $10,000 to gain inside information concerning a contract to design testing devices for aircraft identification beacons. Parkin was promised another $150,000 if he were successful. With Lackner's assistance, Parkin also obtained information from Berlin on a battlefield air traffic control system, which he sold to Hazeltine. "In recognition of the information, Hazeltine lowered its initial bid by $70 million, to about $172 million. Hazeltine won the contract but the contract was voided after the disclosure of the fraud."[19]

Hazeltine Corporation (owned by Emerson Electronics) pleaded guilty to charges of receiving inside information and paid fines totaling $1.9 million (a tiny fraction of Hazeltine's $158 million 1987 profit). On March 22, Berlin pleaded guilty to charges of accepting a bribe and conspiring to defraud the government; on the 27th, Parkin pleaded guilty to charges of bribery, wire fraud, and conspiracy.

On December 8, the Loral Corporation admitted to three felonies of converting government property, conspiracy to defraud the government, and filing false claims. The pivotal figure in this case was a military consultant, William Galvin, who between 1985 and 1988 was paid $578,000 by Loral for inside information. He obtained material from Victor Cohen on how the Pentagon was prepared to evaluate bids to outfit the air force's F-16 fighter aircraft with a new radar system, a contract Loral won. Galvin persuaded Paisley to provide him with similar information on the navy's competition to build a fleet of blimps. Paisley not only gave Galvin data describing the competitive Westinghouse proposal (including cost estimates), he also offered to divide the procurement into areas beneficial to Loral (e.g., an electronics component). Loral lost this bid. The company was assessed $5.8 million in fines, claims, and reimbursements as well as being ordered to deliver F-16 radar equipment (worth about $5.5 million) at no cost.

Galvin was also involved with other firms, such as the Cubic Corporation, to whom he gave Cohen-supplied information on a battlefield reconnaissance system. With Paisley's assistance, Galvin was able to broker a navy missile contract to Mazlat Ltd., an Israeli firm that deposited money in his Swiss bank account. Galvin pleaded guilty to bribery, conspiracy to defraud the government, and tax evasion on March 28, 1990.[20]

The major Ill Wind convictions took place in the summer of 1991. Melvin Paisley pleaded guilty on June 14, claiming that "some of the largest military contractors were eager to offer bribes for confidential information that would give them an advantage in bidding for lucrative contracts." Some of Paisley's payoffs looked a bit peculiar, probably making them a bit harder to discover. He related how Martin Marietta had offered to pay for improvements in the gutter system for his house, while Unisys arranged to buy his Sun Valley condominium at an above-market price (sold one year later at a loss). On August 22, Victor Cohen confessed to bribery and conspiracy to defraud, often in conjunction with Paisley and Galvin.[d] Cohen also structured payments in unorthodox manners; for instance, Galvin purchased Cohen's old Mercedes-Benz for $17,843; a year and many repairs later, Galvin resold the car for $4,225. Galvin also paid a close friend of Cohen's $123,000 from 1983 to 1987. And in September, the Unisys Corporation admitted to criminal charges growing out of its connections to Paisley, Cohen, and others. Unisys agreed to pay a record $190 million in fines.[21]

Conclusions

The principle that underpins the Defense Department's weapons development system is consciously designed with equity in mind, so that in theory, all qualified bidders have an equal opportunity to win a contract. The truly voluminous regulation manuals and procurement bureaucracy exist basically to prevent companies from taking a short-

---

[d] Cohen had remained a civilian employee of the air force during the Ill Wind investigations, although he had been transferred to a position that had no purchasing authority.

cut and circumventing the procedures or being accorded special favor. Unfortunately, when a firm sees its financial solvency (in other words, its very existence) threatened and is faced with what it views as a set of obstructionist procedures, it will go to extraordinary efforts to overcome them. Equity loses some of its appeal when viewed from the perspective of an embattled firm or a harried procurement officer.

Development reforms, in turn, are usually devised either to reduce costs or to expedite development. Either goal can come into conflict with the equity principle, because equal access almost automatically means more time (so that each bid can be treated fairly) and more money. When Lehman, with the assistance of Paisley, attempted to accelerate the navy's development procedure by eliminating its Materiels Command and centralizing the procurement authority within his secretariat, he eviscerated most of the navy's checks and balances against corruption in the R&D process. By so doing, Lehman moved tacitly to replace the equity criterion with efficiency.

Lehman's actions were not carried out naively, nor does he grant any connection. Three months after Ill Wind became public knowledge, he was asked if his management strategies might have led to the scandals uncovered. He reportedly "scoffed" and stated that he did "not see any possibility of any correlation between good, strong management and wrongdoing." To emphasize his point, he admitted that in many respects, the military's acquisition system "doesn't work efficiently" but the blame should be attributed to a "bloated" bureaucracy. He concluded by saying, "I honestly believe we could run our whole defense establishment with half the number of people we have," this after his procurement reforms lay tattered in disrepute.[22]

Lehman's rationale, then, was straightforward in terms of what he wanted to do and the easily potential consequences. Loren Thompson, a former military consultant, succinctly reviewed the benefits and costs:

> Those layers of bureaucracy that prevent you from doing anything efficiently are also what prevent the kinds of abuses that can come when a process that complex is streamlined and placed primarily in the hands of political appointees.[23]

In a sense, Weinberger's and Lehman's efforts to facilitate DoD's development procedures—in part by centralizing the development system in the hands of political appointees[e] and, concomitantly, reducing the bureaucracy, however efficient that might be—served to deny the constitutional checks and balances framework that had produced those very layers and safeguards.[24]

Lehman's management policies still might not have resulted in the Ill Wind scandals except for the fact that most of the defense contractors were in dire financial straits. With the Reagan administration changing contracting rules so dramatically, and the stakes so high, it is little wonder that companies bent the rules to get information that would provide them with a competitive edge. Defense Secretary Carlucci later observed that Weinberger's reforms tended "to provide an incentive for contractors to look for ways, further ways, to intervene in the process."[25] Or, as one defense analyst phrased it, "Cost is the new king [and] clearly information is at a premium."[26] Moreover, the military consultants in the bidding arena did not view themselves as corrupt or "dopers; they considered themselves businessmen," doing what legitimate businessmen do—providing a useful service to a discriminating client.[27]

One should not underestimate the complexity of the weapons systems development process and its countervailing components. Gordon Adams, director of the Defense Budget Project, noted, "My sense of it [reform] historically is that we're dealing with underlying problems here, and they are money and management problems not amendable to easy legislation."[28] Reforms usually add to the confusion; at worst, they add new layers, further micromanagement, and, potentially, argues Edward Luttwak, lead to a debased military.[29] Congressional debate during the Ill Wind indictments indicated that many of the proposed cures and reforms were as susceptible to trouble as those they sought to replace. For instance, congressmen noted that to punish the offending defense contractors too severely by suspending them for some length of time from existing contracts or future bids would strike hardest at their workers and completely innocent suppliers. Or to appoint a centralized DoD acquisition czar would only add new layers of bureaucracy, the very situation that led to Lehman's end-run tactics.[30] What best to do and how to do it presents no tractable resolution.

---

[e] For another example, remember the decisions made by Acting Assistant Secretary Everet Pyatt, going against the advice of his uniformed officers, to favor Wedtech's pontoon bids, for what appeared to be political reasons (Chapter 4, *supra*).

Hence, the history of failures and, in the case prosecuted by Ill Wind attorneys, criminal corruption.

Suzanne Garment's Ill Wind summation is both sympathetic and to the point: when

> The environment for defense contractors is unstable ... [t]hese firms, *like all organizations*, want information in order to reduce these uncertainties and make it possible to plan for the future. The official channels are so cumbersome that it is often very hard to get such information in a timely way through the regular system. Under these circumstances, middlemen will emerge to fill the gap and profit from it as *inexorably* as sidewalk vendors appear ... on the streets of New York City. ...[31]

To be sure, these middlemen—be they military consultants or public officials like Paisley and Cohen—were not serving out of altruistic motives. They were either well paid at the time or compensated after they left the government. However, there are more systemic problems operating here than then-Senator Dan Quayle (R-IN) recognized when he characterized the Ill Wind allegations as "simple greed, bribery, and fraud."[32] Their self-serving financial arrangements should not disguise the fact that all the participants were working in tandem against what they saw to be a dilatory bureaucratic system. Lehman and Paisley were endeavoring to expedite what they viewed as a lethargic, encumbered process unable to produce a quick response when the need arose. The defense contractors were trying to survive in a what they saw as a competitive system with potentially fatal consequences. The military consultants were serving as transition media between the two, ferrying information at both parties' bequests. President Reagan, the fountainhead of his administration's decentralized, incurious management style, was insightful (probably unintentionally) when he replied to a question about the Ill Wind allegations: "I am disappointed and upset [but] I think it should be understandable how such things can happen in something as big as our government." [33]

The Ill Wind disclosures are indicative not so much of personal susceptibilities to corruption but a system in which players are likely to find themselves acting in corrupt ways in order to succeed. We should not overstate this likelihood. In the same competitive environment, Reagan's Department of the Army was notably free of Ill Wind indictments, primarily because of the leadership of its Secretary John O. Marsh. Marsh, early in his tenure, sent a very different message to the army and its contractors than his navy equivalent by establishing a high-level Task Force on Fraud, Waste, and Abuse.[f] The army secretary created his task force

> Because he was repeatedly seeing reports of the Government's losing $50,000 to $100,000. . . . "I became concerned about what was happening to those cases and I wanted to focus attention on them. If we find out about those things and nothing happens, people will think they can get away with it."[34]

The contrast between Marsh's leadership behavior and Lehman's is instructive, not so much in terms of what it did, but, for our purposes, what it prevented. (A comparison of how Wedtech was treated by the army as opposed to the navy, while only one incident, is illustrative.)

Therefore, one can legitimately suspect that the stage for the Ill Wind corruptions might have been set by the intimate relations between public and private personnel or the intensive competitive environment among contractors, but it was Lehman's decision to eliminate the bureaucratic safeguards that made the navy especially prime territory. The clear elevation of efficiency over equity sent a sure signal to all the players that the circumvention of the procurement regulations and their bureaucracy would not only be tolerated but rewarded. Little wonder, then, in light of the prevailing weapons development system, that the lubricating middleman emerged, "inexorably," to corrupt the system.

---

[f]The relative lack of corruption in the army under Marsh's leadership renders suspect Lehman's comments (*supra*) about no "correlation between good, strong management and wrongdoing" and a "bloated" bureaucracy being at fault.

Notes

1. For an academic view of waste, fraud, and abuse, see Jerome B. McKinney, "Fraud, Waste, and Abuse in Government," in James S. Bowman and Frederick A. Elliston, eds., *Ethics, Government, and Public Policy* (Westport, CT: Greenwood Press, 1988), chap. 11; or Jerome B. McKinney and Michael Johnston, eds., *Fraud and Waste in Government* (Philadelphia, PA: Institute for the Study of Human Issues, 1986).

2. Anonymous, "Dividend? What Peace Dividend?" *National Journal*, Vol. 22, No. 28 (July 14, 1990), p. 1699.

3. Kenneth R. Mayer, *The Political Economy of Defense Contracting* (New Haven, CT: Yale University Press, 1991), p. 66.

4. David E. Rosenbaum, "Pentagon Fraud Inquiry: What Is Known to Date," *New York Times*, July 7, 1988, p. A1.

5. Suzanne Garment, *Scandal* (New York: Random House, 1991), pp. 135, 140–141, and 137.

6. Greater detail is provided by J. Ronald Fox, *Arming America: How the U.S. Buys Weapons* (Cambridge, MA: Harvard University Press, 1974); and Jacques S. Gansler, *The Defense Industry* (Cambridge, MA: The MIT Press, 1981).

7. James Fallows, *National Defense* (New York: Random House, 1981), offers several illustrations of these internecine struggles.

8. The most famous controversy was over a joint navy–air force fighter-bomber imposed upon the services by Secretary of Defense Robert McNamara; see Robert F. Coulam, *Illusions of Choice: The F-111 and the Politics of Weapons Acquisition Reform* (Princeton, NJ: Princeton University Press, 1977); and Robert J. Art, *The TFX Decision: McNamara and the Military* (Boston: Little, Brown, 1968).

9. These points are elaborated by Thomas L. McNaugher, *New Weapons, Old Politics* (Washington, D.C.: Brookings Institution, 1989).

10. *Ibid.*, p. 69.

11. John H. Cushman, Jr., "Contractors' Network Led to Questions," *New York Times*, June 20, 1988, p. D4.

12. William C. Rempel, "Procurement Reforms May Have Led Way to Scandal," *Los Angeles Times*, June 20, 1988, Part 1, p. 1.

13. Daniel M. Weintraub and Melissa Healy, "Scandal's Roots Traced to Basic Reagan Policy Goals," *Los Angeles Times*, July 4, 1988, Part 1, p. 16.

14. There is an active debate among military analysts as to the comparative merits of sole-source versus competitive bidding in terms of costs and performance; see Mayer, *The Political Economy of Defense Contracting*, and Fallows, *National Defense*.

15. Quoted in Anonymous, "Navy Has Shifted on Procurement," *New York Times*, June 24, 1988, p. A11.

16. Rempel, "Procurement Reforms," p. 15.

17. See Stephen Engelberg, "Inquiry into Pentagon Bribery Began with a Telephone Call," *New York Times*, June 19, 1988, pp. A1, A21; Philip Shenon, "F.B.I. in Surprise Search of Pentagon and Suppliers," *New York Times*, June 15, 1988, pp. A1, D6; Jeff Gerth, "Untangling One Consultant's Web of Industry and Pentagon Contact," *New York Times*, June 17, 1988, p. D16; John H. Cushman, "McDonnell 'Inside' Information Cited," *New York Times*, June 17, 1988, p. D16; and Rosenbaum, "Pentagon Fraud Inquiry," p. B5. It is important to note that not all the companies and individuals mentioned in the initial Ill Wind news reports would later plead or be found guilty.

18. See John H. Cushman, Jr., "Carlucci Hints Pentagon May Act on Suppliers before Convictions," *New York Times*, June 28, 1988, p. A21; idem., "U.S. Stops Payments on Programs Believed Tainted in Fraud Inquiry," *New York Times*, July 2, 1988, pp. 1, 28; and idem., "Pentagon Resumes Paying Suppliers; Lack of Data Cited," *New York Times*, July 12, 1988, pp. A1, A19.

19. See Philip Shenon, "First Indictment Returned by Jury in Pentagon Fraud," *New York Times*, January 7, 1989, pp. 1, 46; and Michael Wines, "Company Adviser Files Guilty Plea in Pentagon Case," *New York Times*, March 28, 1989, pp. A1, D19.

20. Michael Wines, "U.S. Contractor Cites Two Officials in Guilty Plea," *New York Times*, December 9, 1989, pp. 1, 37; idem., "Guilty Plea in Pentagon Fraud Case," *New York Times*, March 29, 1990, pp. C1, C6; and Michael Lev, "Guilty Pleas in Pentagon Fraud Case," *New York Times*, January 16, 1990, p. C4.

21. Neil A. Lewis, "Guilty Plea Made in Pentagon Case," *New York Times*, June 15, 1991, pp. 1, 36; Richard W. Stevenson, "Guilty Plea in Military Bid Case," *New York Times*, August 23, 1991, pp. C1, C15; and Eric Schmit, "Guilty Plea by Unisys Is Expected," *New York Times*, September 6, 1991, pp. C1, C4.

22. John H. Cushman, Jr., "Former Navy Chief Defends Policies," *New York Times*, September 17, 1988, p. 5.

23. Quoted in Weintraub and Healy, "Scandal's Roots Traced to Basic Reagan Policy Goals," p. 16.

24. McNaugher, *New Weapons, Old Politics*, p. 86.

25. Quoted in David C. Morrison, "Tinkering with Defense," *National Journal*, Vol., No. 36 (September 3, 1988), p. 2179.

26. Weintraub and Healy, "Scandal's Roots Traced to Basic Reagan Policy Goals," p. 18.

27. Engelberg, "Inquiry into Pentagon Bribery Began with a Telephone Call," p. 21.

28. Quoted in Morrison, "Tinkering with Defense," p. 2180; emphasis added.

29. Edward N. Luttwak, "Why We Need More 'Waste, Fraud & Mismanagement' in the Pentagon," *Commentary*, Vol. 73, No. 2 (February 1982), pp. 17–30.

30. John H. Cushman, Jr., "Curbs on Pentagon Fraud in Dispute," *New York Times*, July 10, 1988, Sec. 1, p. 11; and Richard W. Stevenson, "The High Costs of an Arms Scandal," *New York Times*, July 10, 1988, Sec. 3, pp. 1, 8.

31. Garment, *Scandal*, p. 138; emphasis added.

32. Quoted in Morrison, "Tinkering with Defense," p. 2178.

33. Rosenbaum, "Pentagon Fraud Inquiry," p. B5.

34. Richard Halloran, "Army Takes Offensive against Contract Fraud," *New York Times*, January 27, 1989, p. A14. Among those the task force found had overcharged the army was N.W. Avery, the advertising agency that had devised the army's "Be All You Can Be" campaign; Avery refunded $700,000.

6

TOO BIG TO BELIEVE

By most conventional perspectives, the Savings and Loan (S&L) scandals of the late 1980s were simply too large for all but a few persons to comprehend completely their scope and consequences. According to the latest count from the nonpartisan General Accounting Office (GAO), the cumulative costs of the S&L bailout could be over $500 billion, a little over $2,000 for every person in the nation.[1] And this is a cautious fiscal estimate, one that does not include the mounting costs resulting from political reluctance to address the lingering problem in a timely fashion.[2] Furthermore, given the difficulties incurred by the Resolution Trust Corporation (RTC) in rectifying the institutional disasters left behind by the S&L failures, we could easily add sundry RTC expenses to the final tally.

Unfortunately, the simple dollar accounting, however enormous, does not take into account a number of indirect—but scarcely insignificant—costs. For instance, the S&L failures have made banks much more reserved in their lending policies, leading them to restrict access to capital to countless homeowners and businesses, thereby constricting the amount of credit needed for the American economy to function in a healthy manner.[3] These "costs" are impossible to calculate, but their effect would certainly be sizable if, as some builders caution, a recession were to result "in part from a move by federal bank regulators to discourage banks from real estate lending in an attempt to prevent them from falling victim to the same careless practices that bankrupted so many savings institutions."[4] Or, conversely, if lenders are in fact loathe to trust potential applicants, the opposite could be equally true as people elected to put their savings elsewhere (including, not improbably, in a few mattresses), again fueling a recession by restricting the money supply, in particular to the vital housing industry.

A final monetary accounting is less precise but more insidious—the effect of the S&L bailout on the national debt. Although the S&L bailout costs are being carried "off budget" (i.e., they are not being included in the yearly national budget or the accumulating national deficit), one can safely assume that the federal notes being sold to finance the bailout compete in the financial market and thereby absorb resources that might be more productively spent elsewhere. The principal and interest payments on the bailout bonds intended to compensate those individuals whose assets were squandered by reckless S&L executives represent money necessarily spent; but they concomitantly serve to drive the United States economy deeper into its debilitating national debt. And I will not even begin to speculate what other beneficial government programs—both domestic and foreign—could have been financed without the S&L drain on the national treasury and economy.

Nor are dollars the only currency with which to assess the costs of the S&L debacle. There are sizable political notes that must also be paid. For example, we should recognize the distributional pattern of the bailout. A disproportionate number of failed S&Ls were located in the Southwest, but the entire nation is being asked to pay for the bailout, effectively transferring funds from, say, the Northeast to the Southwest and tacitly subsidizing the construction of condominiums and office buildings in Dallas and Phoenix.[a] Professor Edward Hill has calculated that thirteen states will "reap a massive windfall" in this manner while 37 states will lose, some a lot; he estimates that residents of Connecticut could pay $1,237 per capita while Texans gain $4,775 apiece.[5] Thrifty Yankees could justifiably argue that they were being penalized for the excesses of some spendthrift Texans. Political careers have been truncated.[6] The United States Senate has been dragged through prolonged and embarrassing hearings on its ethical standards. Representative Jim Leach (R-IA) described the S&L fiasco as "the single most grievous legislative error of judgment this century."[7] And politi-

---

[a]A more tangible asset is the condominiums and office buildings themselves that will someday attract business to these regions because of their low cost relative to other locales in the nation.

cians of every stripe (congressional and executive), persuasion (Democratic and Republican), and level (national and local) have been smeared by the imbroglio. The S&L scandals have surely exacerbated the already low esteem with which the American voter views the body politic, hardly a healthy symptom.

In short, the S&L crisis dwarfs all other previous corruption crises combined in terms of dollar costs. In a phrase, the S&L debacle gives new credence to the sorry admonishment that the safest way to rob a bank is to buy one.[b] To many, it symbolizes the greed and profligacy of the 1980s political ethos, where staggering amounts of money were made that had virtually no social return; where members of Congress not only neglected their watchdog responsibility, but actually joined in to encourage, then protect, highly dubious activities; where the executive office of the president either pooh-poohed the impending crisis, welcomed the deregulation, hamstrung the government's ability to alleviate the crisis, or, worse, never saw it coming; and where the regulatory agencies were similarly engaged in self- as opposed to public-serving activities. The ultimate irony is that an administration that preached deregulation (almost as a matter of faith) in the thrift industry ended up presiding over its literal decimation at a monumental loss to the taxpayer.

There is no doubt that in many cases, personal greed dictated the widespread failure of the thrift industry; some bankers spent depositors' money without a whiff of conscience, and their prodigal ways led directly to the closing of their S&Ls. Horror stories of marble-laden banks, gourmet excursions, corporate jets, and extravagant bacchanals made respectable media read like supermarket tabloids. The GAO investigated twenty-six large thrifts that were closed between January 1985 and September 1987 and "found egregious conflicts of interest in twenty of them."[8] As the subtitle of their book

---

[b] This is especially true if one measures safety in terms of punishment meted out. As some observers have noted: "The average sentence for an executive who defrauds an S&L and gets sentenced to prison is three years, compared to 13 years for someone who sticks up the same institution. Of the 960 people convicted in federal courts of fraud against lending institutions in one year, only 494 [51%] were sentenced to prison terms; of 795 convicted of embezzling, only 227 [28%] were sentenced to prison terms. But of 996 convicted of robbing banks and S&Ls, 932 [94%] went to prison." Stephen Pizzo, Mary Fricker, and Paul Muolo, Inside Job (New York: McGraw-Hill, 1989), p. 284; emphasis in original.

(*Inside Job: The Looting of America's Savings and Loans*) implies, Stephen Pizzo and his colleagues have diligently and intriguingly limned a network of alleged organized crime participants who were found to be involved in a few of the failed thrifts.[9] Still, there is no reason to exaggerate the pervasiveness of the S&L scandals and, in particular, the role that only a relative few bankers played. Daniel Brumbaugh calculates that the highest closure rate for S&Ls was in 1982, and then only 252 out of the nation's over 3,300 (7.5 percent) failed; by comparison, the worst year for bank failures during the Great Depression was in 1938, when 277 (3.2 percent) of the banks failed.[10] The *Wall Street Journal* estimates that 5 to 10 percent of the S&L costs could be attributed to individual larceny, and Mayer indicates that 20 percent seems to be the accepted figure.[11] Assuming that one out of ten (or as many as one out of five) of the small number of failed thrifts were guilty of committing felonies should scarcely be grounds for the fiscal confidence Americans want to attribute to their bankers, but it is still important to recognize that probably close to 90 percent of the nation's thrifts performed their fiduciary obligations as steadfastly and securely as ever.

A strong case will be made here that while private institutions and individuals were surely the legal culprits, the primary motor behind the S&L breakdown was the political system in which the thrifts operated. As we will see, an extremely stable thrift industry was thrust into an economic pressure cooker and forced by circumstances beyond its control into bankruptcy-threatening conditions. Rather than letting the economy make the inevitable corrections and weed out the weakest, the government responded (or failed to respond) in ways anticipated to permit the endangered thrifts to extricate themselves with a minimum of casualties. What few realized at the time, however, was that the United States was confronted with what Edward Kane has called "zombie thrifts," banks that were virtually dead in terms of assets and should have been permitted to die. However (and high on the list of unintended consequences), the public policies that were designed to resuscitate these zombies instead renewed life to what proved more to be vampires (sucking out precious financial lifeblood) than friendly corner banks. "In effect," wrote Kane, a "zombie [S&L] ... transcended its natural death from accumulated losses by the black magic of federal guarantees."[12]

No public official should be held venally accountable for trying to help a faltering industry, especially a thrift industry so central to the U.S. economy and way of life. As a matter of legal fact, none has been convicted. But just as surely, political officials in the executive branch, Congess, and the regulatory agencies can be held accountable for failing to make hard political choices, to close early on the faltering thrifts as a means of saving the vast majority of the industry (to say nothing of billions of taxpayer dollars). Instead, they passed laws and blocked regulatory reactions that led—inadvertently but directly—to the plundering of the thrift community. Kane's "central message" is to the point: "congressional procedures for budgeting and for overseeing the operations of the deposit-insurance bureaucracy made the regulatory strategy of coverup and deferral *practically irresistible*," or a situation he calls a "federal ponzi scheme."[13] Moreover, and even sadder, when these mistakes were first beginning to surface, the halls of power refused to remedy them, claiming "constituency service." Five U.S. senators questioned the federal investigation into Charles Keating's Lincoln Savings and Loan Association in 1987; their interference pushed back the bank's final closing by almost two years, at an additional cost of over $1 billion to taxpayers.

Moving beyond the actual S&L culprits, whom she quickly dismisses as "massively crooked and colorful," Suzanne Garment focuses on what she terms (with a rather ungainly label) the "nonpersonnel structural factors." These "factors" would include an inattentive White House whose ideological predilections regarding regulation and supervision were unsympathetic (at best) and a Congress with members seemingly fixated on their campaign contributions. More fundamentally, in many ways, the political system was merely reacting to events as they presented themselves, trying to hide and limit the damage rather than addressing the core problem. Kane attributes much of this behavior to what he calls (in an equally ungainly fashion) "incentive-incompatible contracts"—a set of perverse incentives that led the participants to deny and obfuscate—in other words, the actors "effectively put a high price on doing the 'right' thing."[14] If the actors did not respond decisively or accountably, it is because the system itself is not designed to foster those attributes, so it rarely is decisive or accountable. These characteristics led Garment to contend that the "S&L crisis revealed . . . serious and characteristic tendencies toward irresponsibility in our politics and government."[15]

Without neglecting the various bankers, accountants, lawyers, and money managers who contributed so richly to the S&L crisis[16]—and, by extension, to the financial crisis of the nation and its citizens—let us examine how the political system, responding initially to legitimate economic exigencies, aided and abetted the criminal acts that defined the S&L crisis. This exposition will highlight the abundance of available blame and criminality, but still emphasize that many of the programs and decisions concerning the S&Ls began as well-intended actions that unintentionally—although not unpredictably—had disastrous systemic consequences. All these factors combined to create what L.J. Davis has characterized as "not simply a debacle but a series of debacles that made a few people preposterously rich and will leave most of us significantly poorer."[17]

Prelude to a Disaster

To plumb the origins of the S&L fiasco, we need to go back to the traumatic bank failures of the Great Depression, when so many Americans lost their savings. To guard against a recurrence (and to reinstall public confidence in the shattered banking system), Congress passed the Glass–Steagall Act, which created deposit insurance (paid for by the banks themselves) to insure depositors fully for up to a maximum of $10,000 each. The federal government would establish the Federal Deposit Insurance Corporation (FDIC) and later the Federal Savings and Loan Insurance Corporation (FSLIC) to manage the fund. The Federal Home Loan Bank Board (FHLBB)[c] was established at the same time to regulate the charter banks, monitor their condition, and dispense the insurance funds when necessary. President Franklin Roosevelt, initially opposed to the bill, was remarkably prescient in explaining his opposition:

> As to guaranteeing bank deposits, the minute the federal government starts to do that . . . the government runs into a probable loss. We do not wish to make the United States government liable for the mistakes and errors of individual banks and put a premium on unsound banking in the future.[18]

---

[c] Which the mean-spirited have been known to pronounce as "Fizz-Lick" and "flub," respectively.

What Glass–Steagall explicitly did was to remove the risk savers inherently took when they deposited their money in a bank. What the act implicitly did was basically to remove any distinction between good and bad banks, because under the aegis of the federal government's insurance programs, nobody's money—neither the principal nor the interest—was at risk, regardless of the practices of the bank.

For decades, this system worked well; although some banks occasionally failed, their insurance funds covered the losses. Events of the 1960s, however, placed the community-oriented S&Ls under particular hazard. American involvement in Vietnam resulted to serious inflation, with interest rates in the late 1970s reaching close to 20 percent. The S&Ls were placed in a set of monetary scissors. The first blade: to attract new funds, they would have to pay market interest rates; this situation was especially imperative because Americans had recently discovered money market accounts that paid a great deal more interest than the S&Ls were permitted by the FHLBB. The other half of the scissor was that most of the S&Ls' income was from existing loans, many of which had been booked years ago at 6 percent interest. Davis summarizes the dilemma:

> By the late 1970s, the S&Ls were losing depositors by the thousands as customers abandoned the S&Ls, locked into paying 5.5 percent on deposits with inflation at 13 percent, in favor of uninsured money market accounts, newly available to the public from major Wall Street brokerage houses and mutual funds.[19]

Not surprisingly, this condition was cutting sharply into their earnings and, more critically, their very solvency.

Traditionally, S&Ls were very conservative financial institutions. They were mandated to serve their communities, in particular the housing industry as opposed to commerce (the domain of commercial banks). Community trust was extremely important; to ensure this, S&Ls were required to have 400 owners, no single stockholder could own more than 10 percent of the shares, and the stockholders had to live within 125 miles of the institution. More importantly, they were not permitted to compete on an equal basis with other financial institutions, particularly commercial banks, in terms of their investment strategies.

The 1970s were difficult times for the thrifts, as they saw their earnings crash and their access to new funds restricted by their inability to compete in the money market or even among themselves; FHLBB's infamous Regulation Q capped the permissible interest rate within the S&L community.

> The outflow from thrifts quickly reached crisis proportions. In 1972 the nation's savings and loans had a combined worth of $16.7 billion. By 1980, that figure had plummeted to a *negative* new worth of $17.5 billion, and 85 percent of savings and loans were losing money.[20]

While only 2 percent of that 85 percent were actually insolvent by FHLBB definitions, that number was to rise to 7 percent by the end of 1982 and 9 percent by the end of 1983. FHLBB's chief economist later observed that "there was mounting evidence that what was once viewed as an unprofitability problem had become an insolvency problem."[21] Facing the complete collapse of the entire industry, the S&Ls turned to the federal government, which chartered and regulated them, for protection.

Earlier actions, such as permitting market interest rates on Certificates of Deposit (CDs) over $100,000 and negotiated orders of withdrawal (NOW, a type of checking account) did little in the face of the new fiscal exigencies. So in March 1980, Congress passed the Depository Institutions Deregulations and Monetary Control Act. S&Ls could now pay market interest rates, but mortgage rates remained frozen; this effectively and instantly forced the S&Ls out of the home mortgage business. More critically, the act raised the FHLBB insurance coverage from the existing (as of 1974) $40,000 to $100,000. (The Senate had voted to raise the limit to $50,000 when Representative Fernand St Germain, a Democrat from Rhode Island and chairman of the House Banking Committee, proposed a "compromise" limit of $100,000, supposedly at the bequest of the U.S. League of Savings Institutions.) Suddenly a few of the S&Ls realized how to escape from their fiscal bind, and in a hurry; sports metaphors came into currency, as S&Ls were pressed to "throw the Hail Mary pass because if you didn't score a touchdown, you were going to lose," or find "the guys who want to hit home runs. But the cardinal rule of financial services is that there are no home runs."[22] Still, the situation was inviting: to fail to recover quickly would mean almost certain closure.

With the new limits, some S&Ls moved aggressively to attract massive amounts of new capital by advertising jumbo CDs that were now guaranteed up to $100,000 at whatever interest rate the S&L cared to offer. Big money investors such as brokerage houses, insurance funds, and pension funds immediately realized the opportunities and rushed to take advantage of these "brokered accounts." The S&Ls were competing among themselves for the brokered accounts by paying higher and higher interest rates, which brokers indifferently "shopped" because was no risk factor involved for the investors due to the FSLIC guarantee. The administration seemingly concurred. President Reagan's new secretary of the Treasury, Donald Regan, had come to the department from being the CEO of Merrill Lynch, where he was considered by some to be the father of the brokered account. Previously, S&Ls were restricted by the FHLBB to hold no more than 5 percent brokered deposits in their investment portfolios. To reinforce the brokerage option, this restriction was lifted in 1980. Furthermore, banks were no longer required to retain an operating capital (what bankers call "net worth") equal to at least 5 percent of their insured deposits; 3 percent was now defined by the FHLBB as sufficient. In light of these incentives, by 1984 there was more than $34 billion in FSLIC-guaranteed brokered accounts deposited in the S&Ls. The combination—more money to chase high-risk investments—was a sure road to ruin.

Even worse, the malaise was metastatic. Financially sound and conservative S&Ls were forced to advertise nationwide and offer similar interest rates in order to remain competitive, thereby driving down their profit margins and threatening the solvency of the entire industry. Thus, all thrifts were put at risk by the gambling operations of a few; bad apples indeed threatened to rot the entire barrel. But there were few reasons to refuse, given the FSLIC backstop.

Other FHLBB regulations were relaxed under the leadership of President Reagan's appointed director of the Bank Board, Richard Pratt, undoubtedly imbued with the "deregulation Zeitgeist of the 1980s."[23] Pratt quietly removed the various restrictions that made the S&Ls local institutions and, claiming that multiple ownership seemed a "bizarre requirement," declared that an S&L could now have a single owner.[d] Many of the new owners were not only from well outside the immediate community, but also had a variety of checkered back-

---

[d]Even now, Pratt "insists that there was no choice," given the spirit of deregulation and the prevailing economic conditions (Mayer, *The Greatest-Ever Bank Robbery*, chap. 5 at p. 80).

grounds.[24] Alas, with this newly granted flexibility and apparent affluence appeared rampant opportunity; juxtaposed with the incentive to gamble one's way back to profitability with these newfound funds, S&Ls in California, Florida, and the Southwest began to invest in distinctly untraditional ways. The most critical of these changes for the "new wave" of S&Ls was to flee the home mortgage market. The largest of the failed S&Ls, Lincoln Savings and Loan, with twenty-six branches, issued only eleven mortgages during its six-year tenure, and four were to employees. Simply, the interest from mortgages could not provide the money needed to attract the brokered deposits. Other opportunities for potentially higher payoffs were needed to pay the promised high-interest deposits as well as extricate the S&Ls from their insolvency dilemmas.

The most disreputable banks, often found in Texas, California, and other parts of the Southwest, began to find ways to complete "Hail Mary" passes or hit home runs. Unfortunately, their owners were more concerned with personal wealth rather than their institutions' well-being. Aided by generous interpretations of the tax codes that permitted them to increase their capitalizations by reassessing their assets and hide the losses from many of their transactions (e.g., "historic" costs allowed a bank to list a property on its books at the purchase price rather than the usually lower market value), S&Ls started to speculate—and grow— wildly. A typical example: In June 1983, Ranbir Sahni bought a small S&L in Irvine, California, that had declared assets of $11.7 million. Working out of a single office with no banking windows or tellers and never writing a home loan, Sahni's American Diversified attracted brokered deposits from all over the nation by paying the highest return in the country for insured deposits. By June 1988, when American Diversified was finally closed, the *average* account was a little over $80,000 (the nationwide average is about $8,000). Between June 1983 and December 1985, when the California S&L office first issued a cease-and-desist order, American Diversified had grown from $11.7 million to $1.1 billion in declared assets. When it was closed, the loss to FHLBB was close to three-quarters of a billion dollars. To place this in perspective, the cost to the taxpayer for this little-publicized S&L "was roughly as much as the federal government had at risk in the much-debated bailouts of New York City, Lockheed, and Chrysler *put together.*"[25]

In October 1982, Congress passed the Depository Institutions Act sponsored by Senator Jake Garn (R-UT) and Representative St Germain. The act basically liberalized the types of loans an S&L could make—for example, up to 40 percent of a thrift's assets could now be lent for nonresidential real estate loans. According to Martin Mayer,

> Probably the single most damaging provision in the law was the elimination of all regulation of the ratio between what an S&L could lend to a developer and the appraised value of the property for which the loan was made.[26]

This meant that banks could now lend a full 100 percent of assessed value; developers would no longer have to place any of their own money at risk. Moreover, an S&L could now loan all of its capital to one investor. Additional Bank Board regulations made S&Ls more vulnerable; entrepreneurs could now purchase a thrift using "noncash" assets (such as real estate), and loans could be made anywhere in the nation. Land developers were not only permitted to buy S&Ls, they were allowed to lend to themselves, and ADC (acquisition, development, and construction) loans became the rage. One observer neatly captured the resulting debacle:

> . . . when you get a fox in a hen house, you get a lot of dead chickens. That doesn't mean that's a bad fox. That's what a fox will do in a hen house. You give a builder a chance to build with insured deposits he can raise with a phone call whenever he needs some money, and he'll cover the earth with housing.[27]

When President Reagan signed the Garn–St Germain Act, he was fulsome in his assessment, calling it the "most important legislation for financial institutions in 50 years. All in all, I think we've hit the jackpot."[28] President Reagan was probably never more correct, but one must suspect that he never imagined who would be winning this jackpot, or the payoffs or the payees that would ultimately be involved.

S&Ls Turned Loose

Owning an S&L had become virtual child's play, especially when they were only charted by the states (but still protected under the FSLIC).

Apparently some treated the opportunity as if they had been given access to play money, spending it freely on developing real estate and highly speculative investments. A few S&L owners spent their banks' funds even more freely on art, fleets of Rolls-Royces and jet planes, extravagant parties, European gourmet vacations, vacation homes, and stocking the company refrigerators with Dom Perignon campaign.[29] Larger deals and endless expansion were the passwords. Stanley Adams, chairman of Austin's Lamar S&L, even applied to open a branch office on the Sea of Tranquillity, i.e., the moon. And virtually anyone was invited to play with only the most perfunctory background investigation: in California, 235 applications to open an S&L were received between April 1982 and fall 1984.

The most spectacular examples of S&L excesses were found in the Southwest, particularly in California and especially Texas, with land the usual commodity. Empire S&L of Mesquite, Texas, was owned by Spenser Blain, who somehow fell under the influence of land developer D.L. Faulkner. Between the two, they built acres of poorly constructed, unoccupied condominiums and office buildings outside Dallas. Faulkner and a few of his associates would cooperate in what came to be known as a "land flip"—buying and selling a single piece of property, often several times and sometimes in a single day, each time aided by agreeable assessors who happily (and profitably) provided always higher assessed values. Empire and others made out like proverbial bandits:

> Every time a piece of property was sold, the thrift made a new loan to cover the purchase price. Each time a loan was made, the thrift owner or owners pocketed fees—loan fees for negotiating the deal, origination fees for preparing the documents—all of which provided him or them with a handsome and ever increasing income.[30]

Empire's assets grew *eightfold* between September 1982 and September 1983.

To confound any audit, banks could hide bad loans by trading their delinquent loans for another bank's bad loans, thereby giving both banks new assets to post on their books without review for six months, at which time, they would be swapped again. Only in Texas could this picaresque dodge be called "trading dead horses for dead cows." The borrowers made immense profits by inflating their costs and pocketing the difference when they built substandard structures. To make their deals even more irresistible, Empire and its ilk would include the first few years of payments in the loan. And should a loan ever be called due, the borrower would simply return the property to the lender and start all over again. In 1983, Empire was named the most profitable S&L in the nation; the next year, it was closed by the Texas S&L commission.

On May 1, 1983, Edwin Gray was sworn in as the new chairman of the Bank Board. A former press secretary to then-Governor Reagan of California, he had worked on President Reagan's transition team but chose to return to Southern California, where he served as a vice president for public relations for a San Diego S&L. He was well received throughout the S&L community as a man sympathetic to and knowledgeable about the thrift industry, as well as being close to the president. In June, he attended a convention of the Texas Savings and Loan League, delivering a speech entitled "A Sure Cure for What Ails You." This meeting undoubtedly gave Gray the most cordial greeting he would receive from Texas S&L owners.

Shortly after his visit to Texas, Gray began to receive an unmitigated stream of dire warnings regarding the health of the thrift industry and the rapidly closing crisis. Gray was initially concerned about what he thought was an excessive number of brokered deposits. In July 1982, the Penn Square Bank in Oklahoma City went bankrupt, apparently due to too many brokered deposits.[31] Persuaded by staff reports and worried that Penn Square might be an omen for the S&Ls, Gray issued (in conjunction with William Issacs, director of the FDIC) an "Advance Notice on Rulemaking" on January 16, 1984, restricting brokered deposits. Although the regulation was subsequently overturned by the U.S. Court of Appeals, the S&Ls now viewed Gray as an opponent and began to act accordingly.

Gray was soon to find new and even more disturbing evidence to feed his concern and further his distance from the industry he was presumably appointed to support. Most observers argue that March 14, 1984, was his actual defining moment. He was shown a twenty-minute video tape taken by a Dallas appraiser to demonstrate the havoc Empire Savings had brought to the Dallas construction market.

The film introduced Ed Gray to the real world of Empire Savings and Loan of Mesquite.... The condos were built with no regard to the market or economic feasibility, but simply for the sake of building and generating loans.... "I had to turn my head away," said Gray. "I couldn't look at it. It was so shameful."[32]

Empire and its S&L kin had provided Dallas with a twelve-and-a-half-year supply of overconstruction, but the prosperity apparent from reading the S&L's books was literally built on sand, as empty condominiums were littered across the landscape.[e] Mayer estimates in retrospect that by 1985, half of the Texas S&Ls were technically insolvent.[33] In light of the situation, the FSLIC insurance fund could not hope to cover the emerging S&L failures in Texas, let alone nationwide.

Gray at Bay

Faced with what he thought was irrefutable evidence, Gray started to marshall his forces to rein in the "high-riding" (his description) S&Ls using a two-pronged strategy. First, he had to close down a large number of the zombie thrifts; second, he had to increase the FSLIC insurance fund so that the customers of the shuttered thrifts could be reimbursed.

There were, however, two major obstacles to Gray's strategy, one economic and one political. The first dealt with the state of the economy, especially in Texas, where economic hard times brought on by the hyperinflation of the previous years and the crash in the price of oil had rendered the economy extremely vulnerable. More to the point, S&L owners argued that while a number of them were having difficulty remaining solvent, their troubles were a function of the economy rather than their mismanagement; left to their own (deregulated) devices, the argument continued, the thrifts would naturally "grow" out of the crisis. Unfortunately, economic analysis revealed that the S&Ls had introduced an "artificial stimulus" to the Texas economy in the early 1980s, so when the national economy started to recover around 1982–83, Texas banks had already spent their brokered assets, producing a glut of slipshod construction on the market, thus inhibiting the regional economy's recovery.

The political obstacles were far more imposing. There was, for one,

---

[e]A well-traveled Texas real estate joke at the time: What's the difference between venereal disease and condos? You can get rid of VD.

almost constant snipping at Gray from now-Chief of Staff Donald Regan; rumors of Gray's mismanagement or even his resignation were common and said to emanate from "high administration sources." A major shortcoming was that the FHLBB was sorely understaffed (about 700 personnel to monitor 4,000 S&Ls) and underpaid; Kane cites a report finding that

> several hundred FSLIC clients had not been examined even once between January 1984 and July 1986. Among the 2,984 thrifts that were examined in this period, 925 had last been examined in 1984, 1,772 in 1985, and only 277 in 1986.[34]

This lack of staff handcuffed Gray when he ordered large-scale audits; he simply could not muster the necessary manpower. Moreover, the Office of Management and Budget (OMB) under David Stockman refused his pleas for additional staff, proudly citing the merits of deregulation (e.g., fewer rather than more regulators). Gray was able to circumvent this limitation by transferring his auditors to the staffs of the Federal Home Loan Banks (FHLB).[f] These banks were not accountable to OMB and therefore could increase their staffs and the staff salaries. Between July 1985 and the end of December 1986, the examiner staff grew from 747 to 1,524, and their salaries increased by about 50 percent.

By May 1986, Gray had convinced the Reagan administration to request a $15 billion recapitalization of the FSLIC insurance fund, to be paid for by the sale of bonds. According to Mayer,

> the [S&L] industry, interestingly, did not initially oppose the project. Leaders of many established S&Ls felt that higher insurance premiums were a reasonable trade-off for ridding themselves of competition from the zombie thrifts.[35]

The bill crawled through the House of Representatives Banking Committee until, in September, Gray told Chairman St Germain that the FSLIC had approximately $2.5 billion facing a feared $48 billion in

---

[f] There are twelve Federal Home Loan Banks, distributed geographically across the country, that are long-term credit depositories. Owned by the S&Ls in their districts, they are the "principal supervisory agents" for the banks in their regions. For some functions, they report to the FHLBB.

insolvent S&Ls. The bill quickly cleared committee and was scheduled for a September 20 floor vote when it ran into the opposition of House Majority Leader James Wright (D-TX) of Forth Worth.

Wright's ear had been bent by many Texas S&L owners as to how the Bank Board and the regional FHLB were employing Gestapo-like tactics to batter them into submission and seizure. Two bankers stood out in Wright's mind. Tom Gaubert had purchased Independent American S&L in 1982, parlaying its assets from $40 million to $1.9 billion in 1985, but he had been forced to relinquish control of the S&L by the FHLB. Active in Texas Democratic politics, he organized the East Texas First Political Action Committee (PAC), which raised around $100,000 to help Jim Chapman win a local election. This partisan support was particularly appreciated by Representative Tony Coelho (D-CA), Chair of the Democratic Congressional Campaign Committee. Don Dixon brought Vernon S&L, a small, well-established S&L, in 1982. From 1982 until January 1986, its reported assets grew from $82.6 million to $1.3 billion. Dixon, arguably the most notorious of the Texas S&L owners, spent Vernon money on lavish houses in California, *"gastronomique fantastique"* (Mrs. Dixon's description) tours of France with his wife, very expensive automobiles, and a yacht that he docked in Washington for the benefit of Democratic Party functions; he also spent Vernon money on large loans to his own construction company, Dondi Residential Properties, which added to the glut of Texas condominiums. In a truly stellar display of unwavering financial insight, 96 percent of Vernon's loans were classified as "nonperforming" (i.e., just plain bad). By 1985, he had been issued a cease-and-desist order.

For the S&Ls, "June 1986 marked the climax of the most dramatic five years in the history of the Texas thrift industry." [36] In the latter half of 1986, the Dallas FHLB warned at least 100 S&Ls of possible supervisory actions. Not surprisingly, they turned to Representative Wright for relief. On September 15, Gray was invited to Wright's office where, for two hours, Wright and other Texas congressmen complained strenuously about his treatment of their constituents. A few days later, Wright called Gray to complain about the treatment given to Craig Hall of Westwood S&L; specifically, Hall protested about the regulator supervising the Westwood examination, claiming he was not being as "flexible or understanding" as he should, and demanded that he be transferred.

On September 26, Wright removed the FSLIC recapitalization bill from the House calendar, implying that if the Bank Board accommodated Hall, he would release his objections. Gray, admitting that he was buckling under rank political pressure but fearing for the integrity of the insurance fund, reluctantly agreed to replace Hall's objectionable regulator. On October 3, Gray met with Wright to explain how very precarious the situation was and to ask for his help. Although Wright continued to complain about the Bank Board's putative hostile treatment of Texas S&Ls, on October 6 he released his hold on the FSLIC recapitalization bill.

On October 21, Wright returned to Texas for a lunch in Fort Worth hosted by his good friend George Mallick.[g] At the luncheon, he was verbally assaulted by over 100 irate Texas S&L executives and land developers, each vehemently complaining of treatment at the hands of the Bank Board and the Dallas FHLB. A few weeks after the Fort Worth meeting, Wright called Gray, asking him to talk with Tom Gaubert, whose position with Independent American was being threatened by the Dallas FHLB. Even though it was against Bank Board policy to meet with persons the Board might review, Gray met with Gaubert for two hours in order to curry Wright's acquiescence on the recapitalization bill, and agreed to review Gaubert's pending removal from his S&L.[h]

Finally, late that year, Wright returned a telephone call from Don Dixon of Vernon, who railed that the FHLB was about to close Vernon and asked for Wright's intervention. Wright telephoned Gray in San Diego and asked that he investigate Vernon's charge that he was being driven out of business. Gray discovered that the FHLB was trying to serve a "consent-to-merger" agreement, not a foreclosure, on Vernon

---

[g] Wright's various involvements with Mallick were to be the grist of Wright's later House Ethics Committee hearings, hearings that later resulted in Wright's resignation from the House of Representatives.

[h] Wright also began to spread rumors that Joe Shelby, the Dallas FHLB director of enforcement, was a homosexual, and suggested that he be fired. Although Wright strongly denied the allegation, the congressional ethics investigation of Wright found that his request that Gray fire Selby "greatly exceeded the bounds of proper congressional conduct.... An attempt to destroy the distinguished career of a dedicated public servant because of his rumored sexual orientation or because of a wild accusation hardly reflects creditably on the House" (quoted in Pizzo et al., *Inside Job*, p. 219).

and informed Wright's office to that effect. But the proposed mergers did not work out and auditors discovered Dixon and other Vernon executives withdrawing money from the S&L through a number of back doors in anticipation of being shut down. On March 20, 1987, Vernon was closed by the Bank Board and Wright (now Speaker of the House) was furious at Gray for what he perceived to be duplicitous information. Representative Frank Annunzio (D-IL) told the *Washington Post*:

> If [the closing of Vernon] is an attempt to embarrass Jim Wright, then Mr. Gray is lucky that the speaker is an advocate for the homeless because after June [Gray's term expiration date], when Mr. Gray is out of a job, he may be sleeping on a grate.[37]

On April 27, the FSLIC filed civil racketeering lawsuits against Dixon and other Vernon executives, charging them with taking over $540 million out of their S&L.

On January 22, 1987, while testifying before the House Banking Subcommittee, Gray was attacked by the Chair, who later explained to Gray that he was acting under the instructions of the Speaker. In March, St Germain decided to amend his original $15 billion recapitalization bill in favor of a $5 billion version. It seemed likely that the U.S. League of Savings Institutions was now against the recap, arguing that the FHLBB adopt a "forbearance" posture. Forbearance and a smaller FSLIC fund would ensure that the S&Ls could not be foreclosed; that is, if the FSLIC were undercapitalized, it would not have the funds necessary to close down the weak S&Ls. April 28, Speaker Wright publicly agreed to support the recapitalization bill, claiming that Secretary of the Treasury James Baker had requested that he do so. By the time the Comprehensive Equality Banking Act (CEBA) of 1987 was finally passed on August 10, the original $15 billion had been reduced to $10.8 billion with the understanding that it would be spent in thirds over the next three years, thereby affording zombie S&Ls even more time to increase their (ultimately, taxpayer) losses. The S&L bailout was effectively—fatally—delayed by CEBA until after the 1988 presidential campaign, turning "a $30 billion problem into a $300 billion problem."[38]

If Gray thought he was having troubles with the House of Representatives, then the Senate could scarcely be classified as a promenade in the park. Senators too listened to their constituents, especially those who contributed handsomely to their campaign funds. As early as October 1986, Senator David Pryor (D-AR) wrote Gray that

> S&L officials in my state have called to my attention what appears to be a deliberate system of harassment against many institutions in the 9th Federal Home Loan Bank Board District. . . . By forcing examiners to revisit "clean" institutions until they find something to write up, the Bank Board is wasting resources. . . . By keeping those examiners at an institution longer than they need to be, the Bank Board forces the institutions to pay tens of thousands of dollars in costs. . . . Before the Bank Board receives any recapitalization authority from the Congress, you need to assure us that your supervisory resources are being used effectively and fairly. . . . I have put a "hold" on the Senate recapitalization bill and am anxious to receive assurances from you that you will correct the abuses which have been taking place in Arkansas and other states. I was pleased to learn that you have been discussing this problem with the House Majority Leader [Wright].[39]

The key antagonist in Gray's Senate travails was Charles H. Keating, Jr., owner of American Continental Corporation (ACC). In 1984, he applied to buy Lincoln Savings and Loan of Irvine, California. Lincoln had the lowest delinquent mortgage ratio in California and was committed to lending in "mortgage-deprived areas." To gain the California S&L Commission's approval of the purchase, Keating (already under a consent decree from the Security and Exchange Commission for maters in Ohio that should have made his ownership impossible) promised to continue these practices. After the purchase was approved, he fired most of the senior management and ceased writing home mortgages, freeing up his capital for highly speculative investments, including Texas and Arizona real estate, "junk" bonds from Michael Milken of Drexel Burham Lambert and, even worse, unsecured subordinated notes sold directly to the public through ACC. From 1984 to its closing in 1990, Lincoln grew from a $1 billion S&L to one claiming over $6 billion in assets. The bill to the taxpayers is estimated to be approximately $2.5 billion. And this does not include the losses of the investors (pensioners were particularly targeted) who bought the ACC bonds that had no FSLIC safety net.

Keating's investment strategies brought him in conflict with Gray early on. In the February 1985 congressional hearings on Gray's investment restrictions, Keating testified that "To reregulate today is burning the house to roast the pig."[40] At the same hearings, Alan Greenspan (former head to the President's Council of Economic Advisers and current chairman of the Federal Reserve Board), testifying on Lincoln's behalf, named seventeen thrifts that he claimed were prospering; in four years, "15 of the 17 thrifts he'd cited would be out of business and would cost the FSLIC $3 billion in losses."[41]

Keating surely sensed he was skating on legality's thin ice. He retained some of the nation's best lawyers (including Arthur Liman, later the Democrats' Iran–Contra counsel). Arthur Young, one of the nation's most respected accounting firms, audited Lincoln's books, but one needs to question its professionalism. In 1987, one week after giving Lincoln a clean bill of health, Jack Atchinson resigned his Arthur Young post and became an ACC vice president for $900,000 a year. Atchinson repeatedly had written for Keating, vouching for Lincoln's financial stability and complaining to congressmen how FHLB audits were looking at the wrong criteria or using inexperienced examiners. As we just saw, Keating also used renowned economists like Alan Greenspan to argue his case before Congress and regulatory commissions.

Even though most of Lincoln's immediate problems were with the FHLB in San Francisco, Keating apparently considered Gray the key player he had to influence, particularly regarding the FHLBB's restrictions on direct investment, Keating's staple. Through intermediaries, Keating went so far as to offer Gray a position, apparently for a salary of $300,000; Gray refused. In 1986, Keating lobbied widely (e.g., to Chief of Staff Regan) to have a colleague of his, Lee Henkel, appointed to fill a recently opened position as one of the three directors of the Bank Board. Henkel was appointed and assumed an acting position on the Board but resigned because of conflicts of interest when the Senate Banking Committee under Senator William Proxmire (D-WI) disclosed that Henkel and his businesses had borrowed over $133 million from Lincoln and still had $86 million in debt outstanding.

On March 12, 1987, the San Francisco FHLB began a standard audit of Lincoln. On April 1, Henkel resigned from the Bank Board. On April 2, Gray was asked to come without staff to the office of Senator Dennis DeConcini (D-AZ).[42] Senators Alan Cranston (D-CA), John Glenn (D-OH), and John McCain (R-AZ) joined Senator DeConcini. The senators' stated concerns were with the "tough" manner in which the San Francisco FHLB was treating Lincoln and Gray's restriction on direct investment. Keating was already challenging the rule in federal court but also decided to ask the senators to urge Gray to withdraw it. DeConcini, said to have been Keating's primary spokesperson, proffered Gray a deal; they would urge Lincoln to write more home mortgages if the direct investment rule were lifted. Gray refused, explaining that the rule was already under judicial review and, besides that, it was vital to the fundamental health of the entire thrift community. On the matter of the San Francisco FHLB's treatment of Lincoln, Gray urged the senators to talk with the San Francisco personnel directly.[i]

On April 9, Jim Cirona (president of the San Francisco FHLB), Michael Patriarca (his deputy), and Richard Sanchez (the supervisor of the Lincoln audit) met with the four senators. They were accompanied by Bill Black (Gray's deputy and appointed general council to the San Francisco FHLB), who took notes. The four senators were joined by Senator William Riegle (D-MI), soon-to-be-chairman of the Senate Banking Committee—the so-called "Keating Five." The thrust of the senators' charges was summarized by DeConcini: "we have determined that potential actions of yours could injure a constituent." Glenn was to the point: "To be blunt, you should charge them or get off their backs." After Cirona noted that "This meeting is very unusual, to discuss a particular company," Sanchez revealed that Lincoln had "stuffed" its files to make loans look good after the fact: "out of 52 real estate loans Lincoln made between 1984 and 1986, there were no credit reports in the file on borrowers in all 52 cases."

> *Patriarca.* They're flying blind on all their different loans and investments.
>
> *Glenn.* Some people don't do the kind of underwriting you want. [But] is their judgment good?
>
> *Patriarca.* That approach might be okay if they were doing it with their own money. They aren't. They're using federally insured money.

---

[i] When news of the meeting was reported in the press, DeConcini denied that it ever took place. It was not until the *Arizona Republic* printed notes that DeConcini's staff had prepared for him on the meeting that he admitted it had, in fact, occurred. Cranston made similar angry disclaimers but released a statement a month later, admitting that "looking back . . . , I did a pretty stupid thing, politically" (quoted in Adams, *The Big Fix*, p. 254.)

Later Patriarca made the most telling point:

> We're sending a criminal referral to the Department of Justice. Not maybe, we're sending one. This is an extraordinarily serious matter. . . . This is not a profitable institution. Let me give you one example. Lincoln sold a loan with recourse [the buyer had the right to return the property] and booked a $12 million profit. The purchaser rescinded the sale, but Lincoln left the $12 million profit on its books. Now, I don't care how many accountants they get to say that's right, it's wrong.
>
> *DeConcini.* Why would [the accountants] say these things [that the regulators' audit was inordinately long and bordered on harassment]? They have to guard their credibility.
>
> *Patriarca.* They have a client.
>
> *DeConcini.* You believe they would prostitute themselves for a client?
>
> *Patriarca.* Absolutely. It happens all the time.

In Patriarca's words, it was a senatorial "full court press."[43] The meeting ended after two hours.

The San Francisco FHLB finished its examination and, on May 1, recommended that the Bank Board take control of Lincoln, on the grounds that Lincoln had dissipated its assets and operated in "an unsafe and unsound" manner. By the time the recommendation had cleared the appropriate FHLBB offices and legal counsel, it was the end of June and Gray's term as chairman of the Bank Board expired with the month. Gray later explained that rather than "give credence to Mr. Keating's nevertheless absurd allegations that I had a 'vendetta' against him," he left the Lincoln file for the incoming chair, M. Danny Wall.

Wall was well connected in Washington. He had been the staff director for the Senate Banking Committee and the principal author of the 1982 Garn–St Germain bill. "What followed then," Adams argues, "is considered by some highly competent observers to be the biggest scandal of all, an even worse precedent than anything done by Jim Wright and his whole corrupt Texas crew."[44] Keating sued the Bank Board for disclosing sensitive material to a journalist, and demanded to have his case removed to a less-prejudiced venue, the Seattle FHLB. After a full year of hearings and deliberations, Wall's Enforcement Review Committee noted the "seriously adversarial relationship that prevents normal supervisory communications" between Lincoln and the San Francisco FHLB. Seattle vowed that it could not accept jurisdiction over Lincoln, so the Bank Board itself assumed jurisdiction, a procedure it had never undertaken in its fifty-year history. One of Keating's Washington attorneys sent him a "Dear Charlie" letter dated May 11:

> You have the [Bank] Board just where you want them and you should be able to reach an agreement tomorrow which will completely satisfy you. As you know, I have put pressure on Wall to work toward meeting your demands, and he has so instructed his staff. They all know the Wednesday meeting is crucial to their future.[45]

A Memorandum of Understanding was signed on May 20, by which Lincoln was allowed to continue operations under a supervisory agreement, while the Bank Board promised to give it a new, unbiased examination; the new audit team would not even be permitted to see the 1986 audit. In Phoenix, Keating celebrated by throwing a monster party.

By the end of 1988, the Bank Board had decided that San Francisco had been correct and ordered Keating to surrender control of ACC and Lincoln. On April 13, 1989, Keating declared ACC bankrupt; regulators moved against Lincoln the next day and within a few weeks, the Bank Board declared Lincoln's losses at approximately $2.5 billion. In the interim year, Keating had sought to raise new capital (by now, even Drexel Burnham was unwilling to extend Keating credit) through a series of subordinated (i.e., uninsured) notes, which 23,000 investors had purchased for $250 million.

One must add a postscript to the Keating episode, namely, how it was that five U.S. senators felt obligated to interrogate regulators regarding their treatment of a specific company. While undoubtedly elected representatives have an obligation to intervene when they sense a constituent is being mistreated at the hands of an overly bureaucratic process, it is highly unlikely for five senators to involve themselves to the extent described above. The answer almost certainly has to do with Keating's business practice of unabashedly contributing to politicians' campaign funds. When the *Los Angeles Times* reported that he had contributed about $700,000 to thirty-six state and national candidates, Keating responded that he had given money to far more than thirty-six. In the case of the five senators, Keating had contributed generously. DeConcini had received $43,000, plus business support for friends in

Arizona; McCain received $112,000; Glenn apparently got $34,000, plus another $200,000 for a voter registration effort; Riegle received $66,160; and Cranston was given $41,000, plus another $850,000 for a supportive get-out-the-vote organization. Later, Keating was completely candid when questioned about the purpose of his political contributions:

> One question among the many raised in recent weeks had to do with whether my financial support in any way influenced several political figures to take up my cause. I want to say in the most forceful way I can: I certainly hope so.[46]

Conclusions

In many ways, of course, the narrative of the S&L corruption is far from finished. The Reagan administration's efforts to keep the magnitude of the S&L crisis under wraps until after the 1988 presidential election were accepted by Democrats as well as Republicans; neither party was so innocent as to permit the scandals to become a campaign issue. Wall's attempts to salvage the solvency of a few Texas S&Ls (the so-called "Southwest Plan") has drawn its own full share of critics who accuse Wall of making "sweetheart deals," again at the taxpayer's expense.[47] The RTC has come under fire for alleged mismanagement, improprieties, and insensitivity (such as hiring discredited S&L executives[48] and doling out special favors[49]). Even a well-intended plan to make repossessed homes available to low-income citizens has been far more plagued than successful.[50] And, most important, the bailout debt lingers over the American taxpayer while the federal government continues to avoid the problem and will continue to do so well into the next century. But the essential information for our purposes of examining political corruption has been set out above in sufficient detail. We can now turn to the central question of examining the S&L debacles in terms of political corruption.

Needless to say, there were numerous cases in which rank personal greed and extravagance were the principal contributing factors. We can, however, identify a number of systemic factors that also contributed mightily to the S&L crises. For, as Kane cautions us, "It is all too tempting to blame the problem wholly on bad or dishonest management at insolvent S&Ls. But misdiagnosing the roots of the problem means being lured down unproductive paths of reform."[51]

The conditions that led to the S&L crunch in the early 1980s were relatively "objective"; nobody manipulated the economy so basely that the thrifts would fail, leading to the deregulation of the industry. Most observers agree that what happened next was less a question of corruption and more a failure of political nerve. S&Ls that were threatened with insolvency appealed to Washington for relief. Rather than simply let the weak banks, the so-called "zombies," expire (however noisily) and cover those losses with the FSLIC funds, the government enacted laws and regulations to give the zombies another—albeit very long— shot at surviving. Cooperatively, the S&Ls bought and the FSLIC guaranteed the expensive wager that the thrifts could gamble their way back to solvency, thereby rescuing the financial health of both parties. In terms of what we have discussed about political corruption, the various acts and regulations were not the product of corrupt politicians and regulators conspiring to make themselves as well as a few bankers rich. They were an example of bankers seeing their thrift system being racked by the inflation-fighting high interest rates of Paul Volker's Federal Reserve Board and begging for help—asking to have the political system amend the economic system so that they could continue to operate (backstopped by the FSLIC funds) rather than permit the market forces to work their demise. The government accepted the challenge. Mayer summarizes the results:

> What happened to create the disgusting and expensive spectacle of a diseased industry was that the government, confronted with a difficult problem, found a false solution that made the problem worse. This false solution then acquired a supportive constituency that remained vigorous and effective for almost five years after everybody with the slightest expertise in the subject knew that terrible things were happening *everywhere*.[52]

In ruling on a bankrupt S&L in New York, federal judge Jack Weinstein opined that FHLBB's regulations had indeed encouraged the S&Ls to engage in high-risk investments. While this permissiveness did not condone criminal activities, Judge Weinstein apportioned part of the blame to Washington:

> Congress and the Home Loan Bank Board are directly responsible for what happened here. The government, in removing adequate controls

over this bank, led to the activities now complained of. . . . [The S&Ls'
losses are] a result of the failure of the federal government to do what it
should have done in supervising and controlling [thrifts].[53]

William Seidman, a closer observer from his position as Chair of the
FDIC, concurred: "This was a failure of government."[54]

However unfortunate, however rife with unanticipated consequences
these laws and regulations were, their passages and enactments were
not the principal S&L scandal. Where the political corruption really
occurred is when fragmentary audits and news articles revealing the
extent of fraudulent banking practices began to surface. In a sorry
response, virtually nothing was done to rein in the raging Southwest
S&Ls until Gray fired his first shot across their bow, and even then,
government, *including the Bank Board*, seemingly did little to curtail
the criminal and near-criminal activities. The costs of procrastination
were immense: Bert Ely, an acknowledged expert on the subject, "estimates that the S&L bailout would have cost taxpayers $25 billion if the
administration had acted in 1983 and still less than $100 billion by
1986," unquestionably a staggering amount but only 20 percent of the
current calculations, and a cost that could have been largely covered by
the FSLIC funds.[55]

The conventional view of corruption would hold that if the government officials were responsible, it was because they were somehow on
the "take." To a minor degree, the evidence bears this out. Even if the
"take" were not directly into their very wallets, a few congressmen and
senators did benefit from S&L support. And some paid accordingly: St
Germain was defeated for re-election in 1988; Jim Wright and Tony
Coelho resigned from Congress under a pall of charges; and Senator
Cranston was rebuked by the Senate for improper conduct. But the vast
majority of the governmental actors did not benefit. Richard Pratt (of
whom Mayer wrote: "Everybody likes Dick Pratt; and I like Dick Pratt,
too. But if you had to pick one individual to blame for what happened
to the S&Ls and to some hundreds of billions of taxpayer money, Dick
would get the honor without even campaigning"[56]) is now a business
professor at the University of Utah; no one believes he became rich as
the architect of the S&L crisis. His incentive was not personal gain. His
motivation was his perception that the S&L industry could perform
better, more efficiently, if it were freed from the shroud of government
regulation. The 1980 Depository Institutions, Deregulation, and Mone-

tary Control Act and the 1982 Depository Institution Act (which, in retrospect, Wright called a "grotesque error"[57]) both operated with the same set of ideological assumptions against regulation; similar arguments could be couched for Donald Regan's and OMB's refusals to support Gray, because Gray was seemingly impeding the ideological hallmark of the administration (as well as undermining what Regan had created at Merrill Lynch). Gray, although hardly an unbiased party, was on the money when he noted that "The administration was so ideologically blinded that it couldn't understand the difference between thrift deregulation and airline deregulation."[58] These motives and perspectives are hardly the cloth from which the conventional vestment of corruption would be tailored.

In addition to these ideological obstacles, we can identify some critical institutional impediments, the "nonpersonnel structural factors" Garment indicts. These can be largely attributed to a lack of positive incentives to do something constructive as the crisis and evidence emerged. Everything within the system urged a coverup, or at least a short-term coverup that resulted in higher long-term costs. The individual S&Ls had every reason in the world to, first, adopt the "Hail Mary" strategy and then, when that failed, hide their huge losses and impending insolvency in a maze of accounting technicalities. The willingness of the major accounting firms to approve questionable bookkeeping practices reinforced this latter strategy.[59] On the negative side, the condition economists call "moral hazard" erased whatever barriers there were to the S&Ls' "home run" mentality. The taxpayer guarantee to backstop the FSLIC funds meant that shady, worried, and even honest S&L executives could rationalize their gambling tactics knowing that their investors could not lose. Moral hazard—presenting a "heads, we win, tails, FSLIC loses" opportunity—removed whatever downside risk or disincentives that might have prevented the S&Ls from gambling away their fortunes.

Politicians had strong reason to give the S&Ls enough rope to hang themselves: putting off the "moment of truth" would allow them to adopt the "it happened on somebody else's watch" excuse and save them from distasteful hard choices. Last, and most troubling, the regulators had their own institutional reasons to procrastinate. First, to admit to the S&L crisis would be to admit simultaneously to the failure of the Bank Board's supervisory responsibilities. Second, like most regulatory agencies, the Bank Board had been "captured" by the S&Ls.[60]

Relations between the FHLBB and the S&Ls were very close, especially in terms of personnel; for example, Gray was an S&L executive prior to becoming director of the Bank Board. To close down one's friends would undercut one's social and professional standing. Ultimately, this familiarity was overcome, but its effects should not be ignored. And third, regulators are also short-sighted, preferring to leave hard choices to subsequent officials.

In direct contradiction to the usual view that corruption is aberrant behavior, in this case all the institutional dice were loaded in its favor:

> A decapitalized institution faces enormous incentives to undertake go-for-broke financial plays that load potential losses onto uninformed and insufficiently wary taxpayers, while depositors, regulators, and politicians have some incentives to look the other way.... A layered breakdown in incentives—between FSLIC and its clients, between elected politicians and FSLIC, and between politicians and the taxpayers—has turned a horde of zombie deposit institutions loose upon our land.[61]

The incentive to "look the other way" is especially pernicious, for it reinforces the corrupt behavior. The Bank Board's accounting regulations allowed failing S&Ls to hide losses but also permitted the Bank Board and Congress a degree of deniability, shielding themselves from public opprobrium (the short-term perspective in action) and protecting the threatened FSLIC insurance funds. Moreover, by allowing S&Ls to employ accounting games to disguise their true financial conditions, "FSLIC officials strengthened the industry's credibility before Congress and therefore its ability to lobby against more effective regulation."[62]

Congress deserves special attention in this analysis. Although the actions of a few members of Congress were highly questionable, as Garment points out, very few of them were actually illegal at the time of the alleged transgressions, according to the presiding rules of that body. Speaker Wright's behavior was investigated by special counsel Richard Phelan for the House Ethics Committee. Phelan found that the Speaker had violated four House rules in his S&L interventions, which included removing the recapitalization bill from the House schedule in order to pressure the Bank Board regarding Craig Hall, interfering to protect Tom Gaubert, and trying to "destroy [Joe] Selby's career" with charges of homosexuality.[63] The Ethics Committee chose not to accept Phelan's recommendation on these points. Wright's ultimate resignation was based on other charges.

To investigate the Keating Five, the U.S. Senate retained Robert S. Bennett as special counsel to its Ethics Committee. His report specifically addressed the heart of their defense, "constituent service":

> [T]here can be no reasonable doubt that members of the United States Senate can and must have the power to pressure regulators. . . . But . . . there can be no doubt, no reasonable doubt based upon the evidence, that the purpose of these meetings. . . was to pressure the regulators to take action consistent with the wishes of Charles Keating.
>
> . . .
>
> Now simply because constituent service is generally a good thing, it does not mean . . . by merely asserting that "what I did was constituent service". . . that a Senator can erect an impenetrable shield barring ethical inquiry. While important, constituent service cannot be elevated to the status of a religion. And even if it were, it must be remembered that in the history of the world there have been many examples of where many sins have been committed in the name of religion. So, too, many wrongs have been committed in the name of constituent service. . . .[64]

In the end, the ethics panel chastised Senators McCain and Glenn (for "exercising poor judgment"), and DeConcini and Riegle (who "gave the appearance of being improper"), but found that they violated "no rules of the Senate." In DeConcini's case, the committee emphasized that it "did not condone his conduct. The committee has concluded that the totality of the evidence shows that Senator DeConcini's conduct gave the appearance of being improper and was certainly attended with insensitivity and poor judgment." Only Cranston was formally rebuked by the Ethics Committee for engaging "in an impermissible pattern of conduct." In its report to the Senate, the committee held that it "does hereby strongly and severely reprimand Senator Cranston." Cranston defended his actions before the entire Senate, offering his regret but characterizing himself as "singled out"; he warned that if his reprimand held, then all Senators were in "jeopardy" because "everybody does it": "How many of you . . . could rise and declare you've never, ever helped—or agreed to help—a contributor close in time to the solicitation or receipt of a contribution? I don't believe any of you could say 'never.' " Senator Warren Rudman's (R-NH and Vice Chair of the Ethics Committee) strenuous rebuttal aside, Cranston was probably correct.[65]

Garment, largely agreeing with the findings of the Senate Ethics Committee, exonerates Wright, Cranston, and other members of Congress for their activities by contending that while they might have been guilty of errors of judgment, they were not in technical violation of the rules of Congress. Strictly speaking, Garment is correct, even if we would like to think that members of Congress, whom the electorate has entrusted to protect the public good, should somehow not be exploring the gray edge separating legal from illegal. Still, her claim that the "S&L crisis revealed . . . serious and characteristic tendencies in our politics and government" rings true.[66] While it was congressmen per se who contributed to the S&L fiasco, it was the congressional system, in particular the umbrella of constituent service, which most would generally support, that helped create and exacerbate it. The sorry result was a much more discredited Congress and much poorer taxpayer.

In summary, we have seen that the S&L crisis was devised and executed by a number of scurrilous individuals, motivated by little more than the desire to aggrandize their personal wealth. However, this description would be an incomplete reading of the political corruption that fomented and ruinously extended the S&L debacle. We also need to indict the political and regulatory systems that—almost innocently, probably ignorantly—made the looting of the S&Ls possible and, in some cases, even encouraged S&Ls to gamble recklessly. Mayer underscores this theme: "The government was asking to be robbed, and it was robbed—all over the country."[67] Even harsher condemnations need be affixed to the same systems that downplayed, obscured, and condoned the fraud being perpetrated by the S&Ls once the evidence began to accumulate. These shortfalls were more attributable to political corruption than ignorance, as all the major participants conspired to transform a serious embarrassment into a horrible series of debacles. But, as we have seen, there were few incentives in these systems that would have supported the exposure of the crooked S&Ls and many that worked to conceal them. The real corruption, then, was one of trying to protect the system itself, to keep it solvent, rather than the more traditional perspective of making the players rich.

In fairness, the charge of systemic political corruption would be denied by most S&L executives, many regulators, and the majority of the members of Congress. They would claim that the political system was, in fact, only being responsive to its constituents in times of trouble.

Unfortunately, in this case, the constituents were the perpetrators of the problem (S&L owners) rather than the victims (ultimately, the taxpayers). While individuals were the culprits who literally carried out the looting of the S&Ls, in terms of political corruption, the systems in which they operated must stand beside them in the docket.

Notes

1. Stephen Labaton, "New Finance Woes: F.D.I.C. Loss Worse; S.&L. Crisis Deeper," *New York Times*, June 11, 1991, pp. A1, A5; and idem., "Top U.S. Auditor Predicts Banks May Be Headed for Large Bailout," *New York Times*, June 12, 1991, pp. A1, C3. James Ring Adams, *The Big Fix* (New York: John Wiley, 1990), sets the figure at a truly unimaginable $1.5 *trillion* (p. 56).

2. Charles McCoy and Todd Mason, "Audit Report by FDIC Shows Wall's Estimates Were Wildly Low," *Wall Street Journal*, September 14, 1990, p. A12. Secretary of the Treasury Nicholas Brady has estimated that a delay in voting more funds to the bailout efforts is costing taxpayers $4–$6 million a day. Keith Bradsher, "President Urges Congress to Act on S.&L. Bailout," *New York Times*, July 30, 1992, pp. A1, C7.

3. Louis Uchitele, "Bankers Expected to Stay Hesitant to Lend for Years," *New York Times*, July 5, 1991, pp. A1, C4.

4. Iver Peterson, "Builders, Blaming Savings Crisis, See Housing Recession," *New York Times*, July 19, 1990, pp. C1, C3.

5. Neal R. Peirce, "S&L Bailout Ignites Regional Rivalry," *National Journal*, Vol. 22, No. 32 (August 11, 1990), p. 1973; also see David E. Rosenbaum, "Southwest to Get Economic Benefits in Savings Bailout," *New York Times*, June 25, 1990, pp. A1, A9.

6. Richard E. Cohen, "Political Fallout from the S&L Debacle," *National Journal*, Vol. 22, No. 28 (July 4, 1990), p. 1731.

7. Quoted by Steven Waldman and Rich Thomas, "How Did It Happen?" *Newsweek*, May 21, 1990, p. 27. One naturally wonders what legislative errors during the previous century compete for the accolade.

8. The GAO study is cited in Martin Mayer, *The Greatest-Ever Little Bank Robbery* (New York: Charles Scribner's Sons, 1990), p. 53.

9. Stephen Pizzo, Mary Fricker, and Paul Muolo, *Inside Job: The Looting of America's Savings and Loans (New York: McGraw-Hill, 1989)*.

10. These figures do not reflect the size of the losses. In 1986, only fifty-four S&Ls (1.7 percent) failed, but at a loss of $3.239 billion, compared to "only" $1.213 billion in 1982. R. Daniel Brumbaugh, Jr., *Thrifts under Siege* (Cambridge, MA: Ballinger, 1988), Table 1–2, pp. 10–11.

11. Paulette Thomas and Thomas E. Ricks, "Just What Happened to All That Money Savings & Loans Lost?" *Wall Street Journal*, November 5, 1990, pp. A1, A6; and Mayer, *The Greatest-Ever Bank Robbery*, p. 53.

12. Edward J. Kane, *The S&L Insurance Mess: How Did It Happen?* (Washington, D.C.: The Urban Institute, 1989), p. 4.

13. *Ibid.*,p.1; emphasis added. A ponzi scheme is a swindle in which a quick

return (made up of money from new investors) on an initial investment lures the victim into much larger risks.

14. *Ibid.*, pp. 66 and 21; also p. 97.

15. Suzanne Garment, *Scandal* (New York: Random House, 1991), p. 251–252.

16. Charles McCoy, Richard B. Schmitt, and Jeff Bailey, "Besides S&L Owners, Host of Professionals Paved Way for Crisis," *Wall Street Journal*, November 2, 1990, pp. A1, A4.

17. L.J. Davis, "Chronicle of a Debacle Foretold: How Deregulation Begat the S&L Scandal," *Harper's Magazine*, Vol. 281, No. 1684 (September 1980), p. 51.

18. Roosevelt quoted in Adams, *The Big Fix*, pp. 11–12.

19. Davis, "Chronicle of a Debacle Foretold," p. 53.

20. Pizzo et al., *Inside Job*, p. 11; emphasis in original.

21. Mayer, *The Greatest-Ever Bank Robbery*, quotes James R. Barth from a speech delivered in 1988, p. 62.

22. Quoted, respectively, by Larry Martz et al., "Bonfire of the S&Ls," *Newsweek*, May 21, 1990, p. 22, and Mayer, *The Greatest-Ever Bank Robbery*, p. 63.

23. The phrase is from Davis, "Chronicle of a Debacle Foretold," p. 55.

24. Some of the new owners had no experience in the thrift industry; others, more worrisome, had experience in banks that failed under suspicious circumstances; still others, most troubling, had alleged ties to organized crime; Pizzo et al., *Inside Job*, and Adams, *The Big Fix*, elaborate these charges.

25. The illustration of American Diversified is taken from Mayer, *The Greatest-Ever Bank Robbery*, pp. 5–8; quotation on p. 8, emphasis in original.

26. Mayer, *The Greatest-Ever Bank Robbery*, p. 97.

27. Quoted in ibid., p. 55.

28. Pizzo et al., *Inside Job*, pp. 2–3.

29. The resultant and unrelenting horror stories are related in Pizzo et al., *Inside Job*, Mayer, *The Greatest-Ever Bank Robbery*, and Adams, *The Big Fix*.

30. Davis, "Chronicle of a Debacle Foretold," p. 58.

31. Penn Square's closure was due in equal parts to the types of investment, terrible mismanagement, and the inflationary ethos found in Texas and Oklahoma in the 1970s; its fall also threatened other major banks, especially Continental Illinois in Chicago. See Mark Singer, *Funny Money* (New York: Alfred Knopf, 1985).

32. Gray is quoted by Adams, *The Big Fix*, p. 202. The video tape is also described in Mayer, *The Greatest-Ever Bank Robbery*, pp. 128–29, and Pizzo et al., *Inside Job*, pp. 80–81.

33. Mayer, *The Greatest-Ever Bank Robbery*, p. 227.

34. Kane, *The S&L Insurance Crisis*, p. 100.

35. Mayer, *The Greatest-Ever Bank Robbery*, p. 230.

36. Pizzo et al., *Inside Job*, p. 211.

37. Quoted in ibid., p. 225.

38. Adams, *The Big Fix*, p. 233.

39. Quoted in Mayer, *The Greatest-Ever Bank Robbery*, p. 232. Also in Adams, *The Big Fix*, p. 306.

40. Quoted in Adams, *The Big Fix*, p. 240.

41. Pizzo et al., *Inside Job*, p. 266.

42. The most complete account of the April 2 and April 9 meetings with the senators is in Pizzo et al., *Inside Job*, pp. 290–294. All the quotations in the description of these two meetings are from *Inside Job* unless otherwise noted.

43. Patriarca's comments were made before the Senate Ethics Panel investigating the actions of the five senators. Martin Tolchin, "Ethics Panel Told of 'Full Court Press,' " *New York Times*, November 30, 1990, p. A12.

44. Adams, *The Big Fix*, pp. 247–248.

45. The letter, released by the House Banking Committee, is quoted in Mayer, *The Greatest-Ever Bank Robbery*, p. 213.

46. The campaign contributions and the Keating quote are both from Adams, *The Big Fix*, pp. 251 and 254, respectively.

47. See, inter alia, Mayer, *The Greatest-Ever Bank Robbery*, chap. 10; McCoy and Mason, "Audit Report by FDIC Shows Wall's Estimates Were Wildly Low"; Leslie Wayne, "U.S. Renegotiates Some S.&L. Deals to Reduce Costs," *New York Times*, July 29, 1991, pp. A1, C4; and Jeff Gerth, "Questions Raised on Revision by U.S. in S.&L. Asset Deal," *New York Times*, October 7, 1991, pp. A1, C5.

48. Anonymous, "U.S. Paying Ex-Execs of Failed S&Ls," *Denver Post*, May 3, 1990, pp. A1, A19.

49. Testifying before Congress in July 1992, two RTC lawyers stated that "Some Washington officials 'use the agency and its authority as a private playground to reward and protect their favorite friends and supporters.' " Quoted by Steven Wilmsen, "Testimony: 'Politics' Thwarting RTC," *Denver Post*, August 23, 1992, pp. H1, H12.

50. Leslie Wayne;, "Few of Working Poor Get Houses in S.&L. Rescue Plan," and "Housing Earmarked for the Poor Is Enriching Big Investors Instead," both *New York Times*, June 26 and 27, 1991, pp. A1, C6, and A1, C4, respectively.

51. Kane, *The S&L Insurance Mess*, pp. 28–29.

52. Mayer, *The Greatest-Ever Bank Robbery*, p. 27; emphasis in original.

53. Quoted in Kane, *The S&L Insurance Mess*, p. 7; emphasis added.

54. Quoted in an interview with Lou Cannon, *President Reagan: A Role of a Lifetime* (New York: Simon & Schuster, 1991), p. 826.

55. Ely's figures are from an interview with Cannon, *President Reagan*, p. 828.

56. Mayer, *The Greatest-Ever Bank Robbery*, p. 61.

57. Cannon, *President Reagan*, p. 825; it is not clear whether Wright was referring to his role or the act's consequences.

58. Gray is quoted from an interview with Cannon, *President Reagan*, p. 828. Gray concluded his observation with everybody's favorite standard: "I'm not a rocket scientist, but I understand that."

59. Peter Passell, "No Accounting for Bad Banks," *New York Times*, January 16, 1991, p. C2, described accounting standards in some of the failed S&Ls as "more a ritual than a true accounting, one bearing about as much relationship to the real world as a performance of kabuki."

60. See Brumbaugh, *Thrifts under Siege*, pp. 20–21.

61. Kane, *The S&L Insurance Mess*, p. 67.

62. *Ibid.*, p. 69. Kane explains that the regulatory accounting principals (RAP) "adopted in 1982 . . . may exaggerate an institutions's capital by weighing goodwill more generously than [previous methods] and by asymmetrically deferring unrealized losses but permitting unrealized gains to be booked immediately" (p. 77).

63. Pizzo et al., *Inside Job*, p. 315.

64. Bennett's statements were excerpted in the *New York Times*, November 16, 1990, p. A14.

65. See Richard L. Berke, "Ethics Unit Singles Out Cranston, Chides 4 Others in S.&L. Inquiry," *New York Times*, February 28, 1991, pp. A1, A20; and Richard L. Berke, "Cranston Rebuked by Ethics Panel," *New York Times*, November 21, 1991, pp. A1, C19.

66. Garment, *Scandal*, chap. 9, at pp. 251–252; emphasis added.

67. Mayer, *The Greatest-Ever Bank Robbery*, p. 27.

7

PEOPLE WITH THEIR
OWN AGENDA

Unquestionably, the most visible American scandal since the calamitous days of Nixon's Watergate was the product of the confluence of two highly problematic administration foreign policy ventures by the Reagan administration—the selling of arms for hostages to the revolutionary government of Iran and the support of the Nicaraguan rebels (the *contrarrevolucionarios*, or "Contras") in their war to overthrow the Sandinista government. By themselves, both were highly volatile, extremely risky engagements. The administration's support for the Contras had first been limited and then forbidden by the Congress. President Ronald Reagan had repeatedly sworn that he would not deal with terrorist nations (in his characteristic rhetoric, "The American people are not going to tolerate ... these acts from outlaw states run by the strangest collection of misfits, Looney Tunes, and squalid criminals since the advent of the Third Reich"[1]), and had labored to establish a worldwide weapons embargo against the government of the Ayatollah Khomeini. To have publicly violated either of those prohibitions would have been a genuine embarrassment for the administration. But to have it revealed that proceeds from the arms sales to Iran were being secretly "diverted" to support the Contras was, it was widely and legitimately feared in the White House, possible grounds for the president's impeachment. Even though the amount of the diversion was relatively small (congressional investigators later calculated that the Contras only gained $3.8 million from the diversion, much less than the commissions of the arms traders[2]), it was the audacity (maybe the arrogance) of the acts themselves, as well as the diversion, that was considered outrageous. The early, feeble attempts at damage control appeared more like attempts to cover up or deceive, resulting in the president's chagrin and the public's skepticism.

The revelations and maladroit backfilling grievously undermined the public's trust of the Reagan administration, plunging the president's credibility levels to a point where 56 percent of those surveyed thought that this very popular president was lying about his knowledge of the affair, even after his National Security Adviser explained that he had deliberately chosen to keep the president in the dark.[3]

There were, however, more fundamental concerns raised by the Iran–Contra affair, those regarding the administration's apparent willingness to set aside the Constitution's mandate of Congress's right to legislate or, more precisely, Congress's assumption that its legislation would be honored rather than torpedoed. Military officers who had voluntarily sworn to uphold the Constitution and the nation's laws admittedly subverted them with little explanation saving those of convenience and a singular vision of what should be done. To be sure, Congress was not the model of consistency in its legislation regarding Nicaragua, at one time supporting aid to the rebels, then restricting it to humanitarian aid, and later denying aid altogether; as Suzanne Garment notes, "congressional policy towards the Contras bounced from one position to another in a sustained bout of inconsistency and mixed signals."[4] But the lack of consistency was not a gilt-edged invitation to ignore the standing legislation and covertly choose the position that is most compatible with the administration's (in some cases very personal) preference. The acknowledged decision by the perpetrators to hide the diversion from Congress—indeed, from the president himself, even they though testified that they thought he would approve if he knew—clearly signals that they knew what they were doing was setting aside the established processes of government; that is, it was illegal. Theodore Draper emphasizes the conspiratorial nature of such actions and their potential consequences:

> Unauthorized and uncontrolled covert operations put the covert operators in a position to jeopardize the entire government, or even to take its place. Such covert operations become indistinguishable from government by junta or cabal.[5]

President Reagan's reported horror when he was finally told of the diversion by Attorney General Edwin Meese gives further credence to the fact that the Iran–Contra diversion was illegal by virtually everybody's standards.

While there is little question that the revelation of the Iran–Contra diversion resulted in a genuine crisis in the government—surely the most serious faced by the Reagan administration—one can fairly ask if the polices and events that precipitated the crisis constituted an incident of political corruption. Certainly, no members of the administration realized any financial gain from their involvement, and political power never seemed to change hands. However, this chapter will argue that the Iran–Contra affair was every bit as corrupt as the other examples examined, not so much in terms of monetary benefits as political benefits. The carefully developed and recognized constitutional checks and balances were deliberately, even readily neglected to pursue certain self-defined political gains that, to the people who carried them out, were even more valuable than monetary ones. Although political power did not change hands, members of the administration took actions that were consciously sculpted to prevent others from assuming (or even sharing) political power and compromising the suspect causes and activities. While their purposes were far from venal and—in the case of humanitarian support for the Contras and the rescue of American hostages in the Middle East—were surely shared by the president and portions of the American public, their secretive means to these ends, executed without accountability, undermined, that is, corrupted, the American system of government. This type of corruption is just as pernicious as paying off an occasional bidder or official. Given the highest governmental levels at which the Iran–Contra affair occurred, and that it was implemented by officers who admittedly knew better (otherwise, why would they deliberately have kept the commander-in-chief uninformed, a decision totally alien to their military training?), its potential was even more poisonous to the American political system.

We will probably never know the "complete" truth about the Iran–Contra affair, or, in the memorable Watergate words, "who knew what and when did he know it?"[a] The destruction of thousands of docu-

---

[a]Some political wags, faced with President Reagan's unbreachable insistence that he was unable to remember key events, have rephrased the saw to ask, "Who knew what and when did he forget it?"

ments, the reticence of the principal participants to testify, President Bush's executive pardons, and the inability of President Reagan to remember the sequence of events leading up to the discovery of the disclosures remands the truth to history's dustbin. However, the purpose of this chapter to not to assign conclusively any person's legal guilt or moral turpitude. Rather, I hope to show that the blame can largely be attributed to the political system, with individuals only playing what they saw to be their assigned roles as best they could.

Latin American "Freedom Fighters"

The American commitment in Nicaragua can be traced back at least to July 17, 1979, with the victory of the Sandinista National Liberation Front (the "*sandinistas*") over Anastasio Somoza, who had ruled the nation for forty-two years.[b] Although the Carter administration was initially supportive, the new regime began to become more radical in its political orientation; moderates were forced out of the government and Daniel Ortega, called by some the "Nicaraguan Castro," emerged as president. The Sandinistas supported leftist guerrillas in El Salvador, accepted Cuban assistance, and signed various agreements with the Soviet Union. The Nicaraguan plank in the 1980 Republican platform was a clear harbinger of the position a Reagan presidency would assume: "We will support the efforts of the Nicaraguan people to establish a free and independent government."[6] The administration's actual policy was the source of much internal debate. Reagan's personal commitment was nowhere near as robust as it has been portrayed; he was consistently equivocal, thus permitting partisans to interpret his policy pretty much as they preferred. Whatever the course, all agreed that covert aid was preferable. By March 1981, Reagan authorized a covert CIA program against the Sandinistas and on November 17, he signed National Security Decision Directive 17, nominally directing American aid to counter the Sandinistas, who were threatening the government of El Salvador.

American aid to the Contras was extremely controversial. Whatever

---

[b] There is a certain irony about the Sandinistas overthrowing Somoza. The Nicaraguan rebels took their name from Augusto Cesar Sandino, who had been killed in 1934 by the U.S.-trained National Guard led by General Anastasio Somoza, who then established the Somoza dynasty.

the ideological leanings of the Sandinista government, it was a legitimate government, formally recognized by the U.S. government. Just after the Reagan authorization, *Newsweek* magazine ran a cover story entitled "American's Secret War: Nicaragua," tipping off Massachusetts representative Edward Boland to the growing American involvement. The resultant Boland Amendment (passed in the House by 411–0 on December 8) to the Defense Appropriations Bill prohibited the CIA and the Departent of Defense from using any funds "for the purpose of overthrowing the Government of Nicaragua. . . ." The administration's public response was tepid. The president signed the bill and in April explained his position:

> We are complying with the law, the Boland amendment which is the law. . . . But what I might personally wish or what our government might wish still would not justify us violating the law of the land.

And a few days later before a joint session of Congress:

> But let us be clear as to the American attitude toward the Government of Nicaragua. We do not seek its overthrow.[7]

However, the administration's covert actions belied Reagan's public acquiescence. In January 1984, the CIA began to mine Nicaraguan harbors, and in April, American duplicity in what was said to be a Contra act was made public by the *Wall Street Journal*. Congress, and especially the Senate Intelligence Committee, reacted with a furor, Senator Barry Goldwater (R-AZ) stating that the mining was an act of war under international law. The Senate's outrage resulted in an apology by CIA Director William Casey, and the promise that the committee would henceforth be informed *prior* to any covert actions.

Reagan's relatively tolerant public attitude toward the Sandinistas was seemingly changing. In a nationally televised speech on May 9, he described atrocities committed by the Sandinistas and, for the first time, referred to the "Thousands who fought with the *Sandinistas* [who] have taken up arms against them . . . now called the *contras*" as "freedom fighters." Reagan went on to rationalize that "If the Soviet Union can aid and abet subversion in our hemisphere, then the United States has the legal right and moral duty to help resist it."[8]

The Congress, which had funded $24 million of humanitarian aid to the Contras in 1983,[c] now accepted a second Boland Amendment. Boland II, as it came to be known, stated that

> No appropriations or funds made available pursuant to this joint resolution to the Central Intelligence Agency, the Department of Defense, or any other agency or entity of the United States involved in intelligence activities may be obligated or expended for the purpose or which would have the effect of supporting, directly or indirectly, military or paramilitary operations in Nicaragua by any nation, group, organization, movement, or individual.[9]

The congressional debate over Boland II clearly indicated that the amendment was intended to cover all government agencies that used intelligence materials, namely, the National Security Council (NSC).

The Reagan administration adopted different strategic and tactical views than the Congress. The White House was severely riven by the issue. The "pragmatists," led by James Baker and Michael Deaver, wanted to minimize U.S. activities in Latin America; the "ideologues," led by William Casey and Alexander Haig, wanted to engage communism wherever they found it. The question was how this could be done given the manacles of Boland II. A twofold policy evolved. From a strategic perspective, President Reagan decided to support the Contras in whatever ways possible. According to National Security Adviser Robert McFarlane, the president ordered him in 1984 to keep the Contra movement together, "body and soul."[10] In March 1985, Reagan described the Contras as "the moral equivalent of our Founding Fathers and the brave men and women of the French Resistance."[11]

The tactical, how-to-do-it questions were rather thornier. In June 1984, in anticipation of Boland II, Reagan's National Security Planning Group (NSPG) met to discuss the possibility that the U.S. government could solicit funds for the Contras from third parties (both nations and individuals), offering to serve as little more than a conduit to the rebel's bank accounts. Baker warned "that we could not do indirectly what we could not do directly" and that he viewed the proposed action as an "impeachable offense."[12] However, his view was overridden by others, such as Vice President George Bush and Attorney General Meese. The "action" agency would have to be the NSC rather than the more prac-

---

[c] The Boland Amendment was attached to a yearly appropriation bill. Therefore, it had to be reaffirmed each budget cycle.

ticed CIA; the latter, the group reasoned, was enjoined against such action by the language of Boland II, while the NSC was not covered explicitly and, therefore, was implicitly legitimate. That the NSPG's curious logic might have been shaky was indicated by the president's closing remarks that day: referring to the decision to solicit funds from other nations, he remarked, "If such a story gets out [i.e., is leaked], we'll all be hanging by our thumbs in front of the White House until we find out who did it."[13]

The NSC wasted no time. McFarlane informed his NSC aide, Marine Lieutenant Colonel Oliver North, who was the NSC desk officer for Latin America, of the decision to solicit funds from sources outside the U.S. government. The policy came as little surprise. McFarlane later testified to congressional investigating committees that he had considered "the possibility of in effect farming out the whole Contra support operation to another country, which would not provide the funding, but give it some direction."[14] Indeed, without informing Secretary of State George Shultz, McFarlane had approached Israel with such a proposition, which turned him down in April. In May, facing an imminent congressional cutoff of Contra funding, McFarlane turned to the government of Saudi Arabia, which, after some deliberation, agreed to provide a million dollars a month; in February 1985, during a state visit to the White House, Saudi King Fahd told President Reagan that he was increasing the payment to $2 million a month (contributions that would ultimately total $32 million).[d]

North's responsibilities were primarily to put the necessary logistics into operation. For this, he employed a former air force major general *cum* arms trader, Richard Secord, who (with his partner Albert Hakim) established a transportation system as well as the convenient Swiss bank accounts. North also spent considerable time persuading American citizens (such as Nelson Bunker Hunt of Dallas) that they should contribute to the Contra cause through such funds as the American Conservation Trust and the National Endowment for the Preservation of Liberty. President Reagan met with some of these groups to thank individual donors personally. With North's assistance, they ultimately raised a little over $12 million (of which the Contras only received $2,700,000).[15]

---

[d] Other nations that would contribute were Taiwan and, after a sitcom scenario as members of the administration argued over who would entreat the Sultan, Brunei.

The Reagan administration's decision to aid the Contra forces set in place many of the elements that would soon surface in yet another of its foreign policy endeavors—its dealings with the revolutionary government of Iran. The sequestered ways of determining and implementing policies, the willingness to conceal its actions from congressional oversight, and the utter dedication of the principal actors (many of whom were the same) to the policies would soon reappear. What was unexpected was that the two policies would commingle. Let us now turn to a description of American dealings with Iran.

Arms for Hostages

Ronald Reagan's major preoccupation during his presidency was likely over the question of terrorists. He had been elected in 1980 when President Carter was self-imprisoned in the White House Rose Garden because Iran's Revolutionary Guard had seized the American Embassy in Teheran and held sixty-six staff members hostage for 444 days. Reagan had consistently railed against terrorism, rhetoric rendered hollow when he found he could do little to alleviate the situation. The disastrous 1983 American intervention in Lebanon that cost the lives of 241 U.S. marines added salt to this particular wound.

Iran was singled out in this frustration. In the spring of 1983, the Reagan administration initiated Operation Staunch, an international embargo of weapons to Iran. By early summer 1985, seven Americans were known to be held hostage in Lebanon, seemingly by pro-Iranian Shiite groups. In June, a worldwide plague of terrorism erupted. The most noted incident was the hijacking of TWA flight 847 out of Athens; among its 153 passengers and crew were 135 Americans. Ronald Stethem, a U.S. navy diver, was beaten to death by the terrorists and his body dumped on the tarmac at Beirut. As the terrorists made demands for the release of Shiites held captive in Israel, the airplane flew back and forth across the Middle East. Reagan publicly fumed at what became a media circus, but was largely helpless until the Israelis released their Shiite hostages and the TWA hostages were released (June 30). On June 19, seventeen U.S. servicemen were assassinated in San Salvador. On June 23, a bomb exploded on an Air India 747, killing 329 persons. The world was seemingly at the terrorists' whim and the president virtually impotent.

On June 28, during a campaign visit to Chicago, Reagan offered to meet with some of the TWA hostages' family members, as well as the family of Father Lawrence Jenco, who had been kidnapped in January that year. By all accounts, the meeting was viscerally traumatic for the president, and the issue of hostages became even more paramount to him. Robert McFarlane later recalled that "It is just undeniable that Reagan's obsession with freeing the hostages overrode anything else." Donald Regan, Reagan's new chief of staff, was even more graphic in describing Reagan's fixation on the hostages:

> He would see the [hostage] Terry Anderson's sister . . . constantly in the media. . . . He would see that captive. Come back to the actor. Remember, he puts himself into the part. All of a sudden, he's envisioning himself as a captive alone in a dank, damp prison, and where's the president of the United States? What the hell is he doing to get me out of this fucking place? Nothing. . . . Ronald Reagan eats his heart out over this. It worries him. It's with him.[16]

Not surprising, this anxiety was transmitted to his staff. Jeffrey Simon reported that the president "brought up the hostage issue at 90 percent of his briefings."[17]

In this atmosphere, McFarlane was beginning to wonder if the adversarial American policy toward Iran were not ill-advised. He knew that someday the Ayatollah Khomeini would die (probably soon since he was in his eighties) and that Iran was vitally positioned, in a geopolitical sense, to block Soviet expansion into the Middle East oil fields. He hoped to make overtures to some of the "moderate" members of the revolutionary government in order to anticipate an American presence in a post-Khomeini Iran. (Schieffer and Gates suggest that McFarlane viewed this opening rather self-servingly as analogous to the Kissinger-engineered gambit to China in 1971.[18]) At much the same time, CIA analysts were exploring the same possibility. The initial NSC and CIA assessments were that the idea was good but the times not propitious. But the simmering idea warranted McFarlane's regular monitoring and he permitted a NSC consultant to ferret out potential openings through Israeli intelligence, even risking a quarrel with Secretary of State Shultz in the effort.

On July 3, 1985, the idea had a chance to bubble. McFarlane was visited by with the director of intelligence in the Israeli Foreign Ministry, David Kimche, who proposed a possible opening to moderate elements in Iran. Kimche and other Israelis had been approached by Manucher Ghorbanifar, an Iranian exile said still to have connections in Teheran. Ghorbanifar suggested how the ongoing Iran–Iraq war and Operation Staunch had made Iran desperate for weapons replacements and claimed that he could arrange meetings with moderate elements in the Iranian government. Kimche related that these moderates would like to improve U.S.-Iranian relations and would work to obtain the release of the American hostage William Buckley as a sign of their good intentions.[e] In exchange for their risking negotiating with "The Great Satan," these moderates wished to be able to purchase weapons as a symbol of U.S. intentions. McFarlane was understandably interested in the proposition, even after Kimche made it clear that the CIA must not be involved.[f]

McFarlane was a great admirer of Israeli intelligence. Still, he was aware that Israeli and American interests in the Middle East were often at variance. For example, Israel strongly favored Iran in the Iran–Iraq war, so it continued to sell weapons to Iran despite the U.S. embargo; also, Israel was concerned with the safety of 80,000 Jews living in Iran. Yet McFarlane was willing to accept Israel's recommendation that Ghorbanifar be trusted as an intermediary, despite the fact that he had been classified by the CIA as unreliable; indeed, Kimche reportedly was puzzled at McFarlane's reluctance to accept the Israeli verification of Ghorbanifar's bona fide standing. Moreover, Ghorbanifar's hook in this case was something McFarlane wanted very badly—the opportunity to retrieve the American hostages. Finally, Kimche told McFarlane that Ghorbanifar was not asking for a direct sale of American arms but rather to let Israel sell anti-tank missiles to his Iranian contact with the understanding that the United States would then replace the Israeli stock. A July 13 memorandum to Secretary of State Shultz articulated McFarlane's assessment of the offer, especially his reservations regarding the possibility of a double cross:

---

[e] William Buckley had been the CIA station chief in Beirut, so the agency was especially eager to obtain his release.

[f] The somewhat unusual request was easy to understand. The CIA had dealt with Ghorbanifar before; he had failed two agency polygraph tests when he had tried to sell it some information. As a result, the agency had issued a rare "fabricator notice," warning U.S. intelligence agencies that Ghorbanifar "should be regarded as an intelligence fabricator and a nuisance" (cited in Cannon, *President Reagan*, p. 613).

One has to consider where this might lead in terms of our being asked to up the ante on more and more arms and where that could conceivably lead, not just in the compromise of our position, but to the possible eventuality of the Iranians "winning" and where that would put the security of the neighboring Gulf States. Clearly that is a loser. . . . George, I cannot judge the equities on this. . . . [But] On balance my instincts are to see our larger interest in establishing an entree to someone in Iran and the check provided by the Iranian interlocutor's vulnerability to being "blown" as giving us some insurance against perfidy. We could make a tentative show of interest without commitment and see what happens. Or we could walk away. On balance I tend to favor going ahead.[19]

The combination of Ghorbanifar's suggestion that a small amount of American arms would pave the way to Iranian moderates, the strategic opening to the post-Khomeini Iran, the distinct possibility of freeing the captives, and the Israeli willingness to handle the arms transfer (i.e., provide a cover for U.S. involvement) rendered the brew too potent to ignore.

On July 13, President Reagan was admitted to Bethesda Naval Hospital for the removal of a cancerous growth on his intestine. On July 16, McFarlane came to the hospital to brief the president on the Kimche proposal, explaining both the strategic and the hostage elements. Although there is some dispute over the content of McFarlane's briefing and the president's response,[20] President Reagan's July 17 diary entry strongly indicates he grasped the importance of McFarlane's information:

> Some strange soundings are coming from some Iranians. Bud M will be here tomorrow to talk about it. It could be a breakthrough on getting our seven kidnap victims back. Evidently the Iranian economy is disintegrating fast under the strain of war.

This was, in Reagan's recollection, "the beginning of what became known as the Iran–Contra affair."[21] Reagan's orders to McFarlane, according Regan, were direct: "Open it up."[22]

On July 25, Ghorbanifar met with the Israelis and proposed a trade of 100 anti-tank missiles (called TOWs) for "some hostages," even though he warned that the Iranians might retain a few hostages for later leverage. Kimche related this deal to McFarlane on August 2, telling him that Israel would serve as the middleman but that the Israeli government insisted on specific authorization by the U.S. government before it would implement the arms transfer.

On August 6, the president met informally (McFarlane remembered the president attending in pajamas[23]) with his principal national security advisers—Secretary of State Shultz, Secretary of Defense Caspar Weinberger, Vice President George Bush, and Regan. McFarlane briefed the group on the Iranian gambit, setting the exchange rate at 100 TOWs for four hostages. Shultz's notes record that he was strongly opposed to the deal: "I thought this was a very bad idea, . . . that we were just falling into the arms-for-hostages business and we shouldn't do it." Weinberger recalled that he "argued very forcefully against the whole idea, saying that I didn't think it could work . . . that this just shouldn't be done, that this would undercut everything we were going to do in the Mid East. . . ."[24] The president, as was often the case, was noncommittal, which had the unfortunate effect of letting all the participants hear exactly what they wanted to hear:

> Each of the participants was inclined to interpret the President's passivity as a subtle sign of concurrence. Both Shultz and Weinberger left convinced that they had effectively vetoed the deal. McFarlane was just as convinced that Reagan had merely given the Cabinet officers a polite hearing, and that he still wanted to pursue the project.[25]

McFarlane told the Tower Commission and congressional investigators that Reagan telephoned him a few days later and authorized the Israeli sale of TOWs to Iran. In many ways, this was the critical moment of the Iran–Contra affair; everything else flows from this telephone call.[g] Moreover, the date of the decision signifies that the president had knowledge of the arms transfers before they were legally documented.

---

[g]There is some confusion about the telephone call. Testifying before the Tower Commission, President Reagan declared, "I have no personal notes or records to help my recollection on this matter. The only honest answer is to state, try as I might, I cannot recall anything whatsoever about whether I approved an Israeli sale in advance or whether I approved replenishment of Israeli stocks around August of 1985. My answer therefore and the simple truth is, 'I don't remember—period' " (*The Tower Commission Report*, p. 139). McFarlane made no record of the call. Still, the Tower Commission chose to believe McFarlane's version.

McFarlane notified Kimche and on August 20 the Israelis flew ninety-six TOWs to Iran. But no hostages were released. Ghorbanifar explained that the TOWs had been seized by the Revolutionary Guards rather than the intended moderates, so the weapons could not be seen as the prerequisite "symbolic gesture" to the appropriate group. Even though the Iranians, acting through Ghorbanifar, had failed to honor the arrangement, Ghorbanifar asked for another 400 TOWs in exchange for one hostage. McFarlane reluctantly agreed and on September 15, Israel shipped another 408 TOWs to Iran. On the same day, Reverend Benjamin Weir was released.[h] Two patterns were beginning to emerge: first, the United States was almost totally dependent on Ghorbanifar in its dealings with Iran (even if he were thought to be untrustworthy); second, the arms-for-hostages pattern was an acceptable relationship for the United States in spite of its well-publicized statements to the contrary.

In October, despite the disappointment of having only one hostage freed, Ghorbanifar, this time with the assistance of another Iranian, Hassan Karoubi (whom Ghorbanifar introduced as one of the moderates), asked for HAWK anti-aircraft missiles and Phoenix air-to-air missiles. In exchange, Iran would release four hostages. Overcoming severe misgivings, McFarlane agreed that the HAWKs be transhipped by Israel through Portugal to Teheran. On November 17, he put Oliver North in charge of the operation. North recruited his primary Nicaragua accomplice, Richard Secord, even though he later admitted that the use of Secord could potentially have compromised both the Contra and Iranian arms transfers.[26] McFarlane also informed Shultz as to the plan; Shultz related that he objected but "nonetheless expressed [his] hope that the hostages would be released."[27] On November 18, in the midst of Reagan's meetings with Soviet secretary General Mikhail Gorbachev in Geneva, the president, Shultz, and Regan were briefed on the operation by McFarlane.

The November arms shipment was a fiasco beyond belief, virtually a comedy of errors, except that it was not funny. The Israelis could not get landing clearances at Lisbon airport, so North involved the CIA in order to get support from the American embassy to "request clear-

---

[h] When asked to choose an American hostage to release, McFarlane asked that William Buckley, the CIA agent, be freed. Buckley, he was told, was too ill to travel. Later it was discovered that he had died three months earlier.

ances" for the aircraft to land. The cover story was that the airplane contained oil-drilling equipment. The Portuguese, suspicious that a retired American general (Secord) was demanding an urgent flight clearance, refused landing rights and the plane had to return to Tel Aviv. North and Secord were finally able to obtain another aircraft from St. Lucia Airways, a CIA proprietary airline, but even then the horrors continued. It could not hold all 80 HAWKs so only 18 were loaded; then it was discovered that the aircraft was registered in the United States, so it had to be unloaded and another plane found and the cargo reloaded. The HAWK missiles did not reach Teheran until November 25. The final contretemps was when the Iranians discovered that the missiles were not the high-altitude HAWK model they had demanded, rather the older, low-altitude model. Moreover, many were unacceptable because they were inscribed with the Israeli star of David.

All of the parties were furious with one another. Iranian prime minister Moussavi complained bitterly through Ghorbanifar that the HAWKs were useless and demanded money back from Israel, which complied. The Iranians claimed that they had been swindled, so no hostages were released. The Israelis were irate, claiming that Secord and North had bungled the Lisbon flight arrangements. McFarlane and North, irritated that no additional hostages had been released, blamed the Israelis for the fiasco. And the CIA was angry that it had been recruited by North without any semblance of regular channels, as well as having been deceived by North's "oil-drilling equipment" cover story.

It should not have been unexpected that this incredible series of foul-ups was the final incident that drove McFarlane, who had long been talking about leaving the NSC, to offer his resignation to the president, although his fractious relationship with Regan was the principal cause. On December 2, McFarlane resigned and his deputy, Rear Admiral John Poindexter, was appointed in his stead two days later. More critically, McFarlane's departure from the scene left Oliver North in charge of the NSC's dealings with the Iranians. As Lou Cannon notes, "The reclusive Poindexter and the outgoing North would form an odd team."[28] North, a combination of the marines' "true believer" philosophy with a tall talent for deception, was given free rein, a charter that Poindexter's loose management style did almost nothing to restrain. Moreover, Poindexter's virtual paranoia over secrecy was to vitiate any oversight of North. North's other NSC assignment was to supply the Contras. To make him responsible for both was to risk that the two would somehow commingle, a danger nobody saw until it was too late.

Findings and Diversions

One of the damaging by-products of the November fiasco was that of the million dollars the Israelis had paid Secord to facilitate the arms transfers, only $150,000 was returned to them. North, acting on his own initiative and without any approval, simply diverted those remaining funds to a Contra Swiss bank account. He later told congressional investigators that this was his decision, and when the Israelis did not demand the money back, he never returned it. North's unauthorized diversion set the precedent for the later, more expensive diversions. A second damaging result of the November foul-up was that Secord was able to convince North, and hence Poindexter, that the Israelis were the cause of the problem. This perception led to a diminished role of the Israelis, which, in turn, gave North more authority as well as making him more directly dependent on the duplicitous Ghorbanifar.

In late November, Secord met with Ghorbanifar in Paris. On December 4, North prepared a memorandum for Poindexter, reviewing the past incidents and proposing a new, complex exchange. North warned that while all the participants

> agree that there is a high degree of risk in pursuing the course we have started, we are now so far down the road that stopping what has been started could have even more serious repercussions. . . . None of us have any illusions about the cast of characters we are dealing with on the other side. They are a primitive, unsophisticated group who are extraordinarily distrustful of the West in general and the Israelis/U.S. in particular. . . . [To stop the arms sales could] run the risk of never being able to establish a "foothold" for the longer term goals . . . and incur the greater likelihood of reprisals against us for "leading them on." These reprisals could take the form of additional hostage seizures, execution of some/all now held, or both.[29]

North then proposed a quid pro quo strategy that had originated with Ghorbanifar—trading 3,300 TOWs and fifty new HAWKs for the six hostages; the first hostage would be released after the first 300 TOWs were delivered, another after a second 300 TOWs, and so on until the United States had delivered 1,300 TOWs and all the HAWKs. The Iranians would then be given another 2,000 TOWs as a good behavior bonus.

In the meantime, the CIA was increasingly concerned over the legality of its role. The agency's involvement in the November arms shipments was, strictly speaking, illegal without a presidential "Finding." Under the Intelligence Oversight Act (1980), the president was "obligated to 'find' that a covert operation by the CIA was important to the national security of the United States and to report it 'in a timely fashion' to the appropriate committees of Congress."[30] Furthermore, the Finding had to precede the covert action. The deputy director and general counsel of the agency were both bothered that the agency had covertly assisted North without a formal Finding. To remedy this situation, the CIA's general counsel prepared a Finding on November 26 with four items of particular interest: first, it identified the purpose of the Finding as addressing a Middle East arms exchange for American hostages; second, it mentioned only the CIA even though the agency was only acting in support of the NSC; third, the government of Iran was identified as the recipient of the arms; and fourth, it directed "the Director of Central Intelligence not to brief the Congress . . . until at such time as [the president] may direct otherwise." On Poindexter's advice, President Reagan signed the exculpatory Finding on December 5.

This Finding presents strong evidence that the Reagan administration's principal emphasis was on the hostages, not the goal of a strategic opening to Iran as it later claimed. Just as important was the realization that the United States was dealing with the government of Iran, not the putative moderate elements within the government, as, once again, was later claimed. Even more telling was the clause postponing the notification of Congress, a proviso that has proven to be without legal precedent. Lastly, the retroactive nature of the Finding was similarly without precedent. Attorney General Meese later declared that "a finding after the fact of something having been done by the president would be of questionable legality and would certainly raise questions."[31] Indeed, the Finding was so worrisome that when the story was being discovered, Poindexter personally destroyed what he thought was the only copy because he realized that the Finding would, in his words, cause "significant political embarrassment" to the president.[32]

On December 7, President Reagan convened a critical meeting of his foreign policy advisers to permit McFarlane to report on the American initiatives regarding Iran. McFarlane opened with an admission that he no longer trusted Ghorbanifar and that the United States should no longer deal with him. Shultz and Weinberger came fully prepared to argue against any further arms-for-hostages relations. Shultz warned that the exchange would "negate the whole [administration] policy" of not cutting deals with terrorists and, when it became known, would destroy U.S. credibility with the Arab world. Weinberger railed against the policy for almost half an hour, arguing that it violated the Arms Export Control Act as well as Operation Staunch, "that we would be subject to blackmail . . . and that we had no interest whatsoever in helping Iran in any military way, even a minor way, and that in every way it was a policy that we should not engage in and most likely would not be successful." The CIA representative noted that the agency was "unaware of any moderates in Iran, that most of the moderates were slaughtered by Khomeini, that whatever arms we give to these so-called moderates they will end up supporting the Khomeini regime. . . ." Regan was also opposed to continuing the exchange.

Weinberger left the meeting confident that he had carried the field. As he told his military assistant, General Colin Powell, "I believe this baby had been strangled in its cradle, that it was finished." Shultz was hopeful that was the case but less confident, worried that the president still was hung up on the hostage question. When Weinberger had made the point that the initiative might well be illegal, Reagan had retorted, "Well, the American people will never forgive me if I fail to get those hostages out over this legal question," even though he softened his position by saying that if laws were broken and people went to jail, "visiting hours are on Thursday."[33] Later, in his autobiography, Reagan explained,

> I felt a heavy weight on my shoulders to get the hostages home. . . . What American trapped in such circumstances wouldn't have wanted me to do everything I possibly could to set them free? What American *not* held captive under such circumstances would not want me to do my utmost to get the hostages free?[34]

In any case, Reagan articulated no clear decision at the time, except to send McFarlane to London the next day to negotiate with Ghorbanifar and the Israelis. Given the people involved, Reagan's silence was equivalent to giving North a blank check,[i] arguably exactly what the president wanted.

The London meeting between McFarlane and Ghorbanifar was acrimonious, ending with McFarlane yelling at Ghorbanifar to "go pound sand." On the airplane home, McFarlane referred to Ghorbanifar as "one of the most despicable characters I have ever met" and a "borderline moron." All of this caused North, who by now was deeply invested and wanted the affair to continue, some problems, most particularly regarding the reliability of Ghorbanifar. He resolved the dilemma by writing a long memorandum to Poindexter and McFarlane, entitled "Next Steps." The memorandum was, in Draper's words, North's "declaration of independence," in which he "broke decisively with McFarlane's tutelage and represented another large step in the emergence of North as the arbiter of Iran policy."[35] What North proposed was yet another irreversable step in U.S. policy—that the United States eliminate Israel as the middleman, and, employing Secord as North's own agent, work directly with the Iranians through Ghorbanifar. In order to implement the new plans, North asked that Reagan sign a new Finding. The Finding was critical because the Export Control Act mandated notification to Congress of any arms sales over $14 million. Left unspoken was North's hidden agenda; using Secord and his Swiss bank accounts as his media, he could secretly funnel funds to the Contras.

The CIA counsel drafted a revision of the December 5 Finding, again authorizing the covert sale of arms to Iran in exchange for hostages and delaying notification of Congress, but this time acknowledging that contacts with the moderate elements in Iran was the primary intention. "Furthering the release of American hostages held in Beirut" was demoted to third place. Relying on Poindexter's counsel, Reagan signed the second Finding on January 6, 1985.

The next day, the president convened a meeting of his full NSC but never mentioned the new Finding. Weinberger later recalled how the discussants divided:

> I made the same point. George Shultz made the same points. Bill Casey felt that there would be an intelligence gain, and there was also talk of

---

[i]Another irony in the Iran–Contra affair was that North's code word on the NSC computer mail system was, fittingly, "blank check."

the hostages as one of the motivating factors, but not *the* motivating factor, but the responses of the president seemed to me to indicate that he had changed his view and now had decided he wanted to do this.

Shultz concurred, describing that the lack of opposition by everone other than Weinberger and himself "almost seemed unreal."[36] CIA director Casey was the only strong proponent. Although no formal decision was reached, it was clear to all that Reagan had made up his mind. He later wrote that he had chosen "to proceed with the initiative despite a deep division within the cabinet and staff. [Weinberger and Shultz] argued forcefully that I was wrong, but I just put my foot down."[37]

To circumvent the legal restriction, the CIA counsel with North's assistance wrote a third version of the December 5 Finding. The third version was identical to the second except that it now explained the Defense Department would sell arms to an authorized agent of the CIA (Secord, opaquely labeled under "and third parties") who would then move the weapons to Israel for shipment to Iran. Ghorbanifar would act as a purchasing agent for Iran so that the administration could legally say it had not dealt with the Iranian government. Reagan signed the third Finding on January 17; that night, he wrote in his diary, "I agreed to sell TOWs to Iran."[38] Cognizant of their opposition, Poindexter told neither Shultz nor Weinberger about the third Finding.

Plans were immediately drawn up (over Weinberger's muted objections) to transfer 3,500 TOWs and some spare HAWK parts to Iran. North met with Ghorbanifar in London a week later. There, according to North, Ghorbanifar "suggested several incentives to make that February transaction work, and the attractive incentive for me was the one he made that residuals could flow to support the Nicaraguan Resistance." North elaborated to congressional investigators:

> I must confess to you that I thought using the Ayatollah's money to support the Nicaraguan Resistance was a right idea. And I must confess that I advocated that. . . . I still do. I don't think it was wrong. I think it was a neat idea and I came back and I advocated that and we did it; we did it on three occasions.[39]

Poindexter testified that upon North's return, "he [North] said that he thought that he had figured out a way to transfer residual funds from the arms sales that Dick Secord was making to the Contras. . . . I thought about it for several minutes. . . . At the end of the conversation, I told Colonel North to go ahead because I thought it was a good idea." Poindexter, fully aware of his responsibility to his superior, the president, quite consciously chose not to tell President Reagan. As he subsequently explained to Congress,

> So after weighing all these matters, and I also felt that I had the authority to approve it, because I had a commission from the president which was in very broad terms, my role was to make sure that his policies were implemented. In this case, the policy was very clear, and that was to support the *Contras*.
>
> After working with the president for 5.5 years, the last 3 of which were very close . . . I was convinced that I understood the president's thinking on this and that if I had taken it to him that he would have approved it.
>
> Now, I was not so naive as to believe that it was not a politically volatile issue, it clearly was . . . , and it was clear that there would be a lot of people that would disagree. . . .
>
> So although I was convinced that we could properly do it and that the president would approve if asked, I made a very deliberate decision not to ask the president so that I could insulate him from the decision and provide some future deniability for the president if it ever leaked out.[40]

The diversion die was effectively cast. North had proposed the diversion. Poindexter had approved and, quite consciously, chose not to tell the president. From this point on, until the disclosure of the entire sordid deal in November, the Iran–Contra affair was on a beeline toward humiliation. All that was left were the details, some of which were simply bizarre.

A Visit, a Cake, a Terrible Mistake

According to North's plan, the United States would ship the Iranians TOWs, some HAWK parts, and military intelligence pertaining to the Iran–Iraq war. The TOWs would be doled out first but in a step-like sequence, in anticipation of and then in response to the release of American hostages. On February 17, the first shipment of 500 TOWs was delivered via Secord with another 500 ten days later. In between, North and his group (now including CIA Iranian experts) met with Ghorbanifar in Frankfurt, where Ghorbanifar, to validate his reputed standing, introduced Mohsen Kangarlou, whom he said was a member of the Iranian Foreign Ministry. Ghorbanifar also introduced Ali Samii, a Revolutionary Guard intelligence officer. North, believing these new Iranians to be legitimate members of the long-sought Iranian moderate faction, wrote in his notebook, "Major breakthrough w[ith] an honorable religious man who we can trust—Relationship based on honesty."[41] The good news was that the Americans were able to extract a promise from Ghorbanifar's party that they could expect to meet a delegation of high-level Iranian officials in Iran. North's reports to Poindexter were, characteristically, optimistic. The bad news was that after the 1,000 TOWs were delivered to Iran, no hostages were released.

North met again with Ghorbanifar in Paris and then, in April, in Washington to arrange the American visit to Teheran. Ghorbanifar indicated that the Iranian Speaker of the House, Ali Akbar Hashemi Rafsanjani, would be the leader of the delegation. After the second meeting, North felt sufficiently confident that he was able to prepare a memorandum to Poindexter (and, according to North, the president) detailing the schedule by which Secord would ship arms to Iran and the hostages would be freed. Toward the end of the memorandum, he turned to the issue of the "residuals" from the Iranian arms sales, confirming what he had already proposed:

> $12 million will be used to purchase critically needed supplies for the Nicaraguan Democratic Resistance Forces. This material is essential to cover shortages in resistance inventories resulting from their current offensives and Sandinista counter-attacks and to "bridge" the period between now and when Congressionally-approved lethal assistance . . . can be delivered.[42]

After a number of delays, the American delegation, headed by McFarlane (who had been kept abreast of the evolving saga) and including North and two CIA analysts, arrived in Teheran on May 25. Their charter was apodictic; Poindexter had ordered North:

> There are not to be any [weapon] parts delivered until all the hostages are free. . . . None of this half shipment before any are released crap. It is either all or nothing. Also, you may tell them that the president is getting very annoyed at their continual stalling.[43]

Poindexter's instructions made it clear that President Reagan was aware of the Teheran meeting and its intentions.

The Americans arrived with a load of spare parts and, as gifts, two pistols and a chocolate-covered cake they had purchased in Tel Aviv.[j] A jet full of HAWK spare parts was waiting on an Israeli runway with orders to Secord that it take off as soon as he received word of hostages being freed. Almost immediately, the talks were not what the American delegation had hoped, or even expected. The delegation was not officially met at the airport and, even worse, no ranking Iranian leaders were to be found. McFarlane was so angry he refused to talk with the officials the Iranians did provide, tacitly defaulting the leadership of the American delegation to North. The Iranians proved to be resolute negotiators. They argued persuasively that while they worried about the possible Soviet threat, so must the Americans, regardless of what government sits in Teheran. The Iranians did not agree that they had promised to release hostages, although they did say they would try to facilitate their release, but only after the second jet had arrived in Teheran. The Iranians actually added a new demand: the release of a dozen terrorist Shiites held in Kuwait.

The American delegation was not agreed on what was its charge. McFarlane held firm to Poindexter's orders while North was willing to be more flexible. The last night in Teheran, McFarlane went to sleep with the understanding that he would permit Secord's jet to take off from Tel Aviv with the HAWK parts if all the hostages were released during the plane's flight to Teheran. While he slept, the Iranians made a counteroffer to North—two hostages for the HAWK parts now, and two later. North agreed. When McFarlane awoke and was told of North's agreement, which directly disobeyed McFarlane's and Poindexter's orders, he angrily countermanded North's action. The American delegation left the next day with nothing to show for their visit. Reagan wrote in his diary the day after: "It was a heartbreaking disappointment for all of us."[44]

The Americans (and probably the Iranians) were finally beginning to realize that Ghorbanifar, now more than ever, could not be trusted. Unfortunately, the Americans had no other Iranian contacts; Ghorbanifar held the catbird seat. A second error in judgment went unrecognized—that North was willing to devise his own tactics toward his own policy. In this case, he was prepared to sell a plane of HAWK parts to

---

[j]Alas, late May was the Moslem fasting holiday of Ramadan, perhaps a harbinger of things to come.

the Iranians, even though it violated Poindexter's and McFarlane's explicit orders, because he and Secord stood to make a huge profit (they were vastly overcharging the Iranians for the TOWs and HAWKs), much of which would go to support the Contra cause. As North told McFarlane on the way home, "Well, don't be too down hearted. The one bright spot is that the government is availing itself of part of the money in those transactions for Central America."[45]

All Fall Down

Throughout the summer and fall, North met with Ghorbanifar. In October, meeting in Frankfurt, North delivered the now infamous Bible that Reagan had inscribed to Speaker Rafsanjani: "And the Scripture, foreseeing that God would justify the Gentiles by faith, preached the gospel before hand to Abraham, saying 'All the nations of the world shall be blessed in you' " (Galatians 3:8). At roughly the same time, North was trying desperately to eliminate his dependency on Ghorbanifar and open another channel to the much-hoped-for moderate faction in Iran; it was to prove as illusionary as the Ghorbanifar gambit. To worsen matters, the Iranians were legitimately accusing North and Secord of price gouging, even producing a price sheet to bolster their case. They threatened to curtail all further contacts unless their complaints were addressed. North was desperate to continue the sales, however, for now he needed the residuals to sustain the Contras.

Contemporaneously, the NSC was having to deny a growing tattoo of press reports that the White House and North in particular were violating Boland II by sponsoring aid to the Nicaraguan rebels. On July 21, Poindexter stonewalled a congressional request for information, subsequently characterizing his reply as "accurate" but admitting that he had withheld information. As he later explained (although in a contradictory manner): "I have always felt that the Boland Amendment did not apply to the NSC staff and that the NSC staff was complying with the letter and spirit of the law."[46] North unquestionably lied when he testified before the House Intelligence Committee on August 6 that he had in no way violated Boland II, even blaming a Soviet "disinformation campaign" against him. The committee was completely satisfied. Poindexter's memorandum to North regarding his testimony was revealingly to the point: "Well done."

As if all this were not enough pressure, North discovered during the summer that his life had been threatened by the terrorist Abu Nidal because of North's role in pursuing the Nidal-led terrorists who hijacked the cruise ship *Achille Lauro* the previous October. It was North's apparent concern over Nidal's supposed threat that led him to install a $14,000 security system around his Virginia home.[k]

The only good news was that after the May visit to Teheran, Father Lawrence Jenco was released in Beirut in July. The dark cloud to this solitary silver lining soon loomed; three more American hostages were kidnapped in September and October and another one murdered. In short, North's two worlds—his involvements in Iran and Nicaragua—placed him squarely between a geopolitical rock and a hard place. Matters would soon become worse.

The October 6–8 meetings in Frankfurt basically marked the end of the NSC's covert Iran–Contra dealings. In them, North ventured beyond all responsibility. He repeatedly claimed that he was speaking directly and confidentially for the president of the United States (although in truth he never met with the president privately), fabricating that Reagan told him how badly he wanted to terminate the Iran–Iraq war on Iranian terms. He explained how the president had prayed for guidance before quoting Galatians 3:8 in the Bible.[47] And, most important, he proposed another very complex quid pro quo arms-for-hostages exchange. However convoluted the negotiations, North was forced to leave Frankfurt and return to Washington when he was informed that one of Secord's aircraft ferrying arms to the Contras had been downed over Nicaragua; the usual denials were impossible when a crewman was captured by the Sandinistas on October 6. Not wanting to abandon the negotiations at what he considered such a critical juncture, North deputized Secord, a private citizen, to take charge of them; Secord then had to leave as well, so he deputized his business partner, Albert Hakim—a recently naturalized U.S. citizen of Iranian birth—to conduct the negotiations. Cannon neatly captures the untoward nature of the situation:

> The initiative that was supposed to chart the course of U.S.-Iranian relations had been put in the hands of a private citizen who had lived

---

[k]The system was paid for by Secord, thus violating a federal law forbidding government officials from accepting gifts or other gratuities. The relatively minor incident assumed greater importance when North falsified records to hide the transaction.

most of his life in Iran, lacked any background in diplomatic negotiation and stood, by his own estimate, to make "many millions" of dollars from the agreements he was negotiating.[48]

Hakim proceeded to reach an arrangement that North later presented to Poindexter and the president, although North concealed the fact that the arrangements had been negotiated for the U.S. government by a private citizen.

Acting upon Hakim's accords, Secord flew 500 TOWs to Iran on October 28. On November 2, hostage David Jacobsen was released in Beirut. On November 3, a flawed but still accurate description of McFarlane's May trip to Teheran and those negotiations was published in the Lebanese weekly *Al-Shiraa* (the article said it occurred in September 1986); on November 4, the charges were confirmed in a speech by Rafsanjani, although with the same errors. By November 6, both the *Los Angeles Times* and *Washington Post* had lead articles on the arms-for-hostages initiative.

The administration's embarrassment could not have been more acute. Just one month before, Secretary of State Shultz had told a meeting of the United Nations that "We have intensified our efforts to discourage our friends from selling arms to Iran with significant, but not complete success." The White House had been equally adamant in its statements rejecting all deals with terrorists: "We will not negotiate the exchange of innocent Americans for the release from prison of tried and convicted murderers held in a third country. To make such concessions would jeopardize the safety of other Americans citizens and would only encourage more terrorism." And, indeed, the White House's prophecy came true—American Edward Tracy was kidnapped, effectively replacing Jacobsen. All the president could say in response to a question was "no comment" and caution that the controversy was "making it more difficult for us in our effort to get the other hostages free."

The Iran initiative was finished. A cacophonous meeting of the National Security Planning Group (NSPG) on November 10 found Poindexter continuing to dissemble, as he presented a North-concocted chronology that was both inaccurate and incomplete. Shultz and Weinberger were furious when they learned what Poindexter (and, to some extent, Casey) had concealed from them, with Shultz being particularly incensed.[49] After a great deal of debate within the NSPG and facing

obvious public skepticism, it was agreed that the president would address the nation on November 13. Reagan's speech was one of the
worst he had ever given as president; it included the now-famous line
that all the "defensive" weapons and spare parts shipped to Iran "could
easily fit into a single cargo plane" (a claim provided to the president's
speech writer by North and Poindexter[50]). Reagan made the unequivo-
cal statement, "We did not—repeat—did not trade weapons or anything
else for hostages nor will we."

The administration began to splinter, especially after Shultz told a
Sunday morning television news interview show that he, the secretary
of state, could no longer speak for the administration's foreign policy
regarding Iran. Nancy Reagan and Casey both argued to the president
that he should fire Shultz for insubordination. Casey wrote the president a few days later,

> The public pouting of George Schultz and the failure of the State Depart-
> ment to support what we did inflated the uproar on this matter. If we all
> stand together and speak out I believe we can put this matter behind us
> quickly. . . . You need a new pitcher! A leader instead of a bureaucrat. I
> urge you to bring in someone like Jeane Kirkpatrick or Paul Laxalt,
> whom you may recall I recommended for State in 1980. You need this
> to give your foreign policy a new style and thrust and get the Carterite
> bureaucracy in State under your control. Time is short.[51]

McFarlane protested that Regan was blaming him for the initiative, a
charge well within the bounds of their antagonisms. The internal confusion became publicly apparent when Reagan reluctantly held a press
conference on November 19. It was even more disastrous than his
speech, denying, for example, that Israel had been involved even
though Regan had already admitted to the Israelis' participation.
Reagan was unyielding that there was nothing wrong, that there was
no apology to make because there was no mistake to admit. When
asked why he would not say a mistake had been made, he responded testily:

> Because I don't think a mistake was made. It was a high-risk gamble,
> and it was a gamble that, as I've said, I believe the circumstances
> warranted. And I don't see that it has been a fiasco, or a great failure
> of any kind.[52]

In spite of the rampant confusion, North and Poindexter had managed to keep the November 1985 shipments quiet, and nobody had

even hinted at what North called the "secret within a secret," the diversion of Iranian monies to Contra coffers. But the former began to unravel when State Department staff recalled that McFarlane's briefing to Shultz in Geneva had informed the secretary about the HAWK shipment, thus revealing the inaccuracies of Poindexter's chronology. This became especially crucial because Casey was scheduled to testify to Congress on November 21 and was prepared to tell Congress about the November shipment of "oil-drilling" equipment. Despite warnings, Casey gave his testimony, although he soft-pedaled the November shipment information.

During this time, Attorney General Meese was starting to investigate the arms shipment initiative, suspecting that the 1985 transfers could have violated the Arms Export Control Act. Acting under the president's authority, Meese moved carefully, which is to say so slowly that North was able to destroy thousands of potentially incriminating documents; for instance, Meese chose not to seal off North's office. Meese's inaction permitted North to work late at night shredding papers (even breaking down his own shredder) to prevent, by his own admission, Justice's lawyers from finding incriminating material and "to avoid the political embarrassment of having these documents be seen by the Attorney General's staff." [53] Poindexter, on his part, personally tore up what he thought was the only copy of the December 5 Finding.

On Saturday, November 22, two Justice Department officials, while searching North's remaining files for information on the 1985 arms shipments, inadvertently discovered the April 1986 document describing the Iranian arms sales and continuing to note how "$12 million will be used to purchase critically needed supplies for the Nicaraguan democratic Resistance Forces." [54] Without any knowledge about North's use of the Iranian "residuals," they immediately recognized the magnitude of what they had found, the diversion of Iranian funds to the Contras. They told Meese, who personally interviewed North the following day. North dissembled when asked about the diversion. The next morning, Meese warned the president that he had come across some very disturbing information.

On the afternoon of November 24, Meese confronted President Reagan with his information regarding the diversion. Regan's account of the president's reaction to congressional investigators is rather appropriate:

You know, the question has been asked, I've seen it in the paper time and time again: did the president know [in advance about the diversion]? Let me put it this way. This guy I know was an actor, and he was nominated at one time for an Academy Award, but I would give him an Academy Award if he knew anything about this when you watched his reaction to express complete surprise at this news on Monday the 24th. He couldn't have known it.[55]

The next morning, Poindexter was asked to resign. At noon, the president, after again averring "our policy goals to be well founded," announced to the press that "information brought to my attention yesterday convinced me that in one aspect implementation of that policy was seriously flawed." The president announced during his statement that Poindexter had resigned his position and that North would be relieved of his duties. He then turned the meeting over to Meese, who, among other comments, was to implicate North in possible charges of "criminality." Reagan telephoned North later that day and, according to North, told him that he was an "American patriot."[1] The following day, Reagan empaneled the President's Special Review Board chaired by former Texas senator John Tower to investigate and report back to him precisely what had transpired.

Although there were lingering contacts with Iranian negotiators (Schultz refers to "the snake that would not die"), charges of coverup, questions regarding the fallibility of the memories of various participants, highly publicized congressional hearings, and lengthy criminal trials yet to come, the Iran–Contra affair was basically over.

Conclusions

The Tower Commission, after carefully scrutinizing all of the then-available materials and interviewing most of the participants (Poindexter and North, awaiting congressional immunity, declined to be interviewed), came to the conclusion that the principal cause of the Iran–Contra affair was mismanagement. To be more specific, the commission argued that the extant national security system was not wrong,

---

[1] Reagan wrote that he called North just to "wish him well" (*An American Life*, p. 486). But in a telephone interview with *Time* magazine's Hugh Sidney given a week later, Reagan called North a "national hero" (Draper, *A Very Thin Line*, p. 549, and Cannon, *President Reagan*, p. 703).

it just was not operating very well (in the commission's words, "a flawed process") given President Reagan's very relaxed, management-by-delegation style. Reflecting the commission's mastery of understatement, it concluded that the president had not been served well, and recommended no major structural changes in the government's conduct of national security affairs.[56]

With the additional information from Congress's Iran–Contra hearings and the criminal trials of several of the principals, we can arrive at a set of more complete observations focusing on the question of political corruption. This emphasis on corruption will exclude some of the more salacious aspects of Iran–Contra. The most pivotal question of the entire matter, of course, was the degree of the president's involvement. Reagan himself has waffled on his participation, claiming in his early January 1987 testimony to the Tower Commission that he had approved the 1985 arms shipments; in February, he denied any involvement, but a scant ten days later, he changed his mind, writing that "In trying to recall events that happened eighteen months ago I'm afraid that I let myself be influenced by others' recollections, not my own. . . . My answer therefore and the simple truth is, 'I don't remember.' "[57] After giving every indication that he had no knowledge of the diversion, Reagan told a meeting of newspaper editors in May 1987, "As a matter of fact, I was very definitely involved in the decisions about support to the freedom fighters. It was my idea to begin with."[58] It is not particularly central to our discussion whether then–Vice President Bush was "in the loop," which he consistently denies. (There is unmistakable evidence that he knew about the Iranian initiative but apparently chose not to involve himself and has since denied virtually all involvement.[59])

As regards the president's involvement, we can safely infer from his NSPG meetings and three presidential intelligence Findings, Reagan was well aware of the Iranian initiatives (in strategy if not in full detail), although to this day, he persists in his befuddled view that he was not dealing with terrorists, nor trading arms for hostages.[60] The evidence also indicates that he was not informed by Poindexter about the diversion, even if North claims that he was.[61]

The key to viewing Iran–Contra as political corruption is the activities of McFarlane, Poindexter, North, and William Casey (to a lesser extent), aided by Richard Secord and assorted others. All of them showed a remarkable disdain for the American political system of checks and balances, forming a virtual cabal that only answered for its actions to itself. The mindset was presaged as far back as Secord's master's thesis at the Naval War College, in which he wrote: "The unconventional warfare instrument of national policy is so important that bureaucratic obstacles should be dismissed out of hand." [62] The easy implications were perilous.

The facts of the affair unarguably indicate that the NSC support of the Contras violated the Boland II Amendment; that the arms shipments to Iran violated stated American policy; and that the diversion of funds to the Contras was an unauthorized foreign policy act conceived and implemented by a lieutenant colonel, one that almost certainly would have been repudiated as soon as it was discovered (as indeed it was). This constellation of actions had an operational imperative: it could not be disclosed, for revelations would have meant termination. Garment, in her otherwise sympathetic interpretation of the NSC's action, proposes an appropriate imagery:

> By trying to make policy through evasive action against the Hill, Reagan's aides made themselves into yet another guerrilla force [and] adopted a guerrillas' attitude when dealing with Congress and its demands.[63]

Hence, by most standards, the Congress, executing its constitutionally mandated oversight role, was simply lied to—often by omission, occasionally by commission.[m] As Poindexter explained to Congress on July 20, 1987, "I simply did not want any outside interference," and later, "The problem, as I have stated, I didn't want Congress to know the details of how we were implementing the president's policy." [64] North was just as forthright and unrepentant: he told the joint investigating committee, "I will tell you right now ... that I misled the Congress. ... I participated in preparation of documents for the Congress that were erroneous, misleading, evasive, and wrong, and ... I make no excuses for what I did." [65]

The reasoning of Poindexter and North is not difficult to understand. They considered the NSC as part of the president's personal staff,

---

[m]Nor were Poindexter and North the only practitioners. Casey was typically less than forthcoming and Elliott Abrams (under secretary of state for Inter-American Affairs) admitted to having been deliberately misleading in his testimony to Congress; for the latter, see Draper, *A Very Thin Line*, pp. 368–373.

accountable solely to him. For instance, by their reckoning, the NSC was not covered by Boland II because it was not specifically enumerated, regardless of congressional intent. And, in the name of national security, the NSC was not accountable to the Congress, even denying the president's mandated obligation in a Finding to notify the Congress in "timely fashion." Moreover, other national security agencies of the government were equally suspect and kept removed from the president, as exemplified by Poindexter's willingness to keep the Departments of Defense and State, even the CIA, ignorant of North's activities. The danger is patent and not very far removed:

> In effect, Poindexter regarded himself as the head of an American version of a Roman praetorian guard around the president, loyal and responsible to him alone, embattled against Congress and the bureaucracy, invested with the authority to make the "hard decisions" and to see them through.[66]

The Tower Commission tempered its findings but came to much the same conclusion, that, by systematically excluding other agencies, the NSC "deprived those responsible for the initiative of considerable expertise. . . . It also kept the plan from receiving a tough, critical review." Again, "Circumventing the [executive] departments . . . robs the president of the experience and capacity resident in the departments." Still exercising its right to the understated, the Tower Commission found that "The result was a very unprofessional operation." [67] In short, McFarlane and Poindexter's vision of the NSC did not serve their venerated president well.

Furthermore, there was a particularly disturbing contempt in this operation for other branches of government. Even though it meant not availing themselves of others' expertise, North and, implicitly, Poindexter, considered their operations superior to anything else the government could mount. When Albert Hakim was asked during the congressional hearings if it bothered him that "you . . . a private citizen was left with this kind of task of negotiating an agreement in which if it succeeded, you stood to benefit very substantially," his answer manifested a deep contempt of the government: "what bothered me was that we didn't have the competence within the Government to do what I could do. That still bothers me." [68]

Unfortunately, there is evidence (albeit unsubstantiated) that North took his operational charge, his hubris, one step further. An NSC staff member claims he warned North that it is the president "who decides what the government will do, and our job as his staff is to give him the facts and point out the alternatives so he can make an informed judgment." North corrected him: "No, you're wrong. We have to box him in so there's only one way he can go—the right way." [69]

In the abstract, this logic might be relatively harmless. However, in the context of the inattentive Reagan presidency, it was political dynamite. Reagan strongly supported the Contras and gave every sign that he wanted them sustained, even if it meant squeezing past the Boland II restrictions. He even went so far as to meet with private donors and acknowledge the sizable Saudi gifts. He was even more insistent about the hostages; he writes in his memoirs, "Almost every morning at my national security briefings, I began by asking almost the same question: 'Any progress on getting the hostages out of Lebanon?' "[70] Understanding the perspective of the president, is it any wonder that his staff, if they saw an opportunity, would go the extra mile to achieve his goals? [n] McFarlane admits that he manipulated the president by catering to his passions while hiding the more worrisome aspects of the Iranian initiative. When Regan asked Poindexter for his resignation, Regan inquired why he had let the diversion happen. Poindexter's answer reflects his praetorian perspective: "I felt sorry for the Contras. I was so damned mad at [Democratic Speaker of the House] Tip O'Neill for the way he was dragging the *Contras* around that I didn't want to know what, if anything was going on." [71] North defiantly proclaims in his book, *Under Fire*, that the diversion was a wonderful plan.

What is particularly frightening about North and Poindexter's plans is that, in North's words (quoted from their final correspondence), "We nearly succeeded." [72] If an alert member of the State Department staff had not remembered McFarlane's briefing to the president and Shultz in November 1985, Poindexter and Casey might have been able to hide from Congress the 1985 weapons shipments and the specious Findings. The Justice Department lawyers would therefore not have had a reason to search North's files.

---

[n] One is reminded of Henry II's troubles with Thomas à Becket, the archbishop of Canterbury, and his exasperated plea in 1170 to his followers, "Won't anybody rid me of that troublesome priest?" Shortly thereafter, Becket was murdered in his cathedral by knights only executing what they thought to be their liege's desires, much to Henry's political consternation.

Even greater serendipity surrounded their discovery of the "diversion memo," a memorandum that somehow eluded North in his methodical, illegal shredding exercise.

This evidence would easily support charges of arrogance, foolishness, and incompetence but, of course, these all-too-human traits are not synonymous with political corruption. What makes the actions of McFarlane, Poindexter, and North susceptible to the charge of political corruption is that they took it upon themselves to secure political power for themselves by undermining the American system of governance, indeed, consciously subverting the constitutional system of checks and balances. In claiming to have given President Reagan "plausible deniability," Poindexter confessed to Congress that, twisting Truman's famous dictum, "the buck stops here with me." [73] In other words, it was Poindexter who was making presidential decisions. By unilaterally forcing "deniability" upon Reagan, that is, explicitly denying him information on the NSC's activities, Poindexter and North effectively usurped the president's constitutional prerogatives. That they were given an operating license because of the president's naive management practices is hardly an excuse. Some might call it a betrayal, albeit for what they thought were purposes espoused and means sanctioned by the president.

There was no economic benefit to North or Poindexter to reward their corruption (pardoning the relatively minor exception of North's security system paid for by Secord). North claims that he turned down a million-dollar offer from Ghorbanifar in January 1986 and a Persian carpet (valued at $8,000) that November.[74] There were, however, elements of criminality. In legal point of fact, many of the participants have been found guilty of criminal charges. Because of convictions being set aside on legal technicalities, none of the principals have served time in prison. But the lack of financial gain and prison time does not argue that the actions of Casey, McFarlane, Poindexter, and North were not corrupt; it only offers further evidence that corruption does not necessarily lead to prison sentences.

Weinberger fairly described Poindexter and North "people with their own agenda." Draper builds on Weinberger's description:

> This phrase starkly expresses what was most significant about the Iran–*contra* affairs—the takeover of governmental policies by a few strategically placed insiders infatuated with their own sense of superiority and incorruptibility.[75]

Weinberger told the investigating congressional committee, "I think any of these things that attempt to run private operations of this nature become private governments, is totally wrong and I would be totally opposed to it." And Shultz: "I don't think desirable ends justify the means of lying, deceiving, of doing things outside our constitutional processes."[76] To most unpartisan political observers in most political arenas, the actions of North and his colleagues would pass for, arguably define, corruption.

Most portentously, as the Tower Commission quoted from *Satires* by the Latin poet Juvenal, "Who shall guard the guardians from themselves?"[77]

Afterword

On December 24, 1992, President George Bush, acting upon what he described as precepts of "honor, decency, and fairness," exercised his constitutional prerogative and issued executive pardons to Caspar Weinberger, Robert McFarlane, Elliott Abrams, and three CIA officials for their involvement in the Iran–Contra affair. As explanation, President Bush noted that none of them had profited or sought "to profit from their conduct." Bush also observed that "the common denominator of their motivation—whether their actions were right or wrong—was patriotism." Finally and most centrally, Bush declared that "in recent years, the use of criminal processes in policy disputes has become all too common."[78] By granting the presidential pardons, the president manifestly sought to bring an end to independent counsel Lawrence Walsh's six-year investigation of the Iran–Contra imbroglio and thereby close the books on the entire matter, including his own controversial involvement (which had become a campaign issue during the 1992 presidential elections).

However compassionate President Bush's motives may have been, one is hard pressed to deny the appearance they presented. In Walsh's succinct summary,

> President Bush's pardon of Caspar Weinberger and other Iran–Contra defendants undermines the principle that no man is above the law. It demonstrates that powerful people with powerful allies can commit serious crimes in high office—deliberately abusing the public trust without consequences.[79]

Public opinion seemed to concur with the independent counsel. A *USA Today*/CNN poll taken the following week found that 54 percent of those surveyed disapproved of the pardons, with 49 percent of those asked believing that the "main reason" for the Bush pardons was "to protect himself from legal difficulties or embarrassment resulting from his own role in Iran–Contra."[80]

Bush's presidential pardons resonate closely with the prior Iran–Contra analysis as political corruption in three ways. First, he excused the six men because he had seen no element of their personal financial gain. However, as we have argued, to define corruption solely in terms of financial remuneration is naive and shortsighted, for it completely ignores corruption directed toward political goals. Second, he excused them on the grounds that they were acting out of "patriotism," an umbrella with almost infinite elastic proportions that, if stretched, could exculpate just about anybody for virtually any crime. (Recall that the Watergate conspirators were initially thought to be acting on grounds of national security, loosely defined as assuring the re-election of President Richard Nixon.) Surely everybody is a patriot in somebody's eyes, so to offer this as an excuse rather than an explanation is an experiment in baseless logic. Again, we are reminded of Samuel Johnson's aphorism, "patriotism is the last refuge of a scoundrel," but now, the context is no longer eighteenth-century London.

Finally, and most interesting, was the president's explanation that the pardoned six were snared in "a profoundly troubling development in the political and legal climate of our country: the criminalization of policy differences." Bush was simply mistaken here. None of the six was being prosecuted for his actual role in what we have seen to be a foolish policy, silly in plan (if not necessarily in all its objectives) from the very genesis and worse in execution. Rather, they had been indicted (and four of the six had either been found or pleaded guilty to charges brought by Walsh, with the remaining two awaiting trial) for lying to congressional and judicial investigators. The legal issue in the Walsh indictments was *not* the Iran–Contra policy and whether or not the perpetrators violated the second Boland Amendment and arms export restrictions (what Bush had described as "policy differences"), but, most crucially, the subsequent cover-up.

In essence, President Bush flatly refused to "acknowledge that the crimes of which some had been convicted and with which others had been charged were real and serious."[81] His subsequent carping at the press, characterizing media coverage as containing "stupid comments" and "frivolous reporting" reinforced that impression.[82] For reasons known best to Bush—one suspects a strange admixture of decent and self-serving natures—he chose to treat political corruption with its accompanying cover-up as little more than attempts by the Reagan administration (in which he served as vice president) to circumvent the legitimate political system—that is, another case of corruption cum "politics as usual"—even if the policy meant denying the American Constitution.

The Bush pardons emphasize another aspect of political corruption. The Walsh-led investigations have taken over six years and cost well in excess of $30 million and still have left many issues unsettled. Therefore, it was germane when Linda Greenhouse asked in the *New York Times* if "that prosecution was the right place for law and politics to meet." Greenhouse precisely posed the dilemma:

> The Iran–Contra affair was, at its core, an offense against the political system, and the question that remains is whether the criminal justice system is the best vehicle for arriving at what was and what remains the missing ingredient in the whole six-year long saga: political accountability.[83]

Even though Walsh has obtained fourteen indictments and eleven convictions, the feeling persists that such charges as shredding evidence (Oliver North) or deceiving Congress were minor in comparison to what the perpetrators attempted. Political corruption is, above all, a *political* crime. As the Iran–Contra trials demonstrate, the attendant legal infractions are often ambiguous and, more to the point, the legal system cannot always provide the appropriate adjudication. Whether, as President Bush said, "the proper target is the president, not his subordinates; [and] the proper forum is the voting booth, not the courtroom," this assertion was likewise problematic because, in this case, President Reagan was protected by a wall of subordinates' silence and thus from the voters' petition. What was ultimately left were the unsatisfying peripheral charges and the nagging knowledge that this "prosecution was the *right* place for law and politics to meet" only because the political alternative had been eviscerated.

The Iran–Contra corruptions continue then, well past the covert actions of Poindexter, North, and company, past the steadfast refusal of key players to describe honestly what the real chronology of events was, and into the present. The crowning tragedy of the entire sorry affair is that the players—possibly all well-intentioned, albeit toward their own agenda—never realized their actions were fundamentally acts of political corruption on a grand scale, a realization they still gainsay.

Notes

1. From a speech by President Reagan before the American Bar Association on July 8, 1965; quoted in Bob Schieffer and Paul Gary Gates, *The Acting President* (New York: E.P. Dutton, 1989), p. 230.

2. U.S. Congress, *Report of the Congressional Committees Investigating the Iran–Contra Affair* (Washington D.C.: Government Printing Office, November 1987) [hereafter referenced as *Iran–Contra Hearings*], p. 331; cited in Lou Cannon, *President Reagan: A Role of a Lifetime* (New York: Simon & Schuster, 1991), p. 593.

3. From a *New York Times*/CBS News Poll; Richard J. Meislin, "A Majority in New Pool Still Find Reagan Lied on the Iran–Contra Issue," *New York Times*, July 18, 1987, pp. 1, 6; 26 percent responded that they thought the president was telling the truth and 17 percent had no opinion. The margin of error was plus or minus four points.

4. Suzanne Garment, *Scandal* (New York: Random House, 1991), p. 201.

5. Theodore Draper, *A Very Thin Line* (New York: Hill and Wang, 1991), p. 561.

6. Quoted in ibid., p. 16.

7. Quoted in ibid., p. 18.

8. Quoted in Cannon, *President Reagan*, p. 366.

9. Quoted in Draper, *A Very Thin Line*, p. 24.

10. Quoted in Cannon, *President Reagan*, p. 385, and Draper, *A Very Thin Line*, p. 33.

11. Cannon, *President Reagan*, p. 336.

12. See the account of this meeting in Draper, *A Very Thin Line*, pp. 75–77, especially footnote at p. 76.

13. Quoted in Cannon, *President Reagan*, p. 386; also see Draper, *A Very Thin Line*, p. 77.

14. Quoted in Cannon, *President Reagan*, p. 384.

15. Draper, *A Very Thin Line*, p. 67.

16. Both the McFarlane and Regan quotes are from personal interviews with Cannon, *President Reagan*, p. 611.

17. Jeffrey D. Simon, "Misunderstanding Terrorism," *Foreign Policy*, No. 67 (Summer 1987), p. 110. Also see Donald T. Regan, *For the Record* (New York: Harcourt Brace Jovanovich, 1988), pp. 23–24.

18. Schieffer and Gates, *The Acting President*, p. 250–251; Cannon, *President Reagan*, p. 596, indicates that McFarlane's self-comparison to Kissinger and China was manufactured by his critics, such as Secretary of Defense Caspar Weinberger.

19. *Iran–Contra Hearings*; quoted in Draper, *A Very Thin Line*, pp. 143–144.

20. Compare McFarlane's various testimonies to the Iran–Contra investigations, as reported in Draper, *A Very Thin Line*, with those of Regan in his memoirs, *For the Record*, pp. 20–21.

21. Ronald Reagan, *An American Life* (New York: Simon & Schuster, 1990), pp. 501–502. Reagan's telling of this incident is trivialized by his emphasis on his hospitalization. In his testimony to the Tower Commission, he denies any recollection of McFarlane's briefing. John Tower et al., *The Tower Commission Report* (New York: Bantam and [New York] *Times* Books, 1987), p. 129, hereafter cited as *The Tower Commission Report*.

22. Regan's testimony to the Tower Commission, quoted in *The Tower Commission Report*, p. 133.

23. McFarlane's sartorial recollection is noted in *The Tower Commission Report*, p. 139.

24. Shultz from his testimony in the *Iran–Contra Hearings*, in Draper, *A Very Thin Line*, p. 166; Weinberger from his testimony to the Tower Commission, in *The Tower Commission Report*, p. 144.

25. Schieffer and Gates, *The Acting President*, pp. 232–233.

26. Oliver North, *Under Fire: An American Story* (New York: Harper Collins, 1991), writes, "In a perfect world, I would have chosen somebody else. Although Secord was an excellent candidate, he was already absorbed in another covert operation—helping the Contras—and his involvement in a second clandestine activity violated a cardinal rule of covert operations" (p. 30).

27. Shultz testimony to the Tower Commission, *The Tower Commission Report*, p. 159.

28. Cannon, *President Reagan*, p. 627.

29. Memorandum from North to Poindexter, quoted in *The Tower Commission Report*, pp. 166–167; also in Cannon, *President Reagan*, p. 628.

30. Draper, *A Very Thin Line*, p. 212.

31. The definition of a Finding and the subsequent discussion of the Finding are extracted from Draper, *A Very Thin Line*, pp. 213–215.

32. *Iran–Contra Hearings*, quoted in Cannon, *President Reagan*, p. 629.

33. The pivotal December 7 meeting is described in Draper, *A Very Thin Line*, pp. 225–229, Regan, *For the Record*, pp. 510–513, *The Tower Commission Report*, pp. 182–188, and Cannon, *President Reagan*, pp. 630–631.

34. Reagan, *An American Life*, p. 513; emphasis in original.

35. Draper, *A Very Thin Line*, p. 233.

36. Testimony of Weinberger and Shultz in *Iran–Contra Hearings*; quoted by Draper, *A Very Thin Line*, p. 248.

37. Reagan, *An American Life*, pp. 516–517. Reagan acknowledged the correctness of Weinberger and Shultz's positions in an interview with Cannon, *President Reagan*, p. 631, and in his November 19, 1986, press conference.

38. See Draper, *A Very Thin Line*, p. 257, and Cannon, *President Reagan*, p. 638. Reagan, in *An American Life*, makes no mention of any of the three Findings.

39. *Iran–Contra Hearings*, quoted in Draper, *A Very Thin Line*, p. 272 and 274. North also testified that Ghorbanifar offered him a million dollars "if we could make this [1986 arms deal] prosper."

40. Poindexter in *Iran–Contra Hearings*, quoted in Draper, *A Very Thin Line*, pp. 275–276.

41. Quoted from North notebooks by Draper, *A Very Thin Line*, p. 284.

42. Memorandum, North to Poindexter, in Appendix A of *Iran–Contra Hearings*; quoted in Draper, *A Very Thin Line*, p. 302.

43. Poindexter to North, Appendix to *Iran–Contra Hearings*; quoted in Draper, *A Very Thin Line*, p. 306.

44. Reagan, *An American Life*, p. 521.

45. Quoted in *The Tower Commission Report*, p. 337; also North, *Under Fire*, p. 63.

46. Poindexter testimony in *Iran–Contra Hearings*, quoted in Draper, *A Very Thin Line*, p. 344.

47. Draper, *A Very Thin Line*, pp. 421 and 427.

48. Cannon, *President Reagan*, p. 666.

49. Shultz's reaction to this meeting is outlined in George Shultz, " 'Something Is Terribly Wrong Here,' " *Time*, February 8, 1993, pp. 38–48. This article is excerpted from his forthcoming autobiography, George P. Shultz, *Turmoil and Triumph: My Years as Secretary of State* (New York: Charles Schribner's Sons, 1993).

50. North defends the calculation, saying it was verified by the Pentagon. "Regardless of how it was portrayed, this was not an enormous quantity of arms," North, *Under Fire*, p. 311.

51. Casey's letter is quoted by Shultz, "Something Is Terribly Wrong Here," p. 46.

52. Quoted in Cannon, *President Reagan*, p. 61, and Draper, *A Very Thin Line*, p. 483.

53. North, when presented with these characterizations, responded that he did not preclude or deny them; *Iran–Contra Hearings*, in Draper, *A Very Thin Line*, p. 507.

54. Draper, *A Very Thin Line*, p. 505, and Cannon, *President Reagan*, p. 695.

55. Regan's testimony in *Iran–Contra Hearings*, quoted in Draper, *A Very Thin Line*, p. 528. In his autobiography, *For the Record*, Regan described how "The president . . . blanched when he heard Meese's words. The color drained from his face, leaving his skin a pasty white. . . . Nobody who saw the president's response that afternoon could believe for a moment that he knew about the diversion of funds before Meese told him about it. He was the picture of a man to whom the inconceivable had happened" (p. 38). Reagan's own account was remarkably matter-of-fact and nondescript (Reagan, *An American Life*, pp. 530–511).

56. See *The Tower Commission Report*, parts IV and V.

57. Reagan to the Tower Commission, *The Tower Commission Report*, pp. 28–29.

58. Quoted in Draper, *A Very Thin Line*, p. 570, and Cannon, *President Reagan*, p. 717.

59. The least-disputed evidence is that he was present at the August 6 and

January 7 meetings of Reagan's National Security Planning Group; also, he was extensively briefed by Israeli intelligence officers in late July 1986 (see Draper, *A Very Thin Line*, p. 389–391 for details). More recent evidence casts serious doubt on Bush's proclaimed distance; see Anthony Lewis, "The Cover-Up Crumbles," *New York Times*, October 4, 1992, p. A19, Murray Waas and Craig Unger, "Annals of Government: In the Loop: Bush's Secret Mission," *New Yorker*, Vol. 68, No. 37 (November 2, 1992), pp. 64–83, and Shultz, "Something Is Terribly Wrong Here."

60. See Cannon's February 1989 interview with Reagan, in *President Reagan*, p. 631, and Reagan, *An American Life*, p. 512.

61. North, *Under Fire*, p. 12–13. North's evidence is completely conjectural, based on his assumption that the president could *not* have not known.

62. Quoted in Schieffer and Gates, *The Acting President*, p. 253.

63. Garment, *Scandal*, p. 203.

64. Poindexter's testimony in the *Iran–Contra Hearings*, cited in Draper, *A Very Thin Line*, p. 340.

65. North in the *Iran–Contra Hearings*; at his trial, North was somewhat more contrite, admitting, "I was not honest in that [August 6, 1986] meeting. I'm not proud of that. It's not something I feel good about," both quotes from Draper, *A Very Thin Line*, p. 34. In his memoirs, *Under Fire*, North reverts to his unapologetic posture.

66. Draper, *A Very Thin Line*, p. 219.

67. *The Tower Commission Report*, pp. 68, 89, and 73, respectively.

68. Albert Hakim in the *Iran–Contra Hearings*, quoted in Draper, *A Very Thin Line*, p. 432.

69. The staff member was Constantine Menges, a rather controversial member of the NSC staff; quoted in Schieffer and Gates, *The Acting President*, p. 250.

70. Reagan, *An American Life*, p. 492.

71. Regan, *For the Record*, p. 42.

72. North to Poindexter, November 24, 1986, *Iran–Contra Hearings*, quoted in Draper, *A Very Thin Line*, p. 535.

73. Quoted in Cannon, *President Reagan*, p. 590.

74. North, *Under Fire*, pp. 19–20 and 295.

75. Draper, *A Very Thin Line*, p. 563.

76. Weinberger quoted in Draper, *A Very Thin Line*, p. 558; Shultz quoted in Peter deLeon, "Public Policy Implications of Systematic Political Corruption," *Corruption and Reform*, Vol. 4, No. 3 (1989), p. 213.

77. From Juvenal, *Satires*, VI, 347; quoted in *The Tower Commission Report*, p. 102.

78. See David Johnston, "Bush Pardons 6 in Iran Affair, Aborting a Weinberger Trial; Prosecutor Assails 'Cover Up,' " *New York Times*, December 25, 1992, pp. A1, A10; the text of President Bush's pardon is reprinted in *New York Times*, December 25, 1992, p. A10.

79. Walsh's statement is reprinted in *New York Times*, December 25, 1992, p. A10.

80. Other choices (and their percentages) were "to put the Iran–Contra affair in the nation's past" (21 percent), "to protect people he felt acted honorably and patriotically from unfair prosecution" (15 percent), or "to get back at

Iran–Contracutor Lawrence Walsh for bringing charges against Weinberger right before the November [1992] elections" (2 percent). The survey is reported in Adam Clymer, "Bush Criticizes Press Treatment of the Pardons," *New York Times*, December 31, 1992, p. A8, and has a margin of sampling error of plus or minus five percentage points.

81. Meg Greenfield, "Bush's Pardons," *Newsweek*, January 4, 1992, p. 60.

82. Clymer, "Bush Criticizes Press Treatment of Pardons," p. A8. At the same time, however, the president announced that he was retaining legal counsel to represent him in future possible investigations of his role in the arms-for-hostages policy.

83. Linda Greenhouse, "Law Ill-Equipped for Politics," *New York Times*, December 28, 1992, pp. A1, C7, at A1.

Part III
WHAT SHOULD WE DO?

8

PEOPLE AND SYSTEMS

Corruption is the most infallible symptom of constitutional liberty.

—Edward Gibbon,
*The Decline and Fall of
the Roman Empire*

I now return to the main themes of this examination of political corruption, basically to ask and (hopefully) answer two questions: What
do we know? and What should we do about it? The first part of this
chapter reviews the five corruption narratives in light of the ideas
broached in the first two chapters, and is interpretative in nature. The
second asks a hard question and poses some recommendations: if we
can attribute corruption to the political system in which it occurs, the
traditional remedies can be seen as ineffectual; what, then, might we
propose that would make a positive difference?

What Do We Know?

We need first to recognize a difference between political scandal and
political corruption; the first is part of the corruption syndrome but
concerns us only slightly. Here we look upon scandals as *isolated*
incidents that violate political norms and public expectations; often,
but not always, they are illegal. They are usually of a personal and
relatively insignificant nature.[1] Suzanne Garment observes that "a significant part of our current scandals—almost half I would say—in-
volves offenses that in the larger scheme of things simply do not pose

207

any great danger to the republic."[2] Presidential candidate Gary Hart's indiscreet dalliance with model Donna Rice, Bert Lance's questionable financial affairs prior to becoming President Carter's director of the Office of Management and Budget, and the willingness of the House of Representatives bank to honor members' overdrafts are examples. That the scandals are usually insignificant does not mean that they cannot have tragic overtones; Senator Edward Kennedy's (D-MA) presidential ambitions were drowned along with Mary Jo Kopechne in the waters off Chappaquiddick in 1969. In the context of the examples reviewed above, a scandal would be Don Dixon's behavior as the director of Vernon Savings and Loan, DuBois Gilliam's favoritisms at HUD, or Wedtech executives lying on their stock sale registration documents, if these were singular acts. But, in these incidents and numerous others, they were not.

Political corruption, on the other hand, is not an isolated event, but rather a continued, concerted conspiracy—a series or network of scandals in some cases, such as the collapse of the S&Ls and the Ill Wind allegations—in which the purpose is to get around the government's rules and canons of expected behavior. The gains may be personal (as in the cases of HUD Mod Rehab bidders or the Wedtech management) or political (e.g., HUD Secretary Samuel Pierce or Rear Admiral John Poindexter), but the modus operandi is the same—to obtain unsanctioned advantages unavailable to others on a sustained basis. And while the reward might be monetary, the context, influence, and effect are always political, where some variation of political power is the presiding currency.

Political corruption, as we usually view it, is typically perceived as a few or more persons subverting the accepted processes of government for their own financial gain. However, I proposed in the first two chapters and demonstrated in the five subsequent ones that this is an incomplete view of corruption, that people often act in corrupt manners for other, less tangible rewards, such as seeing a controversial policy changed (HUD allocation rules for MRP funds, the White House surreptitiously seeking support for the Contras from private sources or foreign governments, or DoD procurement rules) or, equally likely, continuing an advantageous policy (Congressman James Wright or Senator David Pryor arguing against the enforcement of regulations pertaining to the S&L industry, or the refinancing of the FSLIC insurance fund). The expected benefits, in such cases, would be an ideological gain or political power for other ends, not the usual lucre (filthy or otherwise). Moreover, the losses are much greater and more enduring, ultimately risking the very integrity of the political system,[3] as Theodore Lowi cautions us regarding Big Corruption.

It is important to realize that this reading does not suggest that most people engage in corrupt ways with no financial benefit in sight; the adjective "political" does not preclude money. Quite the contrary, as we saw in the case of the Wedtech management scurrying after undeserved defense contracts so that they could achieve the wealth they chased as the American dream, or the few Texas and California S&L owners "trading dead horses for dead cows" so that they might revel in extravagances almost beyond the ken of that same dream. Surely they were breaking the law for their personal pocketbook gains and have been duly convicted as felons. The military consultants prosecuted in the Ill Wind investigations could contend that they were middlemen—mere cogs in the procurement wheel—who passed ill-gotten information from civilian defense officials to defense contractors, supposedly in the name of enhanced national security. Perhaps. But that argument quickly pales, as the Ill Wind convictions and fines suggest. Certainly then, there is cash involved, sometimes lots of it. But the money model does not adequately explain those cases in which virtually no payments of note occurred—John Poindexter and Oliver North engineering the Iranian arms-for-hostages trade and the Contra diversion, the Small Business Administration (SBA) consistently supporting Wedtech's various machinations, Attorney General Edwin Meese's early championing of Wedtech, or Secretary Pierce and his executive assistant Deborah Gore Dean distributing Section 8 contracts to those with a Republican imprimatur for so little financial benefit to themselves. Money was indeed changing hands, but as we have seen, it was much less the omnipotent "grease" than traditionally supposed.

Money, of course, represents personal gain. If we can agree that persons have engaged in corrupt behaviors for no appreciable monetary gain, we must look elsewhere to understand the actions of North, Meese, Wright, Pierce, and others. In their cases, financial gain can be seen as not necessarily necessary and certainly not sufficient to explain why they engaged in acts of political corruption.

Drawing upon Robert K. Merton's idea of political corruption serving a functional role in governance, such authors as James Scott and Michael Johnston have argued that corruption is nothing more or less than an informal means of dealing with political officials and government procedures.[4] Functional corruption, however, is not a means of governing, but actually a way to circumvent the restrictions implied by being governed. Public policies fluctuate between two poles, representing a dynamic between an exercise of what can be done (e.g., alleviating poverty) and, more often, an exercise of what cannot be done (welfare fraud). Laws, regulations, and bureaucratic interpretations all define citizens' interactions with government, usually in a restrictive manner. One cannot export specified goods without a license, sell to the government without meeting certain standards, or build an office building (even a back porch) without meeting enumerated standards. This is not to suggest that restrictions are deleterious. We can all agree that these regulations and codes are nominally designed to assure the public safety and welfare. But, at the same time, these beneficial regulations can be seen as what we earlier called "bottlenecks," which, by their very design, are meant to ensure a consideration of the public's protection, a consideration that purposefully, invariably impedes the course of business.

Some people refer to such regulations and laws pejoratively as "red tape." We are all reminded of the famous "Grin and Bear It" cartoon, in which an executive announces to his board, "Gentlemen, the bad news is the company is in a state of bankruptcy.... The good news is we have complied with federal rules and regulations."[5] That sentiment would easily resonate with the managements of Wedtech, numerous S&Ls, some military contractors, and even the CIA as the agency worried that it had participated in North's covert arms operation without a presidential Finding. What these critics fail to understand is that red tape did not appear one day by magic, black or white. Rather, it is a direct manifestation of the public's choice that dictates a rule by law based on equal opportunity. However frustrated we might get at bottlenecks and red tape, we need to remember who it was that imposed them upon us. The answer, lest we forget, is, we did; if red tape is a tar baby, it is one of our own conscious making. Nor should we forget why we made that choice. Herbert Kaufman spells out the deliberate rationale:

> A society less concerned about the rights of individuals in government and out might well be governed with a much smaller volume of paper and much simpler and faster administrative procedures than are typical of governance in this country. Americans have adopted a different mix.[6]

Perhaps the origins and reasons for bureaucratic red tape lend themselves to our frustration in dealing with it. To argue against red tape violates our social contract instincts. Tacitly, then, our frustrations condone our attempts to extricate ourselves from the red tape tangles, and we act in a furtive manner assuming that what we do is best for society (or at least society as we prefer to see it). To fight against red tape is to struggle against ourselves. Not surprisingly, in these cases, people are likely to blame the system and picture themselves as well-meaning individuals only trying to make the system more responsive. In fact, by making the system more responsive to their particular needs (as opposed to others'), people are undermining the civic norms and preferences that set those safeguards (or as they would characterize them, obstacles) in place.

In every case reviewed here, an unresponsive or obstructionist political system was seen by the conspirators to be the party at fault. In the eyes of the perpetrators, if Lieutenant Colonel North or John Mariotta or Charles Keating were guilty of anything, it was trying to make a balky system work and allow their worthy projects to proceed unhindered toward a greater good. Remember that John Mariotta told a White House conference how Wedtech could cure ghetto ills if only it had enough business. If that course of unhindered action meant literally lying to Congress, bribing an SBA official, or having U.S. senators interfere with a regulator's duty (which Garment referred to as "organized coercion" and "gorilla" tactics[7]), it was simply because the extant public system failed to work; in its discredited place, individuals operated within another system, one more conducive to their goals. This strategy was made easier because the alternative system—albeit lacking general public approval—was seen to work in supporting the Contra rebels, obtaining defense contracts, and warding off bank closures. To have expected North or Mariotta or Keating to have eschewed the alternatives that they perceived as unfairly forced upon them by the political system would have been naive, even when they knew their actions were stretching the letter of the law.

In all of these cases, corruption was seen to be functional, an alternative, informal, maybe unfortunate means toward what the perpetrators viewed as salutary ends. In Robert Merton's theoretical construct, "the functional deficiencies of the official structure generate an alternative (unofficial) structure to fulfill existing needs somewhat more efficiently." [8] The middlemen prosecuted under the Ill Wind indictments did not consider themselves "dopers," but businessmen trying to reduce the friction in the system, with the goal of a more efficient weapons acquisition process (hence, a more secure "common defense"). They perceived their cause as just but denied justice by an obstructionist procurement system and its guardian regulators. Likewise, S&L executives did not see themselves as corrupt when they lobbied to keep FSLIC underfunded so that their "zombie" thrifts could not be audited or closed.

The clearest illustration of functional corruption was the Iran–Contra initiatives. Poindexter and North unquestionably viewed themselves as patriots working toward freeing hostages and fighting communism; to carry out their plans, they quite consciously kept Congress and possibly the president uninformed and (admittedly) deceived because, in Poindexter's words, "I simply did not want any *outside* interference." [9] That is, he and North did not want the nation's laws and the Constitution hindering their methods of conducting business or derailing their patriotism. They never realized that their secrecy, regardless of how "functional" it might be, was contravening the American system of government checks and balances. As North was lectured by Congressman Louis Stokes (D-OH), "What we seek to do in covert operations is to mask the role of the United States from other countries, not from their own government." [10] As Iran–Contra independent counsel Lawrence Walsh explained when he handed up his indictment against Secretary of Defense Caspar Weinberger,

> It is not a crime to deceive the American public, as high officials of the Reagan Administration did for two years while conducting the Iran and Contra operations, but it is a crime to mislead, deceive and lie to Congress when [it] seeks to learn whether Administration officials are conducting the nation's business in accordance with the law. [11]

Thus, the functional perspective seems to be a viable model for explaining political corruption. Merton is especially cogent to this point: "In this crucial sense, these concepts are not 'merely' theoretical (in the abusive sense of the term), but are eminently practical. In the deliberate enactment of social change, they can be ignored only at the price of considerably heightening the risk of failure." [12]

The problem is not that the corruptions in this book were not functional—they did in fact work, although not as well or as long as the proponents might have liked. Likewise, the problem with corruption as a functional procedure is not that it does not work for the suspicious few—it does. The problem is that it does not work for the law-writing and -abiding many. Indeed, it penalizes them for their adherence to the legal code. For this reason, while political corruption might be beneficial in the interim, to patch together a quick fix or cut a fast deal, in the long run its gains can only prove limited, ephemeral, and counterproductive. Other firms, seeing themselves losing out as the corrupt winning firms are rewarded, will either question the probity of the corrupt firm to the responsible authorities or, worse, adopt similar procedures. The former is precisely what happened as Wedtech wove its corrupt web to obtain defense contracts; a disgruntled loser made inquiries to a congressman that led to a committee investigation. The latter behavior occurred during the S&L crises as solvent banks had to resort to high-risk banking practices in order to stay competitive with the suspect Empires, Vernons, and Lincolns. The consequences of either response can be horrendous: the delays and obfuscations in the S&L crises will cost American taxpayers hundreds of billions of dollars; the Iran–Contra diversion, which Oliver North still thinks was a "neat idea,"[13] virtually destroyed the Reagan presidency, the very office North thought he was serving so well. In both cases, the government's core integrity suffered.

For an instance of the inbred and debilitating nature of functional corruption, let us consider a scenario ripe for fraud, with the important proviso that the scenario is not hypothetical. Rather, it is drawn by Ronald Goldstock, the former director of New York State's Organized Crime Task Force, in his description of the construction industry in New York City:

> Corruption is widespread, especially in Manhattan, because real-estate developers and contractors are "vulnerable to *anyone* who has the power to cause delays" at construction sites.
>
> . . .
>
> Routine construction problems in Manhattan contribute to the delays, increasing pressure on developers to bribe city inspectors or union officials to avoid further slowdowns and to recover their initial investments. The routine problems cited by Mr. Goldstock include assembling real-estate parcels and removing tenants, jurisdictional disputes among unions and traffic congestion.[14]

Another news report regarding Goldstock's Task Force referred to the influence of organized crime: "Its presence is, to a large extent, accepted by developers, contractors and suppliers—in some cases as *a necessary evil* providing stability and predictability, in other instances as an organization which can provide *valuable* services."[15]

The key points here are that these are "routine" situations and problems within the building industry, yet they are ever so conducive and vulnerable to ongoing individual acts of corruption by "anyone" *even when they are expected.* Thus, the Manhattan construction business becomes a fertile setting for corruption—"a necessary evil . . . which can provide valuable services." The remedy is not to roust out the "bad guys," although obviously they cannot be permitted to stay. But then what? Goldstock observed in his interview that

> the elimination of organized-crime racketeering would not alone solve such problems as payoffs to municipal inspectors, bid-rigging among contractors and bribes to union officials for special contract favors and the hiring of lower-paid non-union workers. "Even if you indict and convict every mobster involved in corruption . . . under current conditions, someone else will come along, recognize the potential and become the new predators."[16]

In short, as long as the extant system remains in operation, a set of corruptions providing "valuable service" to "routine" problems will continue. The only result one can expect from "throwing the rascals out" is a new set of rascals who will probably be smarter and harder to detect than the group just rousted, having learned from their convicted brethren's experiences.

A second example of the "routine" nature syndrome is the Ill Wind investigations. When asked about the Ill Wind allegations, Secretary Weinberger (who had resigned a few months before the allegations became public, although the crimes had occurred during his tenure) responded "If there are some procedures that permitted this to happen and it's more than just simple greed and dishonesty, then obviously the procedures need tightening."[17] As we have seen, it was more than "just simple greed and dishonesty," so there is no reason to believe tighter procedures, which would apply to individuals, would be effective. If this were not true, then years of tightening Pentagon procurement procedures would have eliminated fraud and abuse in DoD. Obviously they have not.

We can see that political corruption is more than the result of personal greed. There is also a component of reacting against the public system and, alternatively, ascribing to a less public, nether-system (sometimes inventing one) that can lead more directly, more expeditiously to the desired goals. Melvin Paisley perceived the navy procurement bureaucracy and procedures as delaying Navy Secretary John Lehman's goal of a modernized navy, so he concocted ways around those obstructions. On the other side of the procurement coin, Mariotta likewise saw the navy procurement officers as obstacles, and devised end runs around them, just as Poindexter refused to permit Congress to exercise its constitutional responsibilities in foreign policy. Zombie S&Ls, fighting against a regulatory system they largely designed, turned to political allies to prevent FSLIC from closing their insolvent doors. Similarly, Republican builders and consultants (like James Watt) went over the heads of the HUD bureaucracy to the office of the secretary where they hoped for better treatment. Recall the testimony of developer Judith Siegel before a House subcommittee looking into alleged irregularities at HUD:

> Mr. Chairman, I am sure you recognize that HUD is not an easy agency to work with. It is an agency in disarray, with confused and conflicting policies, and we need someone who could get it to respond. . . . In summary, do I think this selection process was good public policy? No. Do I think a more competitive process would have made better public policy? Of course, but *the system was there*. . . . Developers must not be blamed for the system they neither created nor administered.[18]

The role of the political system in contributing to, conditioning, and actually motivating political corruption goes a long way in explaining the centrality of political corruption in the American political system. It also indicates why the problem seems so ingrained, so intractable, for the system was deliberately constructed to promote and enhance equity and power sharing, a dedication that by its very nature creates and defends the offending bottlenecks that are the basic cause of corruption.

The systemic roots of corruption also suggest why those who say that corruption is more likely during Republican administrations might have their statistics right but their causal inferences wrong. Gerald Seib, writing in the *Wall Street Journal*, asserts that a "pattern" of corruption during Republican administrations is "explained by the philosophical bent of those who tend to work for Republican presidents—a bent that often leads them afoul of the guidelines of government work." Seib quotes the distinguished presidential scholar, James MacGregor Burns:

> Typically, Republican administrations draw people out from the world of big business, a world not necessarily corrupt but one where they are

operating under the rules of business. And they draw people who often are free enterprisers, individual, people who accept the notion that one has to climb up the greasy ladder and don't have to worry about the rules so much to do it.

Likewise, Richard Neustadt suggests that "many Republicans view government with distain and 'hold their noses' while they serve in government posts." The implication is that the Republicans have a general "lack of respect for the intricate rules and regulations that are supposed to steer government employees away from conflicts and ethical breaches," and that Democrats are more aware and respectful of these sensitivities.[19]

If, however, it is the political system—with large bureaucracies and voluminous regulations—that leads to political corruption, then it should make little difference which party occupies the presidency. This book's selection of illustrations drawing upon "Republican" corruption is an artifact of the decision to limit the book's examples to recent cases and the reality that Republican presidents have occupied the White House for the last twelve years. Indeed, the Johnson and Carter administrations had their scandals and corrupt incidents,[a] and congressional Democrats have not abjured an occasional fraudulent moment (for example, the Abscam "sting" in which FBI officers impersonated Arab interests attempting to purchase congressional favor). Furthermore, many of the politicians involved in the S&L imbroglio were of the Democratic stripe.

Nevertheless, it would be myopic not to note that an exorbitant amount of political scandal and corruption did occur on the Reagan watch,[b] largely attributed to the impatient climbers and noseholders described by Burns and Neustadt. The motivation in those cases, however, was less their inherent Republican-ism (assuming we know what that means) than the Reagan administration's abiding faith in the unregulated economy (what Edwin Gray referred to as being "ideologi-

---

[a] Admittedly, nothing that happened during the administrations of Democratic presidents Kennedy, Lyndon Johnson, and Jimmy Carter matches the magnitude of Iran–Contra and the S&L crisis (for which we should be bipartisanly grateful), but those really were special occurrences.

[b] *Time* magazine referred to it as the "scandal-scarred spring of 1987" during which "a relentless procession of forlorn faces assaults the nation's moral equanimity . . ." (Walter Shapiro, "What's Wrong?" *Time*, May 22, 1987, p. 14).

cally blinded" [20]) and the president's decentralized, inattentive management style. In combination, they resulted in an administration that encouraged entrepreneurial behavior unburdened by oversight, in other words, a political environment fertile for fraud and abuse. Judge Stanley Sporkin, when ruling on an S&L case, captured that brittle environment in a nutshell when he held that the entire S&L experience "demonstrates the excesses of a misconceived and misapplied regulatory program along with a group of individuals who were bent on exploiting these excesses." [21]

We should return to an issue addressed in Chapter 2. There I posed the questions "Does corruption extract a sufficient cost from the political system that we need to worry about it?" and "If not, why worry about it?" Earlier, I answered the first question in the affirmative, but in an abstract vein. Now we can see that political corruption is far more destructive than simply bribing an alderman or contributing to a congressional campaign in hopes of favorable legislation. Political corruption that led to delaying closing zombie thrifts will cost American taxpayers billions of dollars; corruptions in the weapons development system led to numerous cases of contracts being given to unqualified bidders; and the Iran–Contra corruptions threatened the constitutional foundations of the American political system. Furthermore, incidents of corruption fed the public cynicism toward government so that even a minor scandal or rumor automatically assumed attention, and often unwarranted prominence.[c] Although the resulting alienation might be easy to quantify in a Gallup-type poll, it is impossible to specify what its effects and their significance might be (a lower voter turnout? more white collar crime?). It is safe to assume, however, that the effects would not be desirable.[22]

---

[c]An example would be the circumstantial evidence linking the late William Casey and, more critically, George Bush, to alleged negotiations with Iranians to delay the release of the American Embassy hostages in Teheran until after the 1980 presidential elections in order to deprive incumbent President Carter of an "October Surprise" that might swing the election to him. See Gary Sick, *The October Surprise: American Hostages in Iran and the Election of Ronald Reagan* (New York: Random House, 1991). Sick was the NSC desk officer during this incident so his analysis cannot be lightly dismissed; however, as he admits, there is little substantive evidence to support his charges. See David Johnston, "80 G.O.P. Hostage Dealings Skirted Propriety, Panel Says," *New York Times*, November 24, 1992, p. A7, and Neil A. Lewis, "House Inquiry Finds No Evidence of Deal on Hostages in 1980," *New York Times*, January 13, 1993, pp. A1, C19.

As these cases demonstrate, to view corruption as a benign (or, at worst, petty) side-show to the American body politic is to permit a dangerous virus entry. Like any virus, corruption might be limited by its own dynamics; but, possibly, the costs could be significant, easily beyond the calculations of the actual perpetrators themselves. Although political corruption might be "functional," its ultimate effect and result are clearly dysfunctional. Indeed, political corruption does warrant our worry. For these reasons—that corruption is neither trivial nor functional and we should therefore look seriously for ways to control it—we shall now turn to a discussion and recommendations as to what might be done.

What Should Be Done?

Before talking about solutions, we need to remind ourselves that some games simply are not worth the candle, some maladies not worth the cure. Edward Gibbon's nineteenth-century warning that "Corruption is the most infallible symptom of constitutional liberty" should be kept in mind. One could conceivably envision a police state so invasively thorough that it could eradicate any and all signs of unsanctioned activity (corruption), although to date we have seen none that has come even close. However, in a democratic system, such an authoritarian regime with its crushing effects on privacy and civil freedoms would be unacceptable. In Garment's words, "a prosecutorial class with no sympathy for human frailties can be a much greater danger to a democracy than the simple peddling of influence."[23] Most Americans would ruefully agree that it would be preferable to accept a limited amount of corruption and democracy's other permissive means inherent in loosely structured, representative government than to risk the consequences of an authoritarian rule. So any recommendations to limit corruption must fall well short of repression.

In suggesting solutions that address the problems and expenses of political corruption, we can assume the two somewhat distinct perspectives addressed above—that of the individual, and that of the system. These distinctions are admittedly more clear-cut in the ambiguity of concept than in the harsh reality of practice, for, in everyday life, individuals must act and interact within a system. Still, the differentiation serves as a valuable cutting edge in proposing different sources and ameliorative courses of action.

The first, or personal, perspective assumes that the basic cause of corruption is the inclination of specific individuals (such as Wedtech's Mariotta and Neuberger, HUD's Pierce and the MRP bidders, or the navy's Paisley) to abandon themselves and their duties to proffered temptations and violate the system's norms. This traditional perspective and its prescribed remedies are intuitively satisfying for at least two reasons. First, they reinforce the comfortable notion that corruption is fundamentally a deviant position—that turning out the occasional ill-mannered scoundrels is all that is needed to keep the body politic healthy, if not immune. Second, it is the apparently aberrant individual who commits the corrupt act. It is the isolated individual, not the system, that should be punished and suffer. Therefore, the solution should be tailored to the person. The rare demon, once exorcised, does not impugn the sanctity of the system, to everybody's sigh of relief.

Alas, these personnel-oriented solutions, while necessary in the operation against corruption, fall short of any durable correction to the ongoing malady because they ignore the systemic roots. In point of historical fact, rascals and reprobates have been booted out of power and position (tossing out the "rotten apple") since the Garden of Eden was surrendered, but with no lasting effect. As long as citizens have had government, there has been some level of corruption; as long as there has been corruption, culprits have been punished and expelled. And, like the mythical dragon Jason slew—whose blood sprouted progeny—corruption crops up again. Corrupt acts have occurred and will continue to occur in spite of social condemnations and severe penalties. We cannot, of course, ignore individuals with their shortfalls and passions. But to propose relief for corruption solely by appeals to disbarments, tighter regulations, inspectors general, and harsh punishment would offer up only chimera. Despite the Ethics in Government Act of 1978, passed as a direct result of the Watergate events, the Reagan administration experienced a myriad of conflict-of-interest cases. Lyn Nofziger, even after he was carefully briefed by the White House counsel on the prohibition of the Ethics Act barring him from lobbying in the White House for a year, was back urging Edwin Meese to support the Wedtech bid for an army contract within a few months of his resignation.

In addition to being ineffective, measures concerned with individual temptations might actually increase the motivations and opportunities for corruption. Under the heading of unintended consequences, a common problem with the corruption remedies that doctor the individual is that they can easily make the vulnerable condition *more* susceptible to corruption. In situations similar to the Wedtech case, additional red tape, tighter codes, and less bureaucratic discretion could exacerbate the condition by making it even more difficult for the government to respond or for companies to obtain government contracts. The increased delay would only make contractors more desperate to expedite the system (i.e., to protect their projected profits) by "greasing" some palms. The vulnerable official would have great control over the now *more* constricted bottleneck and therefore be able to extort a higher "feed me" (market) price. The unintended consequences: the gains are greater and both parties would be more susceptible to graft and corruption.[24] Alternatively and probably worse, the system would become so encumbered by rules that it would be unable to function; cautions Garment, "a network of prohibitions and sanctions tight enough to eliminate all undesirable behavior may also create a government incapable of accomplishing much that is worth doing, in the defense field or any other."[25] Or worst of all, elements of both individual susceptibility and governmental inefficiency would be combined. Even the very best scenario extracts onerous costs: "One of the prices the scandal will enact . . . is that we will be left with a legacy of control that in the name of honesty will make it harder for the government to work efficiently." [26] There are, it would seem, no pleasant outcomes.

Measures leading to increased government inefficiency and questionable progress against corruption would hardly seem to be attractive policy recommendations. Therefore, while actions must unquestionably be taken against the individual "predator" for violating and profiting from the public trust, there should be no illusions that such measures directed exclusively against the suspect individual will result in significant declines in corruption because acts against the individual do not rid the system of the opportunities for ill-gotten gains, a condition others will willingly exploit.

The New Yorker commented on the fallout from the S&L scandal and Iran–Contra:

> the idea that the system itself has problems ... has few champions among the people who are in a position to do something about it. . . .
> It's much more convenient to reduce our political crises to the evil deeds of a few isolated figureheads (Oliver North, with his shredder,

Charles Keating, with his real-estate schemes), and to confine reform to the task of putting away the latest crop of villains—a never-ending task that merely punctuates our scandals rather than resolves them.[27]

For this reason, we must examine the more systemic conditions and incentive structures that incubate and inculcate corruption. If these conditions can be altered so that the opportunities are less available and enticing, then we stand a better chance for reducing graft, bribery, and other such crimes. This approach sounds suspiciously easy. For example, many observers, beginning with the turn-of-the-century Progressives, have called for greater government intervention as a way to stem undesirable and often illegal activities in the private sector. The regulatory commissions are living institutional proof of the government's willingness to accept this challenge. But the effectiveness of such institutions is open to question. Medicare frauds have produced a veritable government oversight industry in the physician's world, but the oversight has had little success in reducing (as opposed to reporting) the plague. A dedicated corps of social workers and mountains of paperwork have not eliminated the immense amount of fraud in federal social services.[28] Nor do these charges reside exclusively in the domain of the financially indigent. The scandals that converged with a vengeance on Wall Street over the last five years have given legitimacy to demands for greater government regulation of the finance markets: "The arrest of prominent investment bankers is not an isolated incident," said former senator William Proxmire (D-WI), "It reveals a *systemic* pattern of abuse." Representative Charles Schumer (D-NY) said, "A year ago, people would say we don't need legislation at all. Now the feeling is that some change is necessary."[29] And, as we have seen, the conventional response to the Ill Wind convictions is yet another layer of oversight.

However, it is far from clear that such changes in the operating environment will have the desired effect in terms of reducing corruption. Medicare snoops have been more successful in uncovering than deterring fraud. In the Wall Street examples, proposed government restrictions on mergers or bond sales could have bearish effects on the economy. Similar shoals cannot be charted in reforming the weapons acquisition process without attending to the dangerous effects on military contractors and to the process's political components.[30] The phenomenon of unintended or unanticipated consequences is further illustrated by the "correction" poses in election financing laws; close one avenue of "abuse" and another appears.[31] The potential is apparent: to tinker with part of the system could have ruinous effects throughout the entire system, some of which might be unpredictable. The result could be the diversion (rather than the correction) of corrupt practices to new, unnoticed, and perhaps more fertile areas and activities. The lesson should be clear: the systemic nature of the problem demands systems responses that, in practical terms, preclude the quick, easy, or lasting fix.

The other side of this argument is often heard. Many believe the converse—that government interference in the private sector inevitably leads to corruption, pointing to health, defense, and welfare frauds as examples. If true, it would follow that the removal of government-imposed bureaucratic obstacles would encourage the market's "hidden hand" to eliminate corruption, for it would no longer be necessary (e.g., nobody to bribe because bribes serve no purpose in a perfectly competitive economy). There is no reason to subscribe to this argument; there are just too many examples in which private sector firms have taken full advantage of a lack of government supervision or latitude to gain a profitable edge. Left to its own devices, the private sector appears to be just as avaricious as, and probably more than, the public sector, if for no other reason than that profit maximization and financial gain are its virtual raison d'être. The curtailment of government controls and involvement might easily result in the privatization (and possible enlargement) of corruption, but there is certainly no reason to expect that it would lead to its elimination or even control. Economist Susan Rose-Ackerman summarized the fallacy of this contention:

> [I]t is often easy to imagine that one may eliminate corruption simply by ending government involvement in one or another area of economic life. But this point of view idealizes the private sector in an entirely illegitimate way. While it is true that *perfect* competition in *all* markets will prevent corruption, deregulation will almost never lead to the resumption of a market resembling the competitive paradigm. Indeed, many of the market failures that justify government intervention are the very same conditions that generate corruption in the absence of intervention. . . . Deregulation may simply mean the substitution of a corrupt private official for a corrupt public one. It is not at all obvious that this is much of an achievement.[32]

One need not look any further than to how portions of the thrift industry resorted pell-mell in widespread corruption when Congress and the FSLIC reduced many of its regulatory constraints, and how the thrifts lobbied industriously to prevent some of these regulations from being reimposed. Likewise, prospective HUD contractors went to expensive lengths to short-circuit the department's bureaucracy, and military contractors made senseless charges (baby-sitting and golfing fees) against their government contracts.[33]

Having reviewed the difficulties inherent in reducing the occurrence of and opportunities for systemic corruption, let us turn to the harder problem of proposing concrete measures that might be effective toward this end. Rose-Ackerman's reservation is pertinent:

> The central question here is whether organizational incentives can substitute for personal honesty in maintaining hierarchical control: Does a realistic model of a stable modern economy require agents who value honesty even when high personal scruples are not rewarded by superiors?[34]

For the sake of the argument, if not the ideal, we must assume the answer is positive. Otherwise, the economy would be morally defenseless, rife with fraud, rendering the point moot. Again, as in Chapter 2, we need to recognize that a total elimination of corruption, even if somehow possible, would be politically and socially unacceptable. Therefore, we must look to partial solutions and assume that the benefits of partial corrections are at least equal to (and possibly greater than) the costs of not acting. Thus, the recommendations and their costs would be commensurate with the resources necessarily expended. At issue, then, is what can be done to reduce the incidence and magnitude of corruption in the public sector. Not surprisingly, the proposed strategy is a mixed one, embracing both the individual and systemic causes of political corruption because individuals are the operating units of the system. Therefore, both must be addressed as a reinforcing tandem.

We need initially to reject the traditional recommendations that more laws or regulations or inspectors general provide the answer. Indeed, one can argue that the only result of more regulations and inspectors would be greater temptation for the vulnerable public servant. This is not to suggest that we do not need closer monitoring, but it is to insist that we need to understand the effect of new regulations and oversight on the system, because the system is the ground in which corruption will either sprout or wither. No place was this clearer than in the juxtaposition of economic conditions and new regulations faced by the S&Ls in the early 1980s. Martin Mayer's December 1982 *New York Times* op-ed essay laid out the consequences in no-nonsense terms; as he later wrote, "The government was asking to be robbed, and it was robbed—all over the country."[35]

Turning first to recommending measures that address the individual level, we need to admit that the existing levels of legal sanctions and financial penalties have been demonstrated to be largely ineffective.[36] The reason in many cases is essentially economic; the prospective gain obtained through corruption (in other words, the product of the payoff times the chance of not being apprehended, or the "expected value"[d]) would exceed the costs of the possible penalty. Wall Street financier Ivan Boesky was fined $100 million for his illegal activities and a minimum prison sentence in a low-security facility, a judgment he quickly accepted because it left him in a few years a free man with a personal fortune of more than $100 million. The key to change would be to write regulations and laws with genuine deterrent power, that is, ones whose penalties, when (not if) enforced, would exceed by significant amounts the marginal value of the corrupt activities. The expected value of the illegal transactions must be sufficiently lowered (by raising either the fine or the risk of discovery[37]) so that they are no longer seen as sustainable, worthwhile "investments." As an example, fines could amount to the illicit gains plus an additional penalty; the treble damages levied in anti-trust convictions could serve as a more potent deterrent. These assessments would apply to both parties in the case of public-private corruption (e.g., kickbacks), so as to reduce the incentives of either party to engage in bribery or payoffs. It goes without saying that the fines should be enforced, as has not always been the case with the penalized S&Ls; GAO testimony reports that of the $83.6 million in fines and court-ordered restitutions, only $365,000, or less than one-half of 1 percent, has been collected.[38]

The simple loss of a public sector position is scarcely an adequate deterrent when alternative positions in the private sector—usually at a

---

[d] For instance, if a person stood to gain $10,000 and perceived he only had one chance in ten of being discovered, the expected value of the fraud would be $10,000 times 0.9 = $9,000.

higher salary—are often available; witness Thomas Saunders, one of the convicted military consultants in the Ill Wind investigations, who lost his position in the navy's Naval Warfare Systems Command for making money in the stock market based on insider information. He simply moved his information service to the private sector and continued trading in propriety information.[39] Wedtech hired many of the government officials (legally, in most cases) who had assisted the company in obtaining government contracts. Conflict-of-interest and ethics in government charges forced the resignation of a large number of Reagan administration appointees, but they were not left positionless, penniless, or even very repentant. For these reasons, penalties should not be restricted to cash fines or mere expulsion. Part of Boesky's willingness to accept his huge fine was the understanding that he would not have to serve an extended term in federal prison, a consequence he seemingly was willing to go to great lengths to avoid, as would most white collar professionals. Michael Milken was not so fortunate; he was sentenced to ten years by Judge Kimba Wood, although Judge Wood later reduced the sentence such that he will only serve a few years.[e]

As noted above, individual financial penalties and possible incarcerations have their limits. They might result in a mere raising of the corruption ante rather than folding one's hand; the opportunity would still exist to fuel the incentives. Furthermore, penalties mattered little to the participants during the Iran–Contra initiatives and even less when we remember that not all corruption is criminal; recall the SBA's support of Wedtech, HUD's Mod Rehab bidders, or the interventions of five U.S. senators to relieve Charles Keating of FSLIC regulatory pressures. We must therefore look to institutional and system changes to cut back on the occasions for corruption, thereby reducing individual temptations. In Garment's words,

> We have invented a [independent counsel] machine that will spend tens of millions of dollars to try to put Oliver North in jail while it strenuously ignores the systemic sores that caused the worst of the Iran–Contra scandal and that continue to fester. [40]

---

[e]Judge Wood's decision to reduce Milken's sentence has been almost as controversial as her original sentence. See James B. Stewart, "Annals of Law: Michael Milken's Biggest Deal," *New Yorker*, Vol. 69, No. 3 (March 3, 1993), pp. 58–71.

In the institutional context, it is apparent that many licensing and permitting bottlenecks present fertile grounds for corruption. Thus, to streamline those procedures and regulations would reduce the number of causes for bribes and, from the official's side, extortions. This streamlining was precisely what Lehman and Paisley attempted to do, but the result of their efforts was far from reducing corruption; so the sought-after results are far from certain. In addition, however appealing in concept, this idea is not a costless proposition. For example, building and food inspectors act as important quality controllers, assuring the public that certain safety standards are met and maintained. To loosen their guidelines as a means of eliminating an indeterminate amount of graft could have a damaging effect in terms of substandard buildings, unhealthy produce, and so forth. More fundamentally, as I argued above, the existence of red tape should be viewed as a deliberately imposed hurdle, one with the public good in mind: in banking, it is meant to protect individuals' savings and investments; in weapons procurement or in HUD contracting, it reflects the nation's dedication to equity and fairness. If we view red tape in terms of the economist's principal agent theory (see Chapter 1), that is, as a means to control subordinate agents, then we might hope to find a perfect game-theoretical mix between control and latitude, but conceptual cures buy little in public reality.

Sanctions that affect the system itself might be devised. For instance, if allegations against defense contractors and consultants were found to be true, penalties might be applied against both the actual culprits and the system as well. In this case, the system encouraged consultants to break the rules, so one might want to punish the entire corps of military consultants (while, naturally, punishing the offending ones more severely). This might appear unjust (why punish an entire industry because of a few isolated felons?) but some form of these overarching sanctions already exist. New Defense Department regulations resulting from the Ill Wind convictions have reduced the number of military consultants and made working the Pentagon more difficult for all the remaining consultants. Similar arguments could be couched for the major regulated industries, such as the thrifts (e.g., pay a higher insurance premium rate). If the systemic penalties were heavy, well advertised, and enforced, they could conceivably produce self-policing and peer pressures against the corrupt parties that would have a greater effect in reducing fraud within the industry (because all stood to suffer) than the dilatory indictments and minor sentencing of a single individual or corporation.

It should go without exception that any regulatory program should have the resources to be closely watched. I say it "should" go without exception for this has proven not to be the case. As we saw in the Wedtech, HUD, and, most notably, S&L corruptions, government auditors were not only insufficient, but were subjected to cutbacks mandated by the Office of Management and Budget at the very moment when their programs were most vulnerable. These cutbacks occurred under the guise of deregulation and the philosophical predilection of the Reagan–Bush administrations, which held that private companies are more efficient than their government counterparts. Even with the Ill Wind convictions, the Defense Audit Contract Agency now has 1,200 fewer auditors than in 1989.[41] A relaxation of government control should not mean a relaxation of government scrutiny.

An alternative to making serious changes within the system would be, of course, to change the system itself. For instance, the United States is the only major industrial nation that permits its military services to design and purchase their own weapon systems. As David Morrison points out, "In Canada, France, Great Britain, and West Germany, procurement is in the hands of agencies organizationally independent of the services."[42] Indeed, after the Ill Wind corruptions, Representative Barbara Boxer (D-CA) argued for system change, claiming that "what Congress has to do is fundamentally change the institution. . . . The military-industrial complex is so intertwined that it has to be broken up."[43] In light of the Iran–Contra abuses, we might wonder if the National Security Council, formed to advise against the exigencies of the Cold War, should continue under its 1947 charter now that the Cold War is history.

If Rose-Ackerman is correct that the political system is particularly vulnerable to corruption at the (admittedly vague) junction of the public and private sectors,[44] then one might consider more radical systemic recommendations designed to reduce the size and number of that union. For instance, this would argue against the current strategy in government toward privatization. In the same vein, one might stem the tide of "bureaucrat bashing" and consider decreasing the number of political appointees who, relative to bureaucrats, are professionally and ethically much closer to the private sector. Clearly these measures are not meant to be draconian in execution, but suggestive of actions that could be implemented at least on a partial basis.

If the system bears a portion of the fault, then members of the

system other than the obvious offending parties must be held accountable. In the cases of the S&L corruptions and Wedtech, two professional groups who should have known better than to engage in
shadowy and costly activities stood out in their irresponsible advice—
accounting and legal firms. Big Eight accounting firms like Arthur
Anderson and Arthur Young approved the books of Keating's Lincoln
and Dixon's Vernon (where 96 percent of the loans were bad), avowing
that they were acting within their professional code of ethics, giving
renegade thrifts and Wedtech every benefit of the doubt and even de-
vising a few new exculpatory twists. Law firms were equally culpable.
Large fines being levied against negligent accounting firms (such as the
$400 million settlement agreed to by Ernst & Young [45]) and law offices
as a result of their professional counsel to failing S&Ls reflect a welcomed move toward this perspective.[46] Again, however, the fines need
to have genuine deterrent value, that is, be both large and certain.[f]

Lastly, we must assume that the public at large prefers its governmental services and processes to be relatively equitable, that is, free
from the "sleaze" that became unfortunately common over the last
decade. It would follow that the greater the insight into the workings of
government, the less the potential for political corruption, almost by
definition because corruption is unsanctioned behavior (i.e., if it were
known and approved, it would not be unsanctioned). This move to what
columnist William Safire calls a "Washington *glasnost*',"[47] is hardly a
novel suggestion. John Dewey wrote, over fifty years ago,

> The essential need is the improvement of the methods and conditions of
> debate, discussion, and persuasion. That is the problem of the public. . . .
> [This] improvement depends essentially upon freeing and perfecting the
> processes of inquiry and dissemination of their conclusions.[48]

True enough, but this observation and its bromidic kin fall far short.
The implementation of such advice requires much more in terms of

---

[f] In the case of Ernst & Young, the $400 million was less imposing than what
many observers had expected. The firm's insurance will pay $300 million. For the
remaining $100 million, the government has given the firm four years to pay the
fine; the firm's 2,000 partners will be allowed to treat the fine for tax purposes as a
business expense. Thus, for partners generally earning over $200,000 per year, the
fine averages roughly $8,000. See Stephen Labaton, "$400 Million Bargain for
Ernst," *New York Times*, November 25, 1992, pp. C1, C10.

substantive policy advice than "better ethical instruction by various mechanisms of society," or "the schools need to restore some study of the responsibility of the individual for honesty, truth, courage, and helping others in government as well as elsewhere in life."[49] It requires more than a president offering vague calls for a code of ethics that is more political than ethical in purpose.[50] Nor is political scientist Patrick Dobel particularly useful when he advises:

> To take corruption seriously is to take civic virtue seriously; to take civic virtue seriously is to demand not just moral education but to demand substantive participation, and economic and political equality.[51]

However important these exhortations might be in global terms, these are offering empty shibboleths in terms of policy, lacking any consensus and offering little in the way of operational recommendations. What do these words mean in terms of laws and programs? To urge disenfranchised ghetto teenagers to "Just Say No" does nothing to combat the temptations and corruption offered by the cocaine syndicates.

In more concrete expressions, what is needed is a greater acceptance of "sunshine"-type legislation and regulation in addition to sustained public attention to the policy process. Neither one is particularly new, but that does not imply a hollow value if their tenets are consistently affirmed. The extensive open hearings that precede most new environmental regulations might be an appropriate model, especially in the early stages of the proposal. We need also to involve some oversight in the implementation of various programs. The excesses of Iran–Contra, the S&L debacles, and the HUD scandals all would have been prevented if their operations had been more public than private, for privacy, of course, is at the very heart of political corruption. Poindexter's suggestion that the *exposure* of the administration's arms dealings rather than the policy itself was the basic problem is illustrative.

Of course, public visibility is nowhere near the complete answer we seek. How, for instance, would this be done? As we have already argued, more oversight would immediately increase the cost of government as well as deny officials the local flexibility they need to deal with peculiar problems. Moreover, it would just drive up the price and temptation of corruption. And who would provide the "sunshine"? The media are less vigilant and fair-minded than one would prefer. They suffer from their own set of corruptions, as indicated by the public skepticism regarding reporters and their practices. The various inspectors general (IG) offices might be vigilant, but as the congressional hearings into the HUD abuses demonstrated, IG reports are not widely read. Nor is the Congress held in hallowed esteem when it comes to protecting the public trust, a perception unfortunately reinforced by the individual peccadillos of representatives James Wright and Mario Biaggi, the institutional shame of the House bank and post office scandals, and Congress's continued refusal to enact meaningful campaign reforms.

In summary, the good news is that there are policies that can be executed to reduce the incidence of political corruption. The bad news is that the easy remedies (usually ascribed to individuals) are not effective and the hard ones (dealing with systemic issues) are difficult to implement. This precaution should not be viewed as a counsel of despair, or buy into Johnston's proposed "strategy of accommodation, a way perhaps to allow us to worry (and to get angry) a bit less,"[52] yet we should not harbor any convenient illusions.

Final Thoughts

We could end without returning briefly to where we began, but it would be wrong. Political corruption, although obviously a recurring phenomenon, is not a major nor debilitating feature of the American political landscape.[g] The overwhelming majority of public officials are trustworthy and conscientious in their workaday duties; similarly, most businessmen openly subscribe (maybe begrudgingly) to the thicket of regulations that tangle their governmental relations without resorting to the low road of corruption. That this book could cover most of the major episodes of the past decade within a few hundred pages when there were innumerable government deals and decisions is a positive indication of the truly small incidence of political corrup-

---

[g] For more horrific examples of politically debilitating corruptions in the industrial nations, see David E. Sanger, "Will Japan Scandal Force Changes in the System?" *New York Times*, April 27, 1989, p. A4; and David E. Sanger, "$50 Million Discovered in Raids on Arrested Japanese Politician," *New York Times*, March 10, 1993; or Alan Cowell, "Broad Bribery Investigation Is Ensnaring the Elite of Italy," *New York Times*, March 3, 1993, pp. A1, A4; and Roger Cohen, "Italian Police Arrest 3 Top Energy Chiefs in Kickback Scandal," *New York Times*, March 12, 1993, p. A5.

tion, that is, in more positive terms, a basic honesty of government, its personnel, and its operations.

But the low number of corruptions should not blind us to the fact that political corruptions have repeatedly occurred, that they were not trivial (again, in Lowi's words, "Every act of Big Corruption puts the state itself at risk"[53]), and that their effects are damaging to the American body politic. And, most important, corruption continues despite the glare of Watergate, Irangate, and all the other "gates," the Ethics in Government Act, independent counsels, and other measures notwithstanding. We cannot seem to rid ourselves of the curse called political corruption. Many of the conditions described above—circumventing Congress and agency regulations as well as the inevitable cover-up—now seem to be surfacing surrounding the Bush administration's covert aid to Saddam Hussein prior to Iraq's 1991 invasion of Kuwait.[54]

The country's natural reaction to this string of corruptions and scandals is increasing skepticism regarding its government and its leaders. President George Bush's disingenuous explanation of his role in the Iran–Contra affair was not believed by 70 percent of the voting public, surely affecting his loss in the 1992 presidential election.[55] Moreover, the affliction is bipartisan: a September 1992 *Time*/CNN poll found that people thought Democratic presidential candidate Bill Clinton was not telling the truth regarding his explanations of his draft status (40 percent responding that he was dishonest), his denial of an extramarital affair (50 percent), and his claim never to have inhaled marijuana (68 percent); 75 percent of those polled think there is less honesty in government than a decade ago.[56] Foreign policy corruptions are no different than domestic ones; Tilley notes and comments, "corruption abroad, as the last six years have shown, invariably leads to corruption at home."[57]

The American political system has weathered serious cases of "corruptionitis" before; nothing today matches the corruptions of the nineteenth century. And, in fact, the nation scarcely missed a beat after Watergate and Irangate. Still, one needs to wonder if any political system can function equitably over the long haul if its citizens are so disenchanted.

The central question concerning political corruption should not be whether it is more or less personal or systemic in nature. Historically it has been ascribed to the former; we have spoken here to the latter. The answer surely lies somewhere in between, depending on the circumstances. The only question should be, will we continue to view corruption as an episodic sideshow of American politics and, accordingly, treat it was an unimportant, isolated event? This book has argued (persuasively, I trust) that it is neither isolated nor unimportant, and so should be treated accordingly. There is no doubt that the necessary reforms in the pivotal public-private nexus, executive-congressional relations, and some government structures—should they be durable—would be politically costly, but the alternative is continued corruption whose costs are equally, if not more, expensive.

Notes

1. Welfare fraud, estimated by the inspector general of the Department of Health and Human Services to be "costing $1 billion a year," is not an insignificant amount of money, but it represents thousands of isolated events and therefore would still constitute a scandal, although a very expensive one. Anonymous, "Fraud in Welfare Put at $1 Billion," *New York Times*, December 7, 1989, p. 17.

2. Suzanne Garment, Scandal (New York: Random House, 1991), p. 283. Garment's book has a very complete list of contemporary political scandals. Unfortunately, she does not identify the 50 percent of the scandals that she guesses would be of "any great danger to the republic." Whatever they might be, given the great number of political scandals she designates, the republic could be in serious danger.

3. Theodore J. Lowi, "The Intelligent Person's Guide to Political Corruption," *Public Affairs*, Series 81, Bulletin No. 82 (September 1978), p. 3.

4. Robert K. Merton, *Social Theory and Social Structure* (New York: The Free Press, 1968 ed.); James C. Scott, *Comparative Political Corruption* (Englewood Cliffs, NJ: Prentice Hall, 1972); and Michael Johnston, *Political Corruption and Public Policy in America* (Monterey, CA: Cole Publishing, 1982).

5. Referenced in Herbert Kaufman, *Red Tape* (Washington, D.C.: The Brookings Institution, 1977), p. 17.

6. *Ibid.*, p. 46.

7. The senators "presented their views to the regulators in a way that suggested organized coercion rather than the more normal inquiries, persuasive devices, and veiled threats of everyday politics. . . . Some of the senators in the Keating case were clearly making gorilla noises," Garment, *Scandal*, p. 256.

8. Merton, *Social Theory and Social Structure*, p. 127, emphasis in original.

9. Congressional testimony by John Poindexter quoted in Theodore Draper, *A Very Thin Line* (New York: Hill and Wang, 1991), p. 340; emphasis added.

10. Quoted in Draper, *A Very Thin Line*, p. 561.

11. Walsh is quoted in Anonymous, "Notes and Comments," *New Yorker*, Vol. 58, No. 26 (August 17, 1992), p. 23; for a more complete report of Weinberger's indictment, see David Johnston, "Jury Charges Weinberger in the Iran–Contra Affair," *New York Times*, June 17, 1992, pp. A1, A14; and Joel Brinkley, "Indictment Clashes with Early Images of Iran Arms-Sale Foe,"

New York Times, June 17, 1992, p. A14.

12. Merton, *Social Theory and Social Structure*, p. 135.

13. Oliver North, *Under Fire: An American Story* (New York: HarperCollins, 1991).

14. Goldstock is quoted by Selwyn Raab, "Anti-Crime Unit Urged for New York Builders," *New York Times*, January 6, 1987, p. 15; emphasis added.

15. Goldstock's report is quoted by John J. Goldman, "Mafia Dominates Building Trade in N.Y., Study Finds," *Los Angeles Times*, May 20, 1988, Section 1, p. 1; emphasis added. Also see Selwyn Raab, "Many Builders See Mafia Benefit, Report Says," *New York Times*, September 9, 1987, pp. 1, 14. Nor is this a new finding; see James Darton, "Construction Industry: The Graft Is Built In," *New York Times*, July 16, 1975, pp. A1, A11.

16. Raab, "Anti-Crime Unit Urged for New York Builders," p. 15.

17. Weinberger in quoted in Philip Shenon, "Weinberger Says Bribery Inquiry May Show Reforms Are Necessary," *New York Times*, June 20, 1988, p. A1.

18. Testimony of Judith Siegel before the United States House of Representatives, (Hearings before the) Employment and Housing Subcommittee of the Committee on Government Operations, *Abuses, Favoritism, and Mismanagement in HUD Programs*, 101st Congress, Vol. 1 (Washington D.C.: Government Printing Office, 1991), May 25, 1989, pp. 164 and 142, respectively; emphasis added.

19. Gerald F. Seib, "GOP's Legacy: From Grant to Reagan, Scandals Seem to Hit Republican Presidents," *Wall Street Journal*, July 16, 1987, pp. 1 and 20. Also see Garment, *Scandal*, chap. 11.

20. Interview with Lou Cannon, *President Reagan: A Role of a Lifetime* (New York: Simon & Schuster, 1991), p. 828.

21. Quoted by Garment, *Scandal*, p. 244.

22. A possible straw in the wind is the cover on *Time* magazine's September 5, 1992, issue: "Lying: Everybody's Doin' It (Honest)," and the cover story, Paul Gray, "Lies, Lies, Lies," *Time*, September 5, 1992, pp. 32–38.

23. Garment, *Scandal*, p. 303.

24. Susan Rose-Ackerman, *Corruption: A Study in Political Economy* (New York: Academic Press, 1978), outlines this thinking with economic rigor.

25. Garment, *Scandal*, p. 141.

26. New York University professor Richard Netzer was analyzing the consequences that might result from the New York City Park Violations Bureau; Michael Oreskes, "New York City Scandals: The Impact," *New York Times*, February 18, 1975, p. 15.

27. Anonymous, "Notes and Comments," *The New Yorker*, Vol. 66, No. 32 (September 24, 1990), p. 34.

28. Anonymous, "Fraud in Welfare Put at $1 Billion."

29. Proxmire and Schumer are quoted by Nathaniel C. Nash, "Calls Mount for Curbs on Markets," *New York Times*, February 14, 1987, p. 21; emphasis added. Also see idem, "Arrests Indicate Get-Tough View of Office Crime," *New York Times*, February 12, 1988, p. A1.

30. John H. Cushman, Jr., "Curbs on Pentagon Fraud in Dispute," *New York Times*, July 10, 1988, Sec. 1, p. A14; Richard W. Stevenson, "The High Costs of an Arms Scandal," *New York Times*, July 10, 1988, Sec. 3, pp. 1, 8; and Thomas L. McNaugher, *New Weapons, Old Politics* (Washington, D.C.:

The Brookings Institution, 1989).

31. See Johnston, *Political Corruption and Public Policy in America*, chapter 6.

32. Rose-Ackerman, *Corruption*, p. 207; emphasis in original.

33. The Sunstrand Corporation, in charges contemporaneous but separate from the Ill Wind investigations, was fined $115 million for conspiracy to overcharge the government. See Philip Shenon, "Military Supplier Fined $115 Million on Fraud Charges," *New York Times*, October 13, 1988, pp. A1, C11; Eric N. Berg, "Sunstrand Destroyed Cost Data," *New York Times*, October 14, 1988, pp. C1, C4; and John H. Cushman, Jr., "Sunstrand Suspended by Pentagon," *New York Times*, October 20, 1988, pp. C1, C6.

34. Rose-Ackerman, *Corruption*, p. 2.

35. Martin Mayer, *The Greatest-Ever Bank Robbery* (New York: Charles Schribner's Sons, 1990), p. 27; his op-ed piece is reprinted on pp. 321–323.

36. The effectiveness of sanctions in deterring criminal activities is empirically disputed; cf., Gary S. Becker, "Crime and Punishment: An Economic Approach," *Journal of Political Economy*, Vol. 78, No. 2 (March/April 1968), pp. 169–217, and Isaac Ehrlich, "Participation in Illegitimate Activities: A Theoretical and Empirical Investigation," *Journal of Political Economy*, Vol. 81, No. 3 (May/June 1973), pp. 521–567, with Brian E. Frost, "Participation in Illegitimate Activities: Further Empirical Findings," *Policy Analysis*, Vol. 2, No. 3 (Summer 1976), pp. 477–492. More vivid arguments on this relationship are found in Gordon Tullock, "Does Punishment Deter Crime?" *Public Interest*, No. 36 (Summer 1974), pp. 103–111.

37. Gary S. Becker and George J. Stigler, "Law Enforcement, Malfeasance, and Compensation of Enforcers," *Journal of Legal Studies*, Vol. 3, No. 1 (January 1973), pp. 1–18, argue that law enforcement would be improved if bounties were paid for culprits apprehended, not unlike commissions (i.e., a payment upon performance system). Both Becker and Stigler are Nobel laureates in economics (1982 and 1992, respectively).

38. Harold A. Valentine, General Accounting Office, Testimony before the Subcommittee on Consumer and Regulatory Affairs, Committee on Banking, Housing, and Urban Affairs, United States Senate, *Bank and Thrift Fraud* (Washington D.C.: Government Printing Office, 1992), p. 11; also see Editorial, "S&L Scandal II: Collecting the Fines," *Denver Post*, February 9, 1992, p. 2H.

39. Stephen Engelberg, "Tale behind Search Warrant: Pentagon Data Believed Sold," *New York Times*, July 1, 1988, pp. A1, B5; and David E. Rosenbaum, "Pentagon Fraud Inquiry: What Is Known to Date," *New York Times*, July 7, 1988, pp. A1, B5.

40. Garment, *Scandal*, p. 289.

41. Keith Schneider, "U.S. Says Lack of Supervision Encouraged Waste in Contracts," *New York Times*, December 2, 1992, pp. A1, A14, reports that a study initiated by Richard Darman, director of the Office of Management and Budget, found that "contractors are squandering vast sums [of money] because Federal agencies fail to supervise how hundreds of billions of dollars are spent each year," with the implicit connivance of the executive branch (which eliminated auditors' positions) and Congress (which approved the budget requests).

42. David C. Morrison, "Tinkering with Defense," *National Journal*, Vol.

20, No. 36 (September 3, 1988), p. 2181.

43. Boxer is quoted by Morrison, "Tinkering with Defense," p. 2181.

44. Rose-Ackerman, *Corruption*, chapter 1.

45. John H. Cushman, Jr., "Accountants Pay 400 Million to U.S. Over S.&L. Audits," *New York Times*, November 24, 1992, pp. A1, C2.

46. See Mayer, *The Greatest-Ever Bank Robbery*, chapter 11.

47. William Safire, "The Voting Trigger," *New York Times*, October 29, 1992, p. A19.

48. John Dewey, *The Public and Its Problems* (New York: Henry Holt, 1927), pp. 208–209; quoted by Johnston, *Political Corruption and Public Policy in America*, p. 186.

49. George C.S. Benson et al., *Political Corruption in America* (Lexington, MA: D.C. Heath, 1978), p. 295.

50. Bernard Weinraub, "Bush Offers Ethics Bill to Set Broad Standards," *New York Times*, April 13, 1989, p. A10; and R.W. Apple, Jr., "The Capital: The Drive for Honesty in Governing: Lasting Change or Politics as Usual," *New York Times*, April 12, 1989, p. A10.

51. J. Patrick Dobel, "The Corruption of the State," *American Political Science Review*, Vol. 72, No. 3 (September 1978), p. 972.

52. Johnston, *Political Corruption and Public Policy in America*, p. 186.

53. Lowi, "The Intelligent's Person's Guide to Political Corruption," p. 3.

54. The current skein of allegations begins with the Italian Bank of Credit & Commerce International and "laundered" money. It grows to include subsidies from the U.S. Department of Agriculture that were used to fund Iraqi purchases of advanced technologies that have weapons applications. Charges now have been leveled at the departments of Agriculture and State, the Central Intelligence Agency, the Justice Department, and, ultimately, the White House. For starters, see Jonathan Beaty and S.C. Gwynne, "The Dirtiest Bank of All," *Time*, July 29, 1991, pp. 42–47; later allegations are reported by Leslie H. Gelb, "Cuddling Saddam," and William Safire, "Obstructing Justice," both *New York Times*, July 9, 1992, p. A15; allegations regarding a possible cover-up are reported by Elaine Sciolino, "Justice Dept. Role Cited in Deception of Iraq Loan Data," *New York Times*, October 10, 1992, pp. 1, 4; and William Safire, "Panic on Ninth Street," *New York Times*, October 12, 1992, p. A19.

55. Jeffrey Schmalz, "Clinton Carves a Wide Path Deep into Reagan Country," *New York Times*, November 4, 1992, p. B1.

56. The *Time*/CNN survey of 1,400 adults was conducted between September 22 and 24, 1992, with a sampling error of 2.5 percent; the surveys are reported in Gray, "Lies, Lies, Lies," p. 37 and 32.

57. Anonymous, "Notes and Comments," *New Yorker*, Vol. 68, No. 26 August 17, 1992, p. 22.

Index

Peter deLeon is Professor of Public Policy at the University of Colorado-Denver. Previously he taught at Columbia University and spent a dozen years on the staff of the RAND Corporation. Dr. deLeon has specialized in policy research on issues of technology development, assessment, and utilization, with substantive expertise in national security and energy. He has also written extensively on the public policy processes, especially program implementation, evaluation, and termination, and served as the editor of the leading journal in the field, *Policy Sciences*. He has twice been named his school's outstanding research scholar; in 1989, he received honorable mention as the University's outstanding research scholar. An adviser to the European Center for Social Welfare (Vienna), the Swedish Colloquium for Advance Study in the Social Sciences, and the Science Center (West Berlin), as well as an invited lecturer in the People's Republic of China, his work has been accorded international recognition. He has been awarded grants from the Ford Foundation, the Alfred J. Sloan Foundation, the German Marshall Fund, the Russell Sage Foundation, the Asia Foundation, and the Swedish Bicentennial Fund.